"Nolo's home page is worth book

—WALL STREET JOURNAL

W9-BMV-433

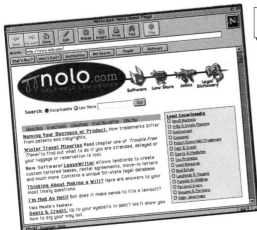

LEGAL INFORMATION ONLINE ANYTIME

24 hours a day

www.nolo.com

AT THE NOLO.COM SELF-HELP LAW CENTER ON THE WEB, YOU'LL FIND

- Nolo's comprehensive Legal Encyclopedia, with links to other online resources
- SharkTalk: Everybody's Legal Dictionary
- Auntie Nolo—if you've got questions, Auntie's got answers
- Update information on Nolo books and software
- The Law Store—over 250 self-help legal products including:
  Downloadable Software, Books, Form Kits and E-Guides
- Discounts and other good deals, plus our hilarious Shark Talk game
- Our ever-popular lawyer jokes
- NoloBriefs.com, our monthly email newsletter

Quality LAW BOOKS & SOFTWARE FOR NON-LAWYERS

Nolo.com legal books and software are consistently first-rate because:

- ⬤ A dozen in-house Nolo legal editors, working with highly skilled authors, ensure that our products are accurate, up-to-date and easy to use.
- ⬤ We know our books get better when we listen to what our customers tell us. (Yes, we really do want to hear from you—please fill out and return the card at the back of this book.)
- ⬤ We are maniacal about updating every book and software program to keep up with changes in the law.
- ⬤ Our commitment to a more democratic legal system informs all of our work.

OUR "NO-HASSLE" GUARANTEE

Return anything you buy directly from Nolo for any reason and we'll cheerfully re-fund your purchase price. No ifs, ands or buts.

An Important Message to Our Readers

This product provides information and general advice about the law. But laws and procedures change frequently, and they can be interpreted differently by different people. For specific advice geared to your specific situation, consult an expert. No book, software or other published material is a substitute for personalized advice from a knowledgeable lawyer licensed to practice law in your state.

CALIFORNIA 13TH EDITION

EVERYBODY'S GUIDE TO

SMALL

CLAIMS

COURT

IN CALIFORNIA

By Attorney Ralph Warner

Illustrated by Linda Allison

Keeping Up to Date

To keep its books up to date, Nolo issues new printings and new editions periodically. New printings reflect minor legal changes and technical corrections. New editions contain major legal changes, major text additions or major reorganizations. To find out if a later printing or edition of any Nolo book is available, call Nolo at 510-549-1976 or check our website at www.nolo.com.

To stay current, follow the "Update" service at our website: www.nolo.com. In another effort to help you use Nolo's latest materials, we offer a 35% discount off the purchase of the new edition of your Nolo book when you turn in the cover of an earlier edition. (See the "Special Upgrade Offer" in the back of the book.) This book was last revised in: **January 2000.**

THIRTEENTH EDITION

Second Printing	January 2000
Illustrations	Linda Allison
Cover	Toni Ihara
Production	Susan Cornell and Amy Ihara
Proofreading	Joe Sadusky
Indexer	Patricia Deminna
Printer	Bertelsmann Industry Services, Inc.

Warner, Ralph E.
 Everybody's guide to small claims court in California / by Ralph Warner. -- California 13th ed.
  p.   cm.
 Includes index.
 ISBN 0-87337-440-1
 1. Small claims courts--California--Popular works. I. Title.
KFC976.Z9W37 1998
347.794'04--dc21   97-35480
                                                          CIP

Copyright © 1978, 1981, 1983, 1987, 1988, 1989, 1991, 1992, 1993, 1996, 1998 and 2000 by Ralph Warner. All rights reserved. Printed in the U.S.A.
No part of this publication may be reproduced, stored in a retrieval system, or transmitted in any form or by any means, electronic, mechanical, photocopying, recording or otherwise without the prior written permission of the publisher and the authors.

For information on bulk purchases or corporate premium sales, please contact the Special Sales department. For academic sales or textbook adoptions, ask for Academic Sales. 800-955-4775, or write to Nolo.com, 950 Parker St., Berkeley, CA, 94710.

Thank You

Nolo is as much family as business. Without the help of many Nolo family members, there would be no books such as this one. For work on the 13th edition, I am particularly grateful to Susan Cornell, whose patient help inspired me to make this a better book.

Over the years, a number of talented friends have read the manuscript of this book and made helpful suggestions for improvement. With enough help, even a tarnished penny can be made to shine. Thanks to David Brown, Robin Leonard, Mary Randolph, Jeanne Stott, Roderic Duncan, Steve Elias, Lisa Goldoftas, Marcia Stewart and Lisa Guerin.

For Toni,

the light, the heart, and the love of my life.

Contents

Chapter 8: Who Can Be Sued?

Chapter 9: Where Can You Sue?

Chapter 10: Plaintiff's and Defendant's Filing Fees,
Court Papers and Court Dates

Chapter 11: Serving Your Papers

Chapter 12: The Defendant's Options

Chapter 13: Getting Ready for Court

Chapter 14: Witnesses

Chapter 15: Presenting Your Case to the Judge

Chapter 16: Motor Vehicle Repair Cases

Chapter 17: Motor Vehicle Purchase Cases

Chapter 18: Bad Debts: Initiating and Defending Cases in Which Money Is Owed

Chapter 19: Vehicle Accident Cases

Chapter 20: Landlord–Tenant Cases

Chapter 21: Miscellaneous Cases

Chapter 22: Disputes Between Small Businesses

Chapter 23: Judgment and Appeal

Chapter 24: Collecting Your Money

Chapter 25: Where Do We Go From Here?

Appendix

Introduction

As we approach the 21st century, Small Claims Court in California is finally getting some of the respect it has long deserved. The maximum amount you can sue for is now $5,000 and would be higher were it not for the fact that in 1997 Governor Wilson caved in to the insurance industry and vetoed an increase to $7,500. Even so, the $5,000 limit is a great improvement over the much lower dollar limits in force just a few years ago. In addition, a series of changes adopted over the last decade has made Small Claims judgments easier to collect. So, while much more could be done to make Small Claims Court a true people's court (see Chapter 25 for some suggestions), it is already an effective place in which the average person can resolve many types of disputes, quickly and inexpensively.

The goal of this book is to give both people bringing a case and those defending one all the step-by-step information necessary to make the best possible use of Small Claims Court. From deciding whether you have a case through gathering evidence, arranging for witnesses, planning your courtroom presentation and collecting your money, you will find everything you need here.

Everybody's Guide to Small Claims Court has now been in print for 20 years. The current edition has been completely updated to reflect the literally hundreds of recent practical and legal changes. My goal is to make it the best possible tool to help you answer such questions as:

"How does Small Claims Court work?"

"Do I have a case worth pursuing or defending?"

"How do I prepare my case to maximum advantage?"

"What witnesses and other evidence should I present?"

"What do I say in court?"

"Can I appeal if I lose?"

"How do I collect my judgment?"

Proper presentation of your Small Claims action can often mean the difference between receiving a check and writing one. This isn't to say that I can tell you how to take a hopeless case and turn it into a blue ribbon winner. It does mean that with the information contained here, and your own creativity and common sense, you will be able to develop and present your legal and factual position as effectively as possible. In short, this book really will show you how a case with a slight limp can be set on four good legs.

Just as important as knowing when and how to bring your Small Claims Court action is knowing when not to. Clearly, you don't want to waste time and energy dragging a hopeless case to court. And even if your case is legally sound, you obviously won't want to pursue it if your chances of collecting from a deadbeat defendant are poor.

As with any book, I have had to make a number of decisions as to the order in which I cover Small Claims issues and the depth in which I cover them. For example, the question of whether an oral contract is valid is discussed in Chapter 2, but not again in Chapter 16 on automobile repairs, where it may also be relevant. So please take the time to read, or at least skim, the entire book before you focus on the chapters that interest you most. Also realize that a very good way to get an overview of the entire Small Claims process is by reading the Table of Contents.

Chapter 24 is the last part of this book designed to help you win your case and collect your money. Chapter 25 is devoted to a different cause—how our court system must be changed to deliver more justice and less frustration. In many ways this material is intensely personal in that it reflects my experience with the inadequacies of our formal, lawyer-dominated legal delivery system over many years. Too often our courts are not really about the affordable resolution of disputes, but instead have become the private fiefdom of lawyers, judges and other professionals who may place their own interests ahead of the common good.

I have included this material because I believe it will be of interest to many people who are considering resolving your own disputes in Small Claims Court. Already you have demonstrated the fortitude necessary to attempt to solve your own legal problem. It follows that you may be interested in enlisting in the ongoing struggle to make California courts both more accessible and fairer, with the idea that there really can be affordable justice without lawyers.

Now a few words about two potentially sensitive subjects. First, when grappling with the ever tricky personal pronoun, I have decided to simply take turns rather than using the cumbersome "he or she" and "his or her." Please bear with me if I inadvertently use one or the other too many times in a single chapter.

Second, it's appropriate to say a few words about my many referrals to other Nolo self-help law books and Nolo's website. Lest you think my only goal is to try to sell you another book, let me make three points. First, Nolo is by far the most comprehensive publisher of self-help law materials in the United States. As a result, there are many legal areas where Nolo publishes the only decent materials aimed at nonlawyers. Second, because a huge variety of legal issues can be litigated in Small Claims Court, information in many other Nolo books and in Nolo's free online legal encyclopedia, may be useful (and is far too voluminous to repeat here). Third, as Nolo's books are available at most American libraries, it shouldn't be hard to look up any needed information at no cost.

■

In the Beginning

A. First Things

The purpose of Small Claims Court is to hear disputes involving small amounts of money, without long delays and formal rules of evidence. Disputes are presented by the people involved and lawyers are normally prohibited. The maximum amount of money that can be sued for in California is $5,000 ($2,500 if you are suing a bonding company or other guarantor). In legal jargon, this is often called the "jurisdictional amount." Unfortunately, however, you are only allowed to bring two lawsuits for more than $2,500 within any calendar year unless you are suing on behalf of a school district or other public entity, in which case there is no case limit. To establish your eligibility for suing for between $2,500 and $5,000, you will have to state as part of your Plaintiff's Claim that you have not already used up your yearly quota.

There are three great advantages of Small Claims Court:

- You get to prepare and present your own case without having to pay a lawyer more than your claim is worth.

- Filing, preparing and presenting a Small Claims case is relatively easy. The gobbledygook of complicated legal forms and language found in other courts is kept to a minimum. To start your case, you need only fill out a few lines on a simple form (that is, "Honest Al's Used Chariots owes me $4,000 because the 1992 Ford Escort they sold me in supposedly 'excellent condition' died less than a mile from the car lot"). When you get to court, you can talk to the judge in plain English without any legal jargon. Even better, if you have helpful documents or witnesses, you can show them to the judge without complying with the thousand years' accumulation of rusty, musty procedures, habits and so-called rules of evidence of which the legal profession is so proud.

- Small Claims Court doesn't take long. Most disputes are heard in court within a month or two from the time the complaint is filed. The hearing itself seldom takes more than 15 minutes. The judge announces her decision either right there in the courtroom, or mails it within a few days.

But before you decide that Small Claims Court sounds like just the place to bring your case, you will want to answer a basic question: Are the results you are likely to achieve in proportion to, or greater than, the effort you will have to expend? Even in Small Claims your case will probably take 10-20 hours to prepare and present and, depending on your personality, may even cause a few sleepless nights.

In order to clearly assess whether your dispute is worth the effort of bringing to court, you will want to understand the details of how Small Claims Court works—being clear about who can sue, where and for how much, is a good start. You will also want to learn a little law so you can make an informed decision as to whether you are entitled to relief, and if so, how do you compute the exact dollar amount to sue for? Finally, and most important, comes the detail that so many people overlook, to their later dismay. Assuming that you prepare and present your case brilliantly and get a judgment for everything you request, can you collect? The ability to get paid seems a silly thing to overlook, doesn't it? Unfortunately, many plaintiffs who go through the entire Small Claims procedure and come out a winner have no chance of collecting a dime because they have sued a person who has neither money nor any reasonable prospect of getting any.

The purpose of the first dozen chapters of this book is to help you decide whether or not you have a case worth pursuing. These are not the chapters where grand strategies are brilliantly unrolled to baffle and confound the opposition—that comes later. Here I am more concerned with such mundane tasks as locating the person you want to sue, suing in the right court, filling out the necessary forms and getting them properly' served. Most California Small Claims forms are uniform for the entire state, although a few local forms may vary slightly from one judicial district to the next. Blank copies of all forms are available at your local Small Claims Court clerk's office.

B. Checklist of Things to Think About Before Initiating or Defending Your Case

Here is a preliminary checklist of things you will want to think about at this initial stage. As you read further, we will go into each of these areas in more detail. Oh, and one more thing: Free Small Claims information sheets are available to you in all counties. In addition, if you have questions, you either have the opportunity to meet with a trained Small Claims advisor in person or talk to one by phone.

QUESTIONS A PLAINTIFF NEEDS TO ANSWER

☐   1.   Do you have a good case? That is, can you establish or prove all key legal elements of your claim necessary to win your lawsuit? (See Chapter 2 for a discussion of what is needed to win contract, debt, property damage and other common types of cases.)

☐   2.   How many dollars is your claim for? If it is for more than the $5,000 Small Claims maximum, do you wish to waive the excess and still use Small Claims Court? (See Chapter 4.)

☐   3.   Have you made a reasonable effort to contact the other party to offer a compromise? (See Chapter 6.)

☐   4.   Is your suit brought within the proper time period? (See Chapter 5.)

☐   5.   Which Small Claims Court should you bring your suit in? (See Chapter 9.)

☐   6.   Whom do you sue and how do you identify this person or business on your court papers? In some types of cases, especially those involving businesses and automobiles, this can be a little more technical and tricky than you might have guessed. (See Chapter 8.)

☐   7.   If mediation is offered or required by your Small Claims Court, do you understand how it works and how best to use it? (See Chapter 6.)

☐   8.   Can you prove your case? That is, do you understand what evidence you need to bring to court to convince a judge you are in the right? (See Chapters 14 through 22.)

☐   9.   Can you make a convincing courtroom presentation? The key here is practice, practice, practice. (See Chapter 15.)

☐ 10.   And again, the most important question—assuming that you can win, is there a reasonable chance you can collect? (See Chapters 3 and 24.)

QUESTIONS A DEFENDANT NEEDS TO ANSWER

1. Do you have legal grounds for a countersuit against the plaintiff? Or put another way, does the plaintiff really owe you money? (See Chapters 10 and 12.)

2. Do you have a partial or complete legal defense against the claim of the plaintiff? Or put another way, has the plaintiff filed a bogus lawsuit? (See Chapters 2 and 12.)

3. Has the plaintiff sued for a reasonable or an excessive amount? (See Chapter 4.)

4. Has the plaintiff brought his suit within the proper time limit? (See Chapter 5.)

5. Has the plaintiff followed reasonably correct procedures in bringing suit and serving you with the court papers? (See Chapters 11 and 12.)

6. If mediation is offered or required by your Small Claims Court, do you understand how it works and how to use it? (See Chapter 6.)

7. Have you made a reasonable effort to contact the plaintiff in order to arrive at a compromise settlement? (See Chapters 6 and 12.)

8. Assuming you'll contest the case in court, you'll normally need proof that your version of events is correct. Can you collect evidence and witnesses to accomplish this? (See Chapters 13 through 15.)

9. Are you prepared to present your side of the case convincingly in court? (See Chapter 15.)

 **Defendants may want to file their own lawsuit.** In addition to their right to vigorously defend themselves, defendants also have the opportunity to file their own case against the plaintiff. (See Chapters 10 and 12.) You will want to do this if you believe that you suffered money damages and the plaintiff is legally responsible for your loss. Defendants' claims commonly develop out of a situation in which both parties are negligent (say in a car accident) and the question to be decided is who was more at fault. If your claim is for less than the Small Claims Court maximum, you can file your Claim of Defendant in Small Claims Court. But if it is for more, you will want to file your case in Municipal Court (up to $25,000) or Superior Court (over $25,000) and then have the Small Claims Court case transferred to this court. (See Chapter 10, Section C.) Before making any decision, read your local rules carefully.

C. Legal Jargon Defined

Mercifully, there is not a great deal of technical language used in Small Claim Courts. But there are a few terms that may be new to you and that you will have to become familiar with. Don't try to learn all of these terms now. Refer back to these definitions when you need them.

Abstract of Judgment: An official document you get from the Small Claims Court clerk's office which indicates that you have a money judgment against another person. Filing it with the County Recorder places a lien on real property owned by the judgment debtor.

Appeal: In the Small Claims context, a request that the Superior Court rehear the case from scratch and reverse the decision of the Small Claims Court. A Small Claims appeal cannot be made by the person who brought the claim in the first place (the plaintiff). That is, only a defendant can appeal on the plaintiff's claim, and only the plaintiff can appeal on the defendant's counterclaim, if she brought one. The appeal is heard in the appellate division of the Superior Court, and the parties may (but do not have to) be represented by attorneys.

Calendar: A list of cases to be heard by a Small Claims Court on a particular day. A case taken off calendar is removed from the list. This usually occurs because the defendant has not been served or because the parties jointly request that it be heard on another day.

California Civil Code (CC) and California Code of Civil Procedure (CCP): Books which contain some of California's most widely used substantive and procedural laws. They are available at all public libraries and law libraries (which are located at the county courthouse and are open to the public). They are also available online by going to http://www.leginfo.ca.gov/calaw.html. Small Claims rules are covered in CCP Secs. 116.110-116.950.

Claim of Defendant: A claim by a defendant that the plaintiff owes him money. A Claim of Defendant, also called a "Defendant's Claim," is filed as part of the same Small Claims action that the plaintiff has started.

Claim of Exemption: A procedure by which a "judgment debtor" can claim that, under federal and/or California law, certain of his money or other property is exempt from being grabbed to satisfy a debt.

Claim of Plaintiff: Also called "Plaintiff's Claim and Order to Defendant," this document is filed with the Small Claims Court to initiate a lawsuit.

Conditional Judgment: When a court issues "equitable relief" (such as the return of a piece of property), it has power to grant a conditional judgment. A conditional judgment consists of certain actions or requirements that are contingent on other actions (for instance, return the property in ten days or pay $2,000).

Continuance: A court order that a hearing be postponed to a later date.

Default Judgment: A court decision given to the plaintiff (the person filing suit) when the defendant fails to show up (that is, defaults).

Defendant: The person or "party" being sued.

Dismissed Case: A dismissal usually occurs when a case is dropped by the plaintiff. If the defendant has not filed a claim, the plaintiff simply files a written request for dismissal. If the defendant has filed a claim, both plaintiff and defendant must agree in writing before a dismissal will be allowed. If a plaintiff does not show up in court on the appointed day, the judge may dismiss the case. Most cases are dismissed "without prejudice," which is legal jargon meaning they can be refiled. But if a case is dismissed "with prejudice," it means that it can't be refiled unless the dismissal is first successfully appealed.

Equitable Relief: There are several legal areas—called "recission," "restitution," "reformation" and "specific performance"—in which a Small Claims Court judge has the power to issue judgment for something other than money damages—that is, to order a party to return "one of a kind" property, end a fraudulent contract, fix a mistaken contract or do one or more of the acts discussed in more detail in Chapter 4, Section E.

Equity: The value of a particular piece of property that you actually own. For example, if a car has a fair market value of $10,000 and you owe a bank $8,000 on it, your equity is $2,000.

Exempt Property: Under California law, certain personal and real property is exempt from being used to pay ("satisfy") court judgments if the debtor follows certain procedures. For example, a judgment debtor's equity in one or more motor vehicles is exempt up to $1,900. (See Chapter 24.)

Formal Court: As used here, this term refers to the regular "lawyer-dominated" state courts. In California, claims of up to $25,000 that are not filed in Small Claims Court are heard in Municipal Court, and claims over that amount are heard in Superior Court. Both of these courts require some knowledge of often confusing legal language and procedure, and you will want to do some homework if you decide to use them. If your claim really is too big for Small Claims Court, see *Represent Yourself in Court: How to Prepare & Try a Winning Case*, by Attorneys Paul Bergman & Sara Berman-Barrett (Nolo Press).

Garnish: To attach (legally take) money—usually wages, or commissions, or a bank account—for payment of a debt.

Hearing: The court trial.

Homestead Declaration: A piece of paper that any homeowner can file with the County Recorder's office which protects the equity in her home from attachment and sale to satisfy most debts. The equity protected is $75,000 for a family; $100,000 for persons who are over 65, blind or disabled, or over 55 with an income under $15,000 ($20,000 for married couples); and $50,000 for a single person. A homeowner is entitled to substantial protection even if a homestead is not filed.

Judgment: The decision rendered by the court. A judgment must be written down and signed by a judge.

Judgment Creditor: A person to whom money is owed under a court decision.

Judgment Debtor: A person who owes money under a court decision.

Judgment Debtor's Statement of Assets: An informational form which accompanies a notice of entry of judgment which must be completed by the losing side unless the judgment is appealed or paid. This form is designed to inform the winning party about such things as where the loser works, banks and owns property. (See Chapter 24.)

Judicial District: California is divided into many judicial areas or districts. Sometimes these are the same as a city or county, but in populous areas especially, there is often more than one judicial district in a county.

Jurisdiction: A Small Claims Court has jurisdiction—or authority—to hear cases involving money damages up to $5,000 where the defendant lives or does business in California. A Small Claims Court may also award several other types of remedies, which order a losing party to do a specific thing (such as return a valuable ring within two weeks). In legal lingo, these "equitable remedies" are called "rescission," "restitution," "reformation" and "specific performance," and are discussed in Chapter 4. (See also "Venue.")

Jury Trial: All Small Claims cases and appeals are heard by judges or commissioners. There is no right to trial by jury in California.

Legal Error: If a judgment is entered which contains a clear clerical or legal error, either party may promptly file a request (motion) with the Small Claims Court asking to have it corrected. (See Chapter 23, Section F.)

Levy: A legal method to seize property or money for unpaid debts under court order. For example, a sheriff can levy on (sell) your automobile if you refuse to pay a judgment.

Lien: A legal right to an interest in the real estate (real property) of another for payment of a debt. To get a lien, you first must get a court judgment and then take proper steps to have the court enter an "Abstract of Judgment." To establish the lien, you then take the Abstract to the County Recorder's office in a county where the judgment debtor has real estate to establish the lien.

Mediation: A process encouraged in many California Small Claims Courts by which the parties to a dispute meet with a neutral person (the mediator) who attempts to help them arrive at their own solution to the problem. If mediation succeeds, it's normally not necessary to argue the case in court; if it fails, the dispute can still go to court to be decided on by a judge.

Motion to Vacate a Judgment: A Motion to Vacate a Judgment is a document typically filed by a defendant who did not appear in court to defend a case on the proper date, with the result that the judge has entered a default judgment. The parties must usually attend a hearing where the judge listens to the defendant's oral presentation as to why he or she missed the first hearing and then decides whether to set aside the default and reopen the case. (See Chapter 10.)

Order of Examination: A court procedure allowing a judgment creditor to question a judgment debtor about the extent and location of his assets.

Party: Lawyer talk for a participant in a lawsuit. Thus the plaintiff or defendant may be referred to as a party—and both together as the parties—to a Small Claims suit.

Plaintiff: The person or "party" who starts a lawsuit.

Prejudice: A term used when a case is dismissed. A case which is dismissed "without prejudice" can be refiled at any time as long as the statute of limitations period has not run out (see Chapter 5). However, a case dismissed "with prejudice" is dead (can't be refiled) unless the dismissal is first successfully appealed.

Process Server: The person who delivers court papers to a party or witness. (See Chapter 11.)

Recorder (Office of the County Recorder): The person employed by the county to make and record important legal documents, such as deeds to real property. The County Recorder's office is usually located in the main county courthouse.

Satisfaction of Judgment: A written statement filed by the judgment creditor when the judgment is paid. (See Chapter 23, Section D.)

Statute of Limitations: The time period in which you must file your lawsuit. It is normally figured from the date the act or omission giving rise to the lawsuit occurs, and varies depending on the type of suit. (See Chapter 5.)

Stay of Enforcement: When a Small Claims Court judgment is appealed to the Superior Court by a defendant, enforcement (collection) of the judgment is stayed (stopped) until the time for appeal has expired.

Stipulation: An agreement to compromise a case which is entered into by the parties and then presented to the judge.

Submission: When a judge wants to delay deciding on a case until a later time, she "takes it under submission." Some judges announce their decision as to who won and who lost right in the courtroom. More often, they take the case under submission and mail out a decision later.

Subpoena: A court order requiring a witness to appear in court. It must be served on the person subpoenaed to be valid. (See Chapter 14.)

Subpoena Duces Tecum: A court order requiring that certain documents be produced in court.

Substituted Service: A method by which court papers may be served on a defendant who is difficult to serve by other means. (See Chapter 11.)

Transfer: The procedure by which the defendant can have a Small Claims case transferred to a "formal court" if she files a counterclaim for a dollar amount larger than allowed in Small Claims Court.

Trial De Novo: The rehearing of a Small Claims case from scratch by a Superior Court judge when an appeal has been initiated by the defendant. In this situation, the previous decision by the Small Claims judge has no effect, and the appeal takes the form of a new trial (trial de novo).

Unlawful Detainer: Legalese for "eviction." Unlawful detainers must be brought in Municipal Court, not Small Claims Court. (See Chapter 20.)

Venue: This basically refers to the proper location (judicial district or court) to bring a suit, and is discussed in detail in Chapter 9. If a suit is brought in the wrong judicial district or court (one that is too far from where the defendant lives or a key event in the case occurred), it can be transferred to the right court or dismissed. If it is dismissed, the plaintiff must refile in the right court. However, the case can be heard even in the wrong court if both parties appear and agree to do so.

Wage Garnishment: After a judgment has been issued (and the defendant's time to appeal has elapsed), the Small Claims Court clerk will issue a writ of execution upon the judgment creditor's request. This may be turned over to a sheriff, marshal or constable with orders to collect (garnish) a portion of the judgment debtor's wages directly from his employer.

Writ of Execution: An order by a court to the sheriff, marshal or constable to collect a specific amount of money due.

D. Legal Research

As part of using Small Claims Court, you may want more information on one or another California law. I refer to many of the most relevant ones in this book, but there are, of course, a great many more than I can possibly list here. If you imagine a child standing on a beach with a pailful of sand, with the sand in the pail representing the laws discussed in this book and the sand on the beach representing the total body of California law, you will have some idea of how many more laws you can sift through if you have the energy.

California laws are roughly divided by subject matter into sets of books called "codes." Thus, there is the Civil Code, the Probate Code, the Penal Code, the Vehicle Code and many more. The majority of California laws, including those having to do with consumer protection (that is, credit cards, landlord/tenant, auto lemon laws, etc.) are found in the Civil Code (abbreviated CC). Other codes that you may want to refer to in preparing a Small Claims case are the Code of Civil Procedure (CCP), which includes the laws having to do with the operation of Small Claims Court (CCP Secs. 116.110-116.950); the Business and Professions Code (Bus. & Prof. Code), which includes rules regarding the collection of professional fees and contractor's license regulations; the Vehicle Code, which contains the rules of the road; and the Commercial Code (Com. Code), which contains information about warranties. To locate a particular law, first locate the correct code and then look up the number. If you do not know if a particular area of conduct is regulated by law, or suspect that a law exists but don't know which code it is in or its number, refer to the master code index, which lists all California laws by subject. In this way you can locate the correct code and number for the law you need.

You can get access to California codes at any large public library or county law library, which are located in main county courthouses (and in some branch courthouses) and are open to the public. You can also gain access to them online by going to Nolo's Self-Help Law Center (www.nolo.com). Once at Nolo's home page, click on the FindLaw box and follow instructions to find California's laws. Small Claims rules are covered in California Code of Civil Procedure (CCP) §§ 116.110–116.950.

Ordinances are passed by cities and counties and have the force of law in that municipality. Among other things, ordinances often include zoning rules, building codes, leash laws, parking restrictions, view and tree-cutting rules and often minor vehicle violations. Usually, you can get copies of local ordinances from city or county offices, and collected sets are commonly available at the public library. In addition, many more populous cities and counties now have their ordinances available online. An easy way to see if yours are available electronically is to go to one of the sites which provide access to local laws. I recommend that you try either http://www.localgov.org/ or http://www.piperinfo.com/state/.

If you do your research at a law library, you will have an opportunity to look up California laws in the annotated codes (published by both West and Matthew Bender). In addition to the basic laws, these codes also list relevant court decisions (called "cases") interpreting each law. If you find a case that seems to cover your fact situation, you will want to read it and, if it still seems relevant (and supports your interpretation of the law), point it out to the judge as part of your Small Claims presentation. If you are confused about how to find and understand a particular case, ask the law librarian for help.

For a more thorough exploration of how to use the law library, see one or more of the following resources, which are available at bookstores and most libraries:

- *Nolo's Pocket Guide to California Law*, by Lisa Guerin, Patti Gima and Nolo editors (Nolo). This alphabetical guide to California law enables readers to quickly and easily look up most laws that apply to them. It gives concise plain-English summaries of the law on children, relationships, renting and buying a house, employment, landlord–tenant questions, contracts, sales, warranties and much more.

- *Legal Research: How to Find and Understand the Law*, by Stephen Elias and Susan Levinkind (Nolo). An invaluable guide to doing your own legal research. This is the only legal research guide written for the nonlawyer and is used as a text at dozens of paralegal schools.

- *Legal Research Made Easy* (Video), Nolo & Legal Star Communications. Surely the best legal research tool available to the nonlawyer. In this 2-1/2 hour video, Law Librarian Bob Berring shows you the books you need to master to do efficient legal research, and explains how to use them. Anyone who ever plans to enter a law library should see it. ■

2

Do You Have a Good Case?

A. Stating Your Claim on Your Court Papers

One of the advantages of Small Claims Court is that when you file your case you are not required to plead theories of law—instead, you simply state the facts of the dispute and rely on the judge to fit them into one or another legal theory of recovery. All you really need to know is that you have suffered real monetary damage and that the person or business you are suing caused your loss.

To illustrate how this works, let's jump ahead and take a look at the form you will fill out when you file your case. Turn to Chapter 10 and find the form entitled "Plaintiff's Claim." Look at Line 1. As you can see, there is no space to state a lengthy legal argument. Indeed, there is barely room to briefly describe your dispute and list the date on which it occurred or began. Depending, of course, on the facts of your case, you will state your claim, more or less like this:

- "John's Dry Cleaners ruined my jacket on December 13, 199_."

- "Defendant's dog bit me on the corner of Rose and Peach Streets in West Covina, California on April 27, 199_."

- "The car repairs that Joe's Garage did on my car on July 11, 199_, were done wrong, resulting in an engine fire."

- "Defendant refused to return the cleaning deposit when I moved out of my apartment on August 11, 199_, even though I left it clean."

- "The used car I purchased from Robert Yee on January 26, 199_, blew a gasket the next day."

- "The $5,000 I lent defendant has not been repaid by November 12, 199_, as promised."

TIME TO GET ORGANIZED

Even before you file your case, you should set up a good system to safeguard key papers and evidence. It's no secret that more than one case has been won (or lost) because of good (or bad) record keeping. One excellent approach is to get a couple of manila envelopes or file folders and label them with the name of your dispute (Lincoln vs. Williams). Use one folder to store all documentary evidence, such as receipts, letters, names and addresses of potential witnesses and photographs. The other is for your court papers. Once organized, make sure you conscientiously store your folders in a safe place.

B. But Is My Case Really Any Good?

If you read the little pamphlets Small Claims Court clerks hand out, you will learn pretty much what I have just outlined in Section A of this chapter. You will be told to:

- briefly state the nature of your dispute,

- organize any evidence and witnesses you think will help back up your version of events,

- come to court on time,

- be polite and

- let the judge decide if your case is any good.

At a very primitive level this is decent advice—you expend little effort or thought and rely on the judge to do the heavy lifting. The only problem with this approach— and something the little pamphlet won't tell you—is that the judge will not decide your case based on who she believes is morally "right," or even whose presentation and witnesses are more convincing. Instead, the judge will apply exactly the same legal rules to your case as would be done if your dispute was heard in a formal court.

Obviously this means there are a number of problems with the "stay ignorant and trust us" approach pushed by Small Claims Court pamphlets. Here are the biggies.

- If you don't understand the legal rules the judge will apply to decide your case, you run the risk of wasting time and energy pursuing an obvious loser.

- If you don't understand the legal realities that underlie your case, you probably won't prepare as sensibly as you otherwise would. In a worst case scenario, you may not even understand—and therefore fail to fulfill—the key legal require- ments necessary to have a judgment entered in your favor.

- If you win—and especially if you lose—you won't know why.

If none of this sounds good to you, perhaps you are open to considering a more informed approach. This consists of taking the time to understand the basic legal issues that underlie your case. Or put another way, it means looking at your case in the same way a judge will ultimately view it.

Assuming you are game, start by reading the rest of this chapter. It contains a discussion of the legal theories most commonly used to establish legal liability in Small Claims Court. In many instances this information will be all you need to understand how to properly prepare your case. But occasionally you will want to do additional legal research, as would be true if the exact wording of a statute or key court decision has a direct bearing on your case. (See Chapter 1, Section D, for more on how to do legal research.)

Below I list the most common legal theories (causes of action) and the requirements (lawyers call them elements) you will need to prove to establish each. In the rest of this chapter, I'll review each key legal theory in detail, so you can see if the facts of your loss fit the requirements of at least one of them.

Defendants need the same legal knowledge as plaintiffs. To defend a case well, a defendant needs to understand the essential legal elements of the case the plaintiff is attempting to prove. Once armed with this information, the defendant will be in good shape to try to convince the judge that at least one key legal element is missing.

- *Breach of Contract:* One or more terms of a valid contract (written, oral or implied) has been broken by the person you are suing. As a result, you have suffered a monetary loss. (See Section C, below.)

- *Bad Debt:* A type of contract case. To prevail, you need to prove the debt exists, its amount, when payment was due, and that the person you are suing hasn't paid it or has only partially paid it.

- *Failure to Return a Security Deposit:* Another variety of contract case that commonly arises between tenants and landlords. As discussed in more detail in Chapter 20, for a tenant to prevail, you need to prove that a deposit was made, that it was not returned (or only partially returned), and that the premises were sufficiently clean and undamaged when you left that the landlord owes you some or all of the amount withheld.

- *Negligence:* The careless behavior of the person you are suing has caused you to suffer a personal injury or property damage resulting in a monetary loss. (Negligence that results in damage to property is covered in Section D1, below. Negligence resulting in a personal injury is covered in Section E, below.)

- *Intentional Harm:* The intentional behavior of the person you are suing has caused you to suffer personal injury or property damage resulting in a monetary loss. (See Section D2 for cases involving property damage and Section E for those involving personal injury.)

- *Personal Injury:* The negligent or intentional behavior of the person you are suing has caused you to suffer personal injury. (See Section E.)

- *Product Liability:* You or your property were injured by a defective product. If so, you qualify for recovery under the legal doctrine of "strict liability," which holds the manufacturer responsible for the damages you suffered, without your having to prove negligence. (See Section F.)

- *Breach of Warranty:* A written or implied warranty extended to you by a merchant has been breached and, as a result, you have suffered a monetary loss—for example, a new or used car suffers mechanical problems while still covered by warranty. (See Section G.)

- *Violation of a Statute:* A right created by statute has been violated and, as a result, you have suffered a monetary loss. This would be the case if a consumer protection law was broken by your opponent, resulting in your being out some money. (See Section H.)

- *Professional Malpractice:* A lawyer, doctor or other professional's failure to use the ordinary skills of members of that profession results in a client or patient being harmed (in the case of a lawyer or accountant, the client must suffer a monetary loss). (See Section I.)

- *Public and Private Nuisance:* Someone's conduct creates a health or safety hazard to you (and perhaps other neighbors or nearby property owners), or does something that interferes with your ability to use and enjoy your property—for example, a factory makes so much noise you and other nearby residents are kept awake all night. (See Section J.)

- *Libel or Slander (Defamation):* To prove a libel or slander case, you must show that the other party said or wrote something untrue about you or your business, that others heard or read it and that it really did damage your reputation. (Public figures must also show that the person defaming them knew the offending statement or writing was false or was made in "reckless disregard of the truth.") (See Chapter 21, Section E.)

Other legal theories exist. The legal theories (lawyers call them "causes of action") listed above are involved in over 98% of Small Claims cases. I have no space to list the technical legal requirements for the dozens of more obscure types of lawsuits. However, if your case isn't covered here, you may sensibly want to do some additional research to determine whether it meets the qualifications (contains the correct "legal elements" or criteria) of some other legal theory (cause of action).

Now, before we consider each of these legal theories individually, here is an example of why it's so important to establish not only that you have suffered a loss, but that the defendant really is legally liable to make it good.

Example 1: *One night someone entered the garage in Sue's apartment complex, smashed her car window and stole a fancy AM-FM radio and tape deck worth $500. Upon discovery of the theft, and after reporting it to the police, Sue promptly filed suit against the landlord in Small Claims Court. As part of preparing for her day in court, Sue got several witnesses to the fact that her car had been vandalized, and obtained a copy of the police investigation report. She also got several estimates as to the cost of repairing the damage to the car window and replacing the tape deck.*

Sue only overlooked one thing. Unfortunately for her, it was a crucial one. Under the circumstances the building owner wasn't liable. He had never promised (agreed by contract, either orally or in writing) to keep the garage locked. In addition, he had never locked the garage or otherwise led Sue to believe that he would do so. Once the judge determined that all the tenants were reasonably on notice that it was easy to gain access to the garage either from inside or outside the building and that there had been no previous crimes committed there, he concluded that in failing to lock the garage the building owner was neither in violation of a contract nor guilty of any negligent behavior. As he explained to Sue when he ruled for the landlord, the legal situation she faced was little different than it would have been if her car had been damaged on the street.

Example 2: *Now let's take this same situation, but change a few facts. Let's assume the lease contract signed by the landlord and tenant stated that the tenant would be assigned a parking place in a "secure garage." Let's also assume that the garage had always been locked until the lock broke seven days before the theft occurred. Finally, let's assume that Sue and other tenants had asked the owner to fix the lock the day after it broke, but that he hadn't "gotten around to it." In this situation, Sue should win. The landlord made a contractual promise to the tenants (to keep the garage locked) and then failed to keep it ("breached the contract," in legal lingo) in a situation where he had plenty of time to fulfill his obligation. The breach of contract allowed the thief access to the car.*

C. How to Approach a Breach of Contract Case

A contract is any agreement between identifiable parties where one side agrees to do something for the other in exchange for something in return. The agreement may be written, oral or implied from the circumstances. Contracts made by minors can be annulled if this is done prior to the minor turning 18. However, in most states, if a contract made prior to age 18 is honored by a person after she turns 18, the contract is valid and can no longer be annulled.

⚠️ **Not all oral contracts are valid.** Most oral contracts are valid and enforceable, assuming, of course, their existence can be established (proved) to the satisfaction of a judge. But there are major exceptions to this rule. Generally speaking, contracts that 1) can't be completely performed within a year or 2) are for the sale of real estate or 3) involve the sale of goods (personal property) worth more than $500 (see Chapter 22) must be in writing. However, because the great majority of consumer-type contracts can be performed in a year (even if it actually takes longer) and involve services, most oral contracts are enforceable in court.

Here are some examples that should help you understand when a valid contract does and does not exist.

Example 3: Marcia tells Steve she is in a bad way financially, and Steve promises to give Marcia $750 on January 1. Later Steve changes his mind because he decides he doesn't like Marcia after all. Can Marcia go to court and sue Steve for the $750? No. This is not a contract, because Marcia has promised to do nothing for Steve in return for his promise to make a loan. Steve has only indicated that he will give Marcia a gift in the future. A promise to make a gift is not enforceable since there is no reciprocal promise or quid pro quo.

Example 4: Steve promises to pay Marcia $750 on January 31 in exchange for Marcia's promise to pay it back with interest (or to clean Steve's office or tutor Steve's oldest son). Under all of these scenarios, this is a valid contract, since each person has promised to do something for the other. If Steve fails to pay Marcia on January 31, Marcia can go to court and get a judgment for the $750, claiming breach of contract.

Example 5: Paul asks Barbara if she wants her house painted. Barbara says "yes." Paul paints Barbara's house but Barbara refuses to pay, claiming that since they never agreed on a price, there was no contract. Barbara is wrong. A court will use the traditional doctrine of "quantum meruit" (as much as is deserved for labor) to rule that when one person does work for another in circumstances where payment is normally expected, and the second person accepts it (consent can be stated, as in the example, or even implied, as would be the case if Barbara simply watches Paul paint her house), a contract exists. In other words, even though one or more technical parts of a contract is missing, when work is involved the law will require that a

person who knowingly benefits from another person's work pay for it, unless it is absolutely
clear the work was donated (the person doing the work was a volunteer).

1. Unpaid Debts

Often a contract that has not been honored involves a failure to pay money. Hardly a
day goes by in any Small Claims Court when someone isn't sued for failing to pay the
phone company, the local hospital, a friend (former, probably) or relative, or even late
fines to the public library. (See Chapter 18 for more on Small Claims suits where money
is owed.) In many situations, getting a judgment for an unpaid debt involves no more
than stating that the defendant committed himself to buy certain goods and services,
that they were, in fact, provided and that a legitimate bill for X dollars has not been
paid.

As a plaintiff, you must normally prove:
- the identity of the debtor;
- the existence of a contract with the debtor;
- that you kept your promises under the deal (normally that you provided the
  goods, services or loan);
- the fact that the debt hasn't been paid.

If you are a defendant and believe you have a good defense, you'll normally need to
prove:
- the goods or services you were supposed to receive were delivered late or not at
  all or were seriously defective (see "Failure to Perform a Contract," just below);
- the plaintiff never lent you the money in the first place;
- you already paid some or all the money plaintiff lent you back; or
- the plaintiff agreed to a subsequent contract to forgive the debt or give you more
  time to pay.

In court, you'll need to convince the judge that the contract existed. If the contract
is in writing, bring it to court. If it's oral, be prepared to prove its existence
through witnesses and circumstantial evidence. Be creative—if you lent money to a
debtor using a check, bring a copy. Along with your own testimony that the borrower
promised to repay you, this should be all you need to establish the existence of a contract.

2.   Failure to Perform a Contract

Sometimes a breach of contract suit results, not from a simple refusal to pay a bill, but because one party claims that the other failed to carry out one or more of the terms of a contract. Such would be the case if:

- A tenant sued an apartment owner who agreed to rent her an apartment but instead rented it to someone else. (Leases and rental agreements are discussed in more detail in Chapter 20.)

- A small business sued a caterer who showed up with the food and drink for an important party four hours late.

- A recently married couple sued a professional wedding photographer who used the wrong film, with the result that all the wedding photos were badly overexposed.

- A freelance writer hired to write an annual report sued the business involved when it failed to provide essential financial information, making it impossible to do the job.

Damages resulting from a breach of contract are normally not difficult to prove. After you show that the contract existed and that the other party failed to meet its terms, you should testify as to the dollar amount of damages you have suffered as a result. And when appropriate, you'll also need to introduce evidence to convince the judge that you really did lose this amount.

Example 6: Justine and Bob planned a June wedding. Since the families of both prospective spouses were widely dispersed, this was to be a combination family reunion and wedding. As a result, the couple planned a large reception with a meal and arranged to have it catered by Top Drawer Deli. A written list of all food and drink orders was prepared by the Deli and signed by Justine. When the big day arrived, everything went swimmingly, until the 200 guests arrived at the reception to find that, while the band was playing cheerfully, Top Drawer had not shown up with the food and bubbly. Fortunately, the best man hopped into his station wagon, drove to the nearest liquor store and was back in less than 20 minutes with ten cases of champagne. (Clearly there was a reason he was picked as best man.) Someone else had the presence of mind to order 30 pizzas. Two hours later, Top Drawer showed up full of apologies. (A key employee called in sick and their van broke down.) Justine and Bob accepted the cake and turned down everything else. When the bill came for the whole works, they paid for the cake and told Top Drawer to eat the rest. Top Drawer sued for $4,000 for breach of contract. Bob and Justine countersued for $5,000 for emotional distress. The judge agreed with the newlyweds that by being two hours *late to a time-sensitive event, Top Drawer had breached its contract and, as a result, Bob and Justine owed them nothing. But the judge also dismissed Bob and Justine's emotional distress claim after remarking that the reception obviously turned into an unforgettable party.*

The fact that many contract cases are easy to win doesn't mean that all result in victory. In fact, I have seen a good number of plaintiffs lose what to them seemed to be open and shut cases. Why? Usually because they:

- failed to show that a contract existed (see Examples 1 and 7);

- failed to sue the right defendant (again, see Example 7);

- failed to show that a contract was broken (see Example 8); or

- failed to establish that they really suffered a monetary loss (see Example 6).

Example 7: *Ben, a landlord, sued John, the parent of one of his tenants, for damages John's daughter and her roommates had caused to their rental unit. John was sued because he had co-signed his daughter's lease. Ben easily convinced the judge that the damage had, in fact, occurred, and the judge seemed disposed toward giving him a judgment for the $980 requested, until John presented his defense. He showed that the lease between his daughter and the landlord had been rewritten three times after he originally co-signed it and that he had not added his signature to any of the revised versions, one of which involved replacing several of his daughter's original roommates with others. The judge agreed that because John had not co-signed any of the subsequent leases (contracts), he wasn't liable. The reason was simple: There was no longer a contract between Ben and John. (Leases and rental agreements, including a detailed discussion of the rights and responsibilities of co-signers, are discussed in more detail in* Every Landlord's Legal Guide, *by Marcia Stewart and Attorneys Ralph Warner and Janet Portman (Nolo Press).)*

Example 8: *Sid sued Acme Dry Cleaners for $650, the cost of replacing a pigskin suede jacket that was ruined (it shrunk dramatically) by Acme. Sid established that he had taken the jacket to Acme for cleaning, and had agreed to pay Acme $80. Since Acme, by accepting the jacket, clearly implied it would properly clean it, there was no question that a contract existed. Sid was very sure of his loss. He stood in the courtroom and slowly tried to wriggle into the jacket. The sleeves barely came to Sid's elbows, and the coat itself didn't reach his waist. The whole courtroom burst out laughing—including the judge, who almost choked trying to keep a straight face. So far so good from Sid's point of view. By putting on the shrunken jacket, he made his point more effectively than he could have with ten minutes of testimony.*

Unfortunately for Sid, he also overlooked two key things—one obvious and one not so obvious. As you have probably guessed, Sid's obvious mistake involved his asking for the full $650 replacement value of a jacket that was eight months old and had been worn a good bit. Valuation is a common problem in clothing cases. (I discuss it in detail in Chapters 4 and 21.) Let's just say that Sid's jacket was probably worth no more than $400 (and probably less) in its used condition. That's because whenever property is damaged or destroyed, the amount of your recovery will be limited to the fair market value of the goods at the time the damage occurred—not their replacement value.

Now let's look at Sid's less obvious mistake. Vijay, Acme Dry Cleaner's owner, testified that when he saw the jacket after cleaning, he was amazed. His cleaning shop specialized in leather goods, and the cleaning process used should have resulted in no such shrinkage. What's more, he testified that he had examined a number of other items in the same cleaning batch and found no similar problem. To determine what happened, he sent the jacket to an "independent testing laboratory." Their report, which he presented to the court, stated that it was the jacket itself, not the cleaning, that was the problem. According to the report, shrinkage occurred because the leather had been severely overstretched prior to assembly.

What happened? The judge was convinced by the testing lab report and felt that Acme had breached no contract as far as the cleaning was concerned. However, the judge also felt that Acme, as a leather cleaning specialist, had some responsibility to notify Sid that the jacket should not have been cleaned in the first place. Therefore, the judge held mostly for Acme, but did award Sid $100. He also suggested that Sid might want to consider suing the store that sold the jacket, claiming that, by selling clothing containing seriously defective material, the store had breached an implied warranty that the goods sold were reasonably fit for the purpose they were designed to fulfill. For information on breach of warranty actions, see Section G, below.

More material concerning contracts:

- How much you should sue for in breach of contract cases (how to value your damages) is discussed in Chapter 4, Section C1.

- Breach of warranty—based on a written or oral contract—is covered in Section G, below.

- Material on how the violation of a state or federal law can make a contract unenforceable is covered in Section H, below.

- Material involving leases and rental agreements—a specialized type of con-tract—is covered in Chapter 20.

- How to collect on contracts involving unpaid bills is covered in Chapter 18.

- If your contract involves fraud, undue influence or a simple mistake ($2,000 was mistakenly written as $20,000), you may have a right to have the contract ended or rewritten or to get your goods back, under the legal doctrine of "equitable relief." (See Chapter 4, Section E.)

D. How to Approach a Case Where Your Property Has Been Damaged by the Negligent or Intentional Acts of Someone Else

The second biggest category of Small Claims disputes involves a plaintiff's claim that a defendant negligently damaged her property. Less often, the plaintiff claims that the defendant intentionally damaged his belongings.

1. Negligence

A technical definition of negligence could—and does—fill entire law texts. But I don't recommend your reading one, since I remember thinking in law school that the more scholarly professors wrote about the subject, the more mixed up they got. Like good taste or bad wine, negligence seems to be easy to recognize, but hard to define.

So let's breeze right past the "ifs," "ands" and "wherefores" and focus on what I'll call a peasant's definition of negligence. If, as a result of another person's conduct, your property is injured, and that person didn't act with reasonable care under the circum-stances, you have a valid legal claim based on his or her negligence. In addition, negligence can occur when a person who has a duty or responsibility to act fails to do so. For example, a car mechanic who fails to check your brakes after you tell him they have been working poorly and he promises to do so would be negligent.

Example 1: Jake knows the brakes on his ancient Saab are in serious need of repair, but does nothing about it. One night, when the car is parked on a hill, the brakes fail and the car rolls across the street and destroys Keija's persimmon tree. Keija sues Jake for $225, the reasonable value of the tree. Jake will lose because he did not act with reasonable care under the circumstances.

Another obvious situation involving negligence would be one where a car or bus swerves into your driving lane and sideswipes your fender. The driver of the offending vehicle has a duty to operate it in such a way as not to harm you. By swerving into your lane, it is extremely likely that he has failed to do so. A situation where negligence could be difficult to show would involve your neighbor's tree that falls on your car while it is properly parked in your driveway. Here you have to be ready to prove that, for some reason (such as age, disease or an obviously bad root system), the tree was in a weakened condition, and the neighbor was negligent in failing to do something about it. That's because if the tree had looked to be in good health, your neighbor probably wasn't negligent since he had no reason to remove it or prop it up. Here are some additional examples where a person or business failed to act with reasonable care and as a result was negligent:

- While playing with his kids in his small back yard, Kevin hits a ball over the fence, smashing a neighbor's window.

- While upgrading Eddie's computer, Bill carelessly installs the wrong chip, which crashes Eddie's hard drive and ruins the computer.

- RapidMail Inc., a local courier service, loses several time-sensitive messages and fails to notify the sender of the problem.

Compound negligence exists where more than one person is responsible for the damages you suffer—for example, if you are injured because you fall down a staircase with no hand railing after someone who is not paying attention to where she is going runs into you. When dealing with a situation such as this, in which more than one person may have contributed to your loss, Rule #1 is to sue them all.

Example 2: Sandy comes home from work one day to find her new fence knocked over and Fred's Chevy Blazer in the middle of her front lawn. Fred admits his vehicle knocked over the fence when his brakes failed. To Sandy, this may at first seem like a simple case involving filing suit against Fred. But what if Fred had just picked up his car from Atomic Auto Repair, where he had his brakes worked on? Fred's liability may range from minimal (Atomic is only 50 feet away; he just left the shop with the assurance that the brakes were fixed) to extensive. (Atomic is located across town. At the last two stop signs, Fred's brakes acted "funny" but he continued to drive anyway.) Although Sandy may not know all these details, if she learns that Fred recently had his brakes worked on, she would be well-advised to sue both Fred and Atomic and let the judge sort out who is most at fault.

Example 3: *Now suppose that Fred's brakes are fine, but he claims he was rear-ended at the stop sign by Dana, whose pick-up truck pushed his vehicle through Sandy's fence. Again, Fred's liability may be minimal (Dana was drunk and speeding), or it may be extensive (Fred ran a stop sign while turning and was rear-ended by Dana, who had the right of way). Again, Sandy would be wise to sue both parties and let the judge sort out who was most at fault.*

Negligence concepts are tricky: Don't try to be a judge. There is often no fool-proof way to determine in advance whether someone will be judged to be negligent. In fact, when it comes to accidents, it's often so close a factual and legal question that lawyers regularly arrive at the wrong conclusion. So if you have suffered a real loss and think someone else caused it, bring your case, present as much evidence supporting your point of view as possible and let the judge decide.

Here are a couple of questions, the answers to which may help you make a decision as to whether you have a good case based on someone else's negligence.

- Did the person whose act (or failure to act) injured you behave in a reasonable way? Or to put it another way, would you have behaved differently if you were in her shoes?
- Was your own conduct a significant cause of the injury?

If you believe that the person who caused you to suffer a monetary loss behaved in an unreasonable way (ran a red light when drunk) and that you were acting sensibly (driving at 30 mph in the proper lane), you probably have a good case. If you were a little at fault (slightly negligent), but the other fellow was much more at fault (very negligent), you can still recover most of your losses, since courts follow a legal doctrine called "comparative negligence." This involves subtracting the percentage of your negligence from 100% to find out how legally responsible the other party is. Thus, if a judge finds that one person (drunk and speeding) was 80% at fault, and the other (slightly inattentive) was 20% at fault, the slightly inattentive party can recover 80% of her loss.

How to get more information about negligence. If, despite my advice to keep it simple, you want to get into the gory details of negligence theory, go to your nearest law library and get any recent hardbound legal text on "torts" (wrongful acts or injuries). Or, even easier, if you are near a law bookstore, buy a copy of one of the several competing paperback course summaries covering torts that law students rely on to get through their torts exams. One good one, *The Gilbert Law Summary of Torts*, is available from Nolo's bookstore in Berkeley.

2. Intentional Acts

Not all injuries to people or property are accidents. You also have the right to recover money damages if you or your personal property have been intentionally damaged by someone. (I cover personal injuries in Section E, below.)

Example: Basil and Shirley are neighbors who can't stand the sight of each other, despite, or perhaps because of, the fact that both are prize-winning rose growers. When Basil took first place in the local garden club contest for his exotic roses, Shirley, who was angry, frustrated and jealous, intentionally left her hose running and drowned all of Basil's roses. By bringing a Small Claims case, Basil should be able to recover the value of his rose bushes from Shirley.

In theory, at least, it is also possible to recover punitive damages if you are damaged by the malicious conduct of someone else. However, in part because public sentiment is running strongly against punitive damage awards , they are seldom awarded in Small Claims Court. Nevertheless, based on Shirley's bad conduct, Basil might be tempted to sue Shirley for more than the cost of replacing the roses. No problem, but of course the most Basil can sue for is $5,000. This might be plenty in a case involving drowned rose bushes, but obviously would not be nearly enough in a typical fact situation where punitive damages might be awarded. In short, most cases requesting punitive damages should be filed in Municipal Court (claims up to $25,000) or more likely, Superior Court (claims over $25,000).

More material concerning property damage:
- To determine how much to sue for, see Chapter 4, Section C2.

E. How to Approach a Personal Injury (and Mental Distress) Case

I treat personal injury cases in this separate section because so many people look at them as being a different kind of lawsuit. In fact, most personal injury cases are based on a claim that someone has been negligent (and a few are based on claims of intentional injury). The legal theories involved are the same as set out in Section D, above. To prevail, you must show that your injury was caused by someone's negligent or intentional behavior (unless your injury was caused by a defective product, in which case the legal doctrine of strict liability applies—see Section F, below).

Start by understanding that most personal injury cases involve amounts of money that are clearly over the Small Claims maximum and should therefore be pursued in formal court. However, occasionally a minor personal injury case will be appropriate for Small Claims.

Example 1: Jenny and Karen are playing softball in a picnic area of a park, where many families are picnicking in the sun. Jenny, never a star fielder, misses a batted ball that hits seven-year-old Willie in the face while he is sitting on a blanket eating lunch. Willie suffers a chipped tooth. With the help of his parents, Willie sues Jenny and Karen for the $500 it will cost to repair his tooth. Jenny and Karen claim they were just playing a game and shouldn't be held liable. How will a judge decide this case? Almost surely in favor of Willie, who was eating lunch in a picnic area where he had a right to be. By contrast, Jenny and Karen almost surely were careless (negligent). Why? Because as a society, we have decided that picnic areas are for picnickers—not ballplayers—and since Jenny and Karen's game was inappropriate and dangerous to others, they are going to have to pay for their negligence.

Example 2: Now, assume that Jenny and Karen move over to a nearby ball field. Their skills haven't improved and Jenny again misses the ball. And again it hits poor Willie—who has escaped his parents and wandered onto the field unobserved—in the mouth. Are Jenny and Karen still liable to pay to fix Willie's tooth? Probably not. Jenny and Karen took reasonable precautions to avoid hitting picnickers by playing on the ball field. While they may have a responsibility to get little Willie off the field if they spot him, they are probably not legally responsible—that is, negligent—in a situation where he wanders onto the field unnoticed.

Consider not only your loss, but whether the other party acted reasonably under the circumstances. Before you sue someone for an injury, consider whether it was really caused by their negligence. If so, the person is legally liable to make good your loss. If not (you trip and fall down a perfectly safe set of stairs), you have no right to recover, no matter how serious your injury (again, one major exception to the rule that you must demonstrate the other side's negligence applies when you are injured by a defective product—see Section F, below). If in doubt, go ahead and sue, but be prepared to deal with the negligence question, as well as simply showing the extent of your injury. In Chapters 14 and 15 I give you some practical advice as to how to prove your case.

As discussed in more detail in Chapter 4, you do not have to suffer a physical injury to successfully recover in court as a result of someone else's negligent or intentionally obnoxious behavior. Invasion of privacy and the intentional infliction of mental distress are but two of the types of lawsuits that can be based on nonphysical injuries.

Example: *Suppose your landlord enters your apartment without notice, permission or good legal reason. You make it clear that this behavior is highly upsetting and ask her to cease invading your privacy. She nevertheless persists in entering your apartment with no good reason, causing you to become genuinely upset and anxious. You file a Small Claims case based on the intentional infliction of mental distress. Assuming you can convince the judge that you were truly and seriously upset, your chances of winning are good.*

Obviously, not every instance of obnoxious behavior that makes you mad qualifies as being serious enough to bring a successful lawsuit. Generally, to recover, the other person's actions must:

- be truly obnoxious;
- violate a state law or local ordinance (the invasion of a tenant's privacy qualifies, since statutes in most states prohibit a landlord from entering without notice, except in an emergency.) For more on this see *Tenants' Rights*, by Myron Moskovitz & Ralph Warner (Nolo);
- continue after you have asked the person to stop (it's best to do this in writing and to do it more than once).

In addition, you must be able to convince a judge that you have genuinely suffered mental distress as a result of the other person's conduct. (A bill from a therapist or perhaps testimony about your inability to sleep would be good evidence to present to the judge.)

One area in which the number of Small Claims cases is growing involves sexual harassment in the workplace. As a precondition of going to court, a formal complaint must first be filed with the federal or California Equal Employment Opportunity Commission. Since these agencies get far more complaints than they can cope with, this usually results in your receiving a rejection letter. Fine, now you can go to court. And because it can be very difficult to get a lawyer unless truly outrageous conduct can be proven, you may choose to scale back your claim to $5,000 so that it will fit into Small Claims Court, assuming, of course, you have suffered real provable damages.

By far the best book on how to handle a job-related sexual harassment claim, including a thorough review of your non-court options, is *Sexual Harassment on the Job,* by Attorneys William Petrocelli and Barbara Kate Repa (Nolo).

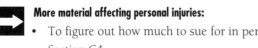

More material affecting personal injuries:
- To figure out how much to sue for in personal injury cases, see Chapter 4, Section C4.

F. How to Approach a Case When You Are Injured by a Defective Product (Doctrine of Strict Liability)

Under a legal concept called "strict liability," there is usually no need to prove negligence if you are injured as a result of a defect in a product. (This legal area is often referred to as "products liability.") The point is, if your vacuum cleaner, hair dryer, steam iron, lawnmower or other product malfunctions and you are injured as a result, you are entitled to recover from the manufacturer or other defendant (usually the person you bought or rented the product from) without having to prove negligence. When an injury is serious, product liability cases are always filed in formal court. Now and then, however, a defective product will cause a more minor—but still real—injury, in which case filing in Small Claims Court may be appropriate. If you find yourself in this situation, it is best to sue both the manufacturer and seller of the defective product. Be prepared to prove both that the product really did malfunction and that you were injured as a result.

G. How to Approach a Breach of Warranty Case

In Chapter 17, I discuss warranties as they apply to problems with new and used cars, as well as the California Lemon Law.

First you need to understand that warranty law is extremely confusing, even to lawyers. A principal reason for this is that three separate and distinct warranty laws can apply to the retail sale of goods. The unhappy result is that, short of presenting you with a major legal treatise, it's impossible to thoroughly explain warranty law. The best I can do in this short space is to review the basic rules:

✔ **Written Warranties:** If a new or used product comes with a written warranty, you have the right to rely on its terms.

✔ **Oral (Express) Warranties:** If a seller makes written or oral statements describing a product's features (for example, "these tires will last at least 25,000 miles") or what it will do ("it will work for two years"), and you rely on them as part of making your decision to purchase the product, an "express" legal warranty exists. It is important to understand that this is true even though a more limited written warranty printed on the package states there are no other warranties.

✔ **Implied Warranties:** In most situations, an implied warranty of general fitness for the intended use or "merchantability" is also present (for example, that a lawn-mower will cut grass, a tire will hold air and a calculator will subtract). This warranty exists in addition to the written and oral (express) warranties discussed just above. Again, it's important to understand that it applies even though there is a statement (often called a "warranty disclaimer") printed on the product or packaging saying no warranties exist beyond the express written warranty, or that no warranty exists at all, or that all implied warranties are specifically disclaimed.

In California, implied warranties apply to new products of all kinds except clothing and consumables. (CC Sec. 1793.35.) Under California law (CC Secs. 1790–1795.8), they normally last for the same time period as the written warranty, but in no case longer than one year or shorter than 60 days. Under the California Commercial Code (Com. Code Secs. 2313, 2315) and the Federal Code, Magnuson-Moss Act (15 USC 2302), implied warranties may last for a longer time under some circumstances. Implied warranties apply to used products only in transactions in which a written warranty is given, and then only last for as long as the written warranty, but no shorter than 30 days or longer than 90 days.

If you believe any warranty has been breached—for example, a TV set with a six-month warranty on parts and labor breaks the day after purchase—you should notify the seller and manufacturer in writing, keeping copies of both letters. Give them a reasonable chance to make necessary repairs or replace the defective product. Thirty days to accomplish this is usually considered to be reasonable. If they fail to do so, it's time to think about filing in Small Claims Court.

In considering whether and how to pursue a breach of warranty case, realize that Small Claims Court judges evaluate warranty disputes based on their own broad view of what is fair under the circumstances. In other words, if you purchase goods that are clearly defective or do not accomplish the task the seller claimed they would accomplish (either in an advertisement or a personal statement to you), and you have made and documented a good faith effort to have the seller or manufacturer either fix or replace the goods or refund your money, your chances of winning are excellent as long as you can establish (prove) that the warranty existed in the first place. However, realize that this can sometimes be difficult when the promises were made orally and the other party will likely deny he ever made them.

Example: *Alan purchases a computer and some expensive accounting software from ABC Computer. He thoroughly explains his specialized bookkeeping needs to the salesperson and is assured that the computer and software will do the job. The computer contains a written warranty against defects in parts and labor for 90 days. The warranty statement says that all implied warranties are disclaimed. The software contains no written warranty statement. It is apparent to Alan after a couple of days' work that the software simply is not sophisticated enough to meet the bookkeeping needs he had explained to the salesperson and that the salesperson didn't know what he was talking about when he said it was "perfect for the job."*

Two days later the computer breaks. Alan calls ABC and asks for the computer to be fixed or replaced and for his money back on the software. When ABC ignores him, Alan sues in Small Claims Court. Alan should have no problem recovering for the price of the computer—it failed within the written warranty period. But the software raises a tougher problem. Here Alan is claiming a breach of an oral or "express" warranty (that he relied on the salesperson's state-ment that the software would meet his needs), as well as the implied warranty of general fitness or merchantability (to succeed on the second claim, Alan must show the software really does fall below the reasonable standard for sophisticated small business accounting packages). However, this second claim will probably be hard to prove—especially if the software is in wide use and is generally considered to be adequate to accomplish most accounting tasks. In short, Alan would be smart to focus on trying to prove that in making his decision to purchase the software he relied on the salesperson's oral statements that the software would meet his specific bookkeeping needs.

How should he do this? If Alan had given the salesperson a written specification detailing his accounting needs and still has a copy, he should show it to the judge. Even better, if he has a witness who heard the salesperson's overly optimistic promises, he should ask this person to testify in court or at least write a letter stating what happened. Unfortunately, if Alan has no convincing evidence as to the salesman's statements, the Small Claims hearing is likely to come down to his word against the salesperson's, with the judge left to decide who appears to be telling the truth.

H. How to Approach a Case When Your Rights Under California Law Have Been Breached

There are thousands of California laws designed to protect consumers. (I list a number of the most important ones in the Appendix.) Everything from the construction of home swimming pools, to regulation of retail sales, to the moving of household goods, to the types of contracts that you can be offered by a health studio are covered. These laws are far too numerous to outline here; however, you should be aware that if a provider of goods or services has violated a consumer protection law, you may be able to cancel your deal with no obligation to pay. If you think one of these laws may apply to your situation, be sure to look it up. (For information on how to do legal research, see Chapter 1, Section D.)

Californians commonly complain that they were misled by false or deceptive advertising. Fortunately, California Bus. & Prof. Code Sec. 17500, which prohibits this type of advertising, also provides that Californians may recover any money spent for goods or services advertised in this fashion.

Another common type of consumer protection law relevant in Small Claims disputes involves the imposition of a mandatory cooling-off period—usually a three- to five-day time window during which you can cancel certain types of purchase contracts. For example, the Federal Trade Commission imposes a three-day cancellation period for all door-to-door sales of more than $25 (16 C.F.R. Sec. 429.1). You must be given notice of your right to cancel and a cancellation form when you sign the purchase contract. If you don't get the form, your cancellation right extends until the seller sends it to you, even if it takes months. Very similar legal protection for door-to-door sales is also contained in California law. (CC Sec. 1689.7.)

In addition, California has adopted laws that also provide consumers with cancellation rights for a number of other types of contracts. (See table below.)

Contracts You Can Cancel Under California Laws

Code Section	Contracts You Can Cancel Under State Cancellation Laws	Time to Cancel
CC 1689.14	Home improvement work following a federal, state or local disaster	7 days
CC 1689.20	Seminar sales	3 days
CC 1694.1	Dating service	3 days
CC 1694.6	Weight loss	3 days
CC 1695.4	Houses sold immediately before foreclosure sale	5 days, or until 8 a.m. of the day of the sale, whichever is earlier
CC 1812.54	Dance lessons	180 days; must pay for lessons received
CC 1812.303	Membership camping	3 days
CC 2982.9	Motor vehicle financing from lender at a rate specified in purchase contract	number of days in contract you have to secure financing

The point is simple: if you believe that the person you have a claim against has violated a California law and that this violation is directly related to the monetary damage you have suffered, call the judge's attention to the law in question as part of your oral presentation in Small Claims Court.

Example: Steve purchased a set of cookware from a very persuasive door-to-door salesperson. That afternoon he checked at a discount store and found a very similar cookware set for half the price. Realizing that he had been talked into a bad deal, Steve wondered if he had any rights to cancel the door-to-door purchase. On the way home he stopped at a local library and looked up door-to-door sales in the index to the West California Codes. He found nothing. Being a persistent sort, Steve next looked up the word "home." Sure enough, he found an entry for "Home Solicitation Contracts," and under that a subheading for "Cancellations." He was referred to Section 1689.6 of the Civil Code. Looking up this section, Steve read, "…the buyer has the right to cancel a home solicitation contract or offer until midnight of the third business day after the day on which the buyer signs an agreement or offer to purchase…." The notes that accompanied the statute also indicated that the Federal Trade Commission requires a similar three-day cooling-off rule. Steve immediately wrote a letter canceling his contract and asking the sales company to refund his money and pick up the cookware. When it refused to do so, Steve filed an action in Small Claims Court for the full amount he paid for the cookware.

When he had his day in court, Steve showed the judge the statute and the Federal Trade Commission rule. He was promptly awarded a judgment for the amount of the purchase plus court costs.

In addition to the specific consumer protection rights embedded in literally thousands of California laws, there are several helpful legal rules you should know about. Perhaps the most important covers fraud. (CC Sec. 1572.) Generally speaking, if fraud is present as part of a transaction (contract or sale), the deal can be canceled. Fraud can take the form of intentional misrepresentation (a deliberate, false statement about a product or service), negligent misrepresentation (a statement about a product or service made without adequate information that it is true), fraudulent concealment (suppression of the truth), a false promise (a promise with no intention to perform) or any other act designed to deceive. If you think you have been defrauded, make sure the judge knows about your contention. If she agrees, the judge has the power to "rescind" (cancel) the sale or other contract or order that your money be refunded, along with any damages you have suffered as a result of the fraud.

I. Professional Malpractice

An increasing number of Small Claims cases are being filed against doctors, lawyers, accountants and other professionals. The main reason is that it can be difficult or impossible to get lawyers to represent you in a formal court action. (Lawyers accept only one in 20 medical malpractice cases, according to one study.) As a result, the injured person must decide to either file without a lawyer in formal court or scale down the dollar amount of her claim to fit into Small Claims Court.

As with all lawsuits (legal claims), to succeed with a malpractice claim, you must establish all its required legal elements as part of presenting your case. These normally consist of:

- *Duty:* The lawyer, doctor, dentist or other professional owed you a duty of care. This one is automatically taken care of as long as you were a patient or a client.

- *Carelessness:* The professional failed to use at least ordinary professional skills in carrying out the task (unless he claimed to be a specialist, in which case the standard is higher). This one can be tougher to prove, since unless the mistake is breathtakingly obvious, you'll normally need to get the opinion of one or more other professionals (experts) to the point that your professional screwed up. In theory, you can do this via a letter, but since the professional you are suing will almost surely be in court denying all wrongdoing, far better to have your expert witness testify in person.

- *Causation:* The professional's carelessness directly caused the harm or injury you suffered. For most types of malpractice, showing that the professional caused your injury isn't a problem (if a dentist stuck a drill through your cheek, for example). But in the legal field, the causation issue can be tricky. That's because you typically will need to show not only that the lawyer's mistake caused you to lose, but that you would have won if no mistake had been made. In other words, to be eligible to recover money damages, you need to convince the judge your underlying lawsuit was a winner.

- *Damages:* The harm you suffered at the hands of the professional resulted in actual economic loss to you.

Example: *You consult a lawyer about an injury you suffered when you tripped and fell at a store. The lawyer agrees to file a lawsuit on your behalf, but forgets to do so before the one-year statute of limitations runs out. Several malpractice lawyers you consult won't represent you in suing the incompetent lawyer because your injuries were fairly minor and they aren't sure that even if malpractice is established, you will be able to prove that you would have won your case against the store. (In other words, they believe you may not have been harmed by your lawyer's mistake in failing to file your case on time because your case wasn't so hot in the first place.) You sue your lawyer in Small Claims Court. His failure to file your case on time is clearly an act of carelessness (a lawyer using ordinary legal skills would have filed on time), but to win you'll also have to show that your lawyer's careless act resulted in monetary harm to you. This means convincing the judge that, in fact, your case against the store was a winner and that your injuries were serious enough to qualify for at least the amount of money you are requesting.*

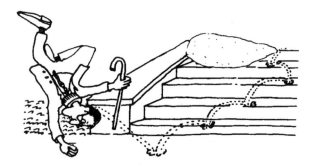

Further reading on malpractice cases:

- *Mad at Your Lawyer,* by Attorney Tanya Starnes (Nolo). Contains an extensive discussion about what is involved in suing an attorney for malpractice.

- *Represent Yourself in Court: How to Prepare and Try a Winning Case,* by Attorneys Paul Bergman and Sara J. Berman-Barrett (Nolo). Explores how to bring a malpractice case in formal court.

J. How to Prove a Nuisance Case

Sorry to use arcane terminology like "nuisance," but when you deal with legal theories (causes of action), gobbledygook usually comes with the territory. Start by understanding that a private nuisance occurs when someone prevents or disturbs your use or enjoyment of your property. For example, if your neighbor lets his dog bark all night, preventing you from sleeping, that's a private nuisance. If after asking that the dog be kept quiet, the barking persists and causes you real discomfort, you can sue.

A public nuisance, by contrast, consists of someone's act that causes a group of people (residents of a particular neighborhood, for example) to suffer a health or safety hazard or lose the peaceful enjoyment of their property—for example, lots of noisy airplanes suddenly begin flying low over a residential area, or a chemical plant lets toxic fumes drift over neighboring property. Public nuisance suits are often initiated by groups of individuals all filing Small Claims suits at more or less the same time. One fairly common example of this phenomenon involves the filing of multiple Small Claims lawsuits against drug-selling neighbors or their landlords. (See Chapter 7, Section E, for more about these so-called class actions.) If you want to know more about the law of nuisance generally, locate one of the several law student's course summaries on the field of torts. These are available at specialty law book stores and from Nolo's stores in Berkeley and San Jose, California.

Try mediation before filing a lawsuit against a neighbor. It is very difficult to put a dollar value on lawsuits against neighbors for anti-social acts, no matter how annoying. In addition, filing suit usually makes long-term relationships worse. For these reasons, I believe disputing neighbors should always try mediation before turning to Small Claims Court. (See Chapter 6 for more on mediation.)   ■

3

Can You Recover If You Win?

This is the shortest chapter in the book, but one of the most important. At bottom, it involves your asking yourself a very simple question: If I win my Small Claims case, can I collect the judgment? Unfortunately, it is easy to get so caught up in thinking about suing the bastard who did you wrong that you forget to think about how you'll collect. This is a bad mistake that can easily result in your compounding your loss by wasting valuable time obtaining a judgment against a person or business that will never pay it.

Collecting from solvent individuals or businesses isn't usually a problem, since most will routinely pay any judgments entered against them; and if they don't, there are a number of legal ways you can use to force them to do so. But unfortunately, in a small but nevertheless significant percentage of situations, people and businesses sued in Small Claims Court are either broke (lawyers say "judgment proof") or so adept at hiding their assets that collecting your winnings is likely to prove impossible. And where a deadbeat debtor won't pay voluntarily, collecting your judgment can be difficult. That's because the existence of debtor protection laws means you can't seize and sell many types of property, including the food from her table, the clothing from her closet and the TV from her living room. And in many instances it will even be impossible to seize and sell her car, since a debtor's motor vehicle(s) is protected from being sold to satisfy a debt if the amount of equity in the vehicle is $1,900 or less. And if the vehicle is used as a part of the debtor's business (is a tool of her trade), the car is exempt from being grabbed and sold as long as the equity is $5,000 or less. (CCP Secs. 704.010, 704.060.)

What should these facts mean to you? Again, that a significant percentage of Californians who are not homeless are nevertheless "judgment proof." You can sue and get judgments against these deadbeat defendants until red cows dance on a pink moon, but you won't be able to collect a dime.

It follows that a big part of deciding whether or not to file a Small Claims case should be determining in advance whether you can collect any judgment you win. The first thing you should investigate is whether the defendant has a job, since if a person fails to pay a judgment voluntarily, the easiest way to collect is to garnish up to 25% of his wages (the wages of very low income workers are exempt from garnishment—see sidebar). But you can't garnish a welfare, Social Security, unemployment, pension or disability check. So if the person sued gets her income from one of these sources, red flags should definitely be flying unless you can locate other non-exempt assets.

WAGE GARNISHMENTS IN A NUTSHELL

In California a creditor with a judgment can't take more than 25% of a judgment debtor's net earnings, or the amount by which the debtor's net earnings exceed 30 times the federal minimum wage, whichever is less. (Net earnings are total earnings less all mandatory deductions for such items as withheld income taxes and unemployment tax.)

The sheriff or marshal's office in your area can supply you with detailed rules. Strategies to cope with wage garnishment are covered in *Money Troubles: Legal Strategies to Cope With Your Debts* by Robin Leonard (Nolo).

What about other collection sources? Can't a judgment be collected from assets other than wages? Sure, real estate, bank accounts, stocks and bonds and motor vehicles are other common collection sources. And where a business is the judgment debtor, you can often collect by ordering the sheriff or marshal to take the amount of the judgment right out of the debtor's cash register. But remember, as mentioned above, many types of personal property are exempt from attachment. For example, you can't effectively get at the judgment debtor's equity in a residence unless the debtor is single and the equity exceeds $50,000 (homestead protection is $75,000 for families and $100,000 if the debtor is over 65, blind or disabled, or over 55 and earning under $15,000 ($20,000 if married)). And again, as mentioned above, most furniture, motor vehicle(s) with $1,900 or less in equity and the tools of a person's trade valued up to $5,000 ($10,000 if used by spouses in the same occupation) are exempt from being grabbed to satisfy debts. (See Chapter 24 for the details of many California debtor protection laws.)

Here are some positive indicators that you probably will be able to collect a Small Claims judgment.

•   The person or business you wish to sue is solvent and likely to voluntarily pay a court judgment.

•   The defendant has a decent-paying job or is likely to get one in the not too distant future, as might be the case with a student. (California allows a judgment to be collected for ten years from the date it is entered, and you can apply to have this period extended (see Chapter 24).)

•   You can identify other assets—not protected by California's debtor exemption laws—that you can levy on, such as a bank account or real property (preferably other than the place where the person lives).

•   If a business is involved that may not voluntarily pay its debts, you can identify a readily available cash source you can collect from—the best source is a cash register. Another good one is a valuable piece of equipment or machinery owned by the judgment debtor, which you can order sold to pay off your judgment.

•   Your lawsuit is against a contractor who has a current license. In this situation, if your judgment isn't paid, you can file it with the State of California. If the contractor doesn't pay it off or post a bond, he faces losing his license. (See Chapter 24.)

•   A person who is broke now but is very likely to be solvent in the future. Judgments can be collected for ten years (this period can usually be renewed) and accrue interest as long as they are not paid. In short, if you are willing to take a chance that a destitute college student will eventually get a job, win the lottery, inherit money, win a personal injury lawsuit or otherwise become solvent sometime in the next few years, go ahead and sue. You'll have to sit on the judgment for awhile, but eventually it should be collectible.

⚠ Beware of bankruptcy. If a person or a business declares a straight bankruptcy (under Chapter 7 of the Federal Bankruptcy Act) and lists you as a creditor, your right to recover a Small Claims Court judgment is cut off, along with most of his other debts (but if your judgment was based on a secured loan, you do have the right to recover the property pledged as security). One big exception to this general rule exists if your judgment was obtained because you or your property were injured by the malicious behavior of the defendant. In this situation, your right to collect your judgment should survive the bankruptcy (but you may need to intervene in the bankruptcy proceeding). An example of malicious behavior would be someone getting drunk and then attacking and injuring you.

Now let's look at some situations where you are likely to have a problem collecting:

- The defendant has no job or prospect of getting one.

- You can't identify any property to use as a collection source (for example, your opponent has no real estate, valuable car or investments).

- If a business is involved, it's a fly-by-night outfit with no permanent address or obvious collection source such as a cash register or owned fixtures or equipment (remember, lots of businesses lease business equipment or take out a secured loan to purchase it, which means you're out of luck).

- A contractor you want to sue is unlicensed and hard to track down.

In Chapter 24, we deal in detail with the mechanics of collecting after you get your judgment. If you still think that collection may pose a problem, please skip ahead and read this chapter.

■

4

How Much Can You Sue For?

The maximum amount for which you can sue—or be sued—in Small Claims Court is $5,000 (except guarantors such as insurance companies that write performance bonds can only be sued for $4,000). But you can only bring two cases in the same calendar year for amounts over $2,500 (unless you are a governmental entity, in which case there is no restriction). With a few exceptions, Small Claims Court does not hear cases unless they are for money damages. Thus, you can't use Small Claims Court to get a divorce, collect child support, stop ("enjoin") the city from cutting down your favorite neighborhood oak tree, change your name or do any of the thousands of other things that require a solution other than one side paying money to the other.

One exception to the "money only" rule involves equitable relief. This is legalspeak for a court's power to order a party to perform a specific act, such as return a uniquely valuable piece of property or change a contract that contains an obvious mistake. Often called by their centuries-old names, "rescission," "restitution," "reformation" and "specific performance," these remedies are discussed in Section E of this chapter.

A. Cutting Down a Claim That's Over the Limit to Fit Into Small Claims Court

It is legal to reduce an excessive claim so that it will fit into Small Claims Court. Thus, you could take a $5,600 debt and bring it into Small Claims Court, claiming only $5,000. (Costs for filing and serving papers are recoverable in addition to the dollar limit.) But if you do this, you forever waive the $600 difference between $5,000 and $5,600. In legal parlance, this is called "waiving the excess." Why might you want to do this? Because the alternative to Small Claims Court involves filing your suit in a formal court with dozens of complicated rules and the likelihood that you'll need to hire a lawyer, who will surely charge considerably more than $600 to represent you.

It is possible to represent yourself in Municipal Court (for cases up to $25,000) or Superior Court (for cases over $25,000), but doing so requires a good bit of homework and the fortitude to walk into an unfamiliar and sometimes hostile arena. Fortunately, Nolo publishes *Everybody's Guide to Municipal Court*, by Roderic Duncan, an invaluable guide to many types of routine Municipal Court cases. If you do plan to go it alone in Superior Court, by far the best book ever published on handling your own case is *Represent Yourself in Court: How to Prepare & Try a Winning Case*, by Paul Bergman and Sara Berman-Barrett (Nolo), which explains in detail how to present your case in formal court.

B. Splitting Small Claims Court Cases

It is not legal to split an over-the-limit claim into two or more pieces to fit each into Small Claims Court. Taking the $5,600 figure we used above, this means you couldn't sue the same person separately for $1,100 and $4,500. (Defendants' claims that are over the $5,000 limit are discussed in Chapters 10 and 12.) As with most rules, however, a little creative thought can sometimes point the way to an exception. Start by understanding that it's perfectly okay to bring multiple suits against the same person as long as they are based on different claims, and that there is often a large gray area in which it is genuinely difficult to differentiate between one divided claim and several independent ones. This, of course, is where the creativity comes in.

If you can reasonably argue that a $5,600 case actually involves two or more separate contracts or injuries to your person or property, you may as well try dividing it.

The worst that will happen is that a judge will disagree and tell you to make a choice between taking the entire claim to Municipal Court or waiving any claim for money in excess of $5,000 and staying in Small Claims.

Remember, though, that Small Claims Court limits you to bringing only two suits involving claims of over $2,500 during the same calendar year. So even if you decide that your present case actually involves two or more separate contracts or injuries, you still could be kept out of Small Claims Court if you have already used up your annual quota of two lawsuits for more than $2,500.

Example 1: One morning, a man in the private telephone business come into Small Claims Court with two separate lawsuits against the same defendant for a combined total of $6,100. One claim, he said, was for failure to pay for the installation of a number of new phones, and the other was for failure to pay for moving phones to a different location. The man claimed that each lawsuit was based on the breach of a separate contract. The judge, after asking a few questions, told the man that he was on the borderline between one divided (not acceptable) and two separate (acceptable) claims, but decided to give him the benefit of the doubt and allowed him to present each case. The man won both and got one judgment for $2,600 and a second for $3,500.

Example 2: Another morning a woman alleged that she had lent a business acquaintance $4,000 on two separate occasions and was therefore bringing two separate suits, each for $4,000. The defendant objected, claiming that she had borrowed $8,000 to be repaid in two installments. A different judge, after briefly listening to each side of the argument, agreed with the defendant and told the plaintiff that only one claim was involved and that if she didn't want to waive all money over $5,000, she should go to Municipal Court, which had a top dollar limit of $25,000. (Note that if the judge let the woman bring the two suits, she would consequently be prohibited from bringing another suit for more than $2,500 for one year.)

Think twice before filing separate but related claims on the same day. If you split an over-the-limit claim, you may want to file your two or more separate claims a few weeks apart, since this will result in their being heard on different days, and, in most metropolitan areas, probably by different judges. Unless the defendant shows up and argues that you have split one claim, you will likely get your judgments without difficulty. There is, however, one possible drawback to this approach. If you bring your claims to court on the same day and the judge rules they are really only one claim, he will normally give you a choice as to whether to waive the excess over $5,000 or go to a Municipal Court.

However, if you go to court on different days and the question of split claims is raised on the second or third day, you may have a problem. If the judge decides that your action in splitting the claims was improper, he may throw the second and third claims out of Small Claims Court without giving you the opportunity to refile in Municipal Court. This is because you have already sued and won, and you are not entitled to sue the same person twice for the same claim.

C. How to Compute the Exact Amount of Your Claim

Usually determining the amount to sue for is fairly easy. But for some types of cases it can be a little tricky. Before we get to the tricky part, let's start with a basic rule: When in doubt, always bring your suit a little on the high side. Why? Because the court has the power to award you less than you request, but can't give you more, even if the judge feels that you are entitled to it. But don't go overboard—if you sue for $2,500 on a $1,000 claim, you are likely to spur your opponent to furious opposition, ruin any chance for an out-of-court compromise and lose the respect of the judge.

Ask to amend your claim if you belatedly discover you should have requested more. If you find yourself in court and belatedly realize you have asked for too little, request that the judge allow you to amend your claim on the spot. Some judges will do this and, at the same time, offer the defendant extra time to prepare to defend against the higher claim. Other judges will allow you to dismiss your original case (without prejudice) and start over, which is fine as long as your time to file hasn't run out. (See Chapter 5.)

1. Computing the Exact Amount—Contract Cases

To arrive at the exact figure to sue for in contract cases, compute the difference between the amount you were supposed to receive under the contract and what you actually received. For example, if Jeannie Goodday agrees to pay Homer Brightspot $4,200 to paint her house, but then only pays him $3,000, Homer has a claim for $1,200 plus the cost of filing suit and serving Jeannie with the papers. (Court costs which can be added to your judgment are discussed in more detail in Chapter 15.) The fact that Jeannie and Homer made their agreement orally does not bar Homer from suing. As discussed in Chapter 2, Section C, oral contracts are generally legal as long as they can be carried out in a year and don't involve either the sale of real estate or of goods (personal property) worth $500 or more. (Also see Chapter 22 for a discussion of the relatively relaxed written contract requirements for the sale of goods.) Of course, since people who are embroiled in a dispute almost always remember the details of any oral contract differently, they can be hard to prove in court. This is one of several good reasons why it is always wise to reduce agreements to writing, even if only by use of an informal note or letter agreement dated and signed by both parties.

Unfortunately, some claims based on breach of contract are harder to reduce to a dollar amount. This is often due to a legal doctrine known as "mitigation of damages." Don't let the fancy term throw you. As with so much of law, the concept behind the mumbo jumbo is simple. "Mitigation of damages" means that the person bringing suit for breach of contract must, himself, take all reasonable steps to limit the amount of damages he suffers. Let's take an example from the landlord–tenant field. Tillie the tenant moves out three months before the end of her lease (remember, a lease is a contract). Her monthly rent is $950. Can Larry the landlord recover the full $2,850 ($950 x 3 months) from Tillie in Small Claims Court? Maybe not. Larry must try to limit (or mitigate) his damages by taking reasonable steps to attempt to find a new tenant. If Larry can immediately rerent the apartment to someone else for $950 or more per month, he has suffered little or no damage (he has fulfilled his responsibility to "mitigate damages"). More typically, it might take Larry several weeks or months (unless he had plenty of advance notice, or Tillie herself found a new tenant) to find a suitable new tenant. For example, if it took Larry one month and $75 worth of newspaper ads, he could recover approximately $1,025 from Tillie, assuming the judge found that Larry had taken reasonable steps to find the new tenant.

The mitigation of damages concept applies to most contracts in which the person damaged has the opportunity to take reasonable steps to limit her losses. In the earlier house painting example, if Jeannie Goodday had agreed to pay Homer Brightspot $300 per day for seven days to paint her house and then had canceled after the first day, Homer would be eligible to sue her for the remaining $1,800, based on Jeannie's breach of the contract. However, in court, Homer likely would be asked whether he had earned any other money during the six days. If he had, it would be subtracted from the $1,800. But what if Homer refused other work and slept in his hammock all week? If Jeannie could show that he had turned down other jobs, or had refused to make reasonable efforts to seek available work, the judge would likely consider this a failure to mitigate damages and reduce Homer's recovery.

a. Loan Contracts

How much should you sue for if you lent money to a person who promised to repay it but failed to do so? Bring suit for the total you are currently owed, including any unpaid interest (assuming it doesn't result in your claim exceeding the Small Claims maximum). I have seen several disappointed people sue for the exact amount of the debt (say $500) and not include interest (say $50), thinking they could have the judge add the interest when they got to court. This normally can't be done—the judge doesn't have the power to make an award larger than the amount you request.

Don't invent interest if none was provided as part of the loan. As a general rule, you can only recover interest when it is called for in a written or oral contract. For example, if you loaned a friend $1,000, but never mentioned interest, you can sue only for the return of the $1,000.

Understand special rules for installment loans. If you are owed money under the terms of a promissory note (contract) that calls for repayment to be made in installments, you are normally only entitled to recover the amount of the payments that have already been missed (that is, what you are currently owed) and not those that aren't yet due. And this is true even if you are sure future installments will never be paid. But there is an important exception to this rule: You can sue for the entire loan amount plus any interest your contract calls for if your installment contract contains what lawyers call an "acceleration clause"—language which states that the entire amount of the loan is immediately due if one payment is missed.

b. Extra Damages for Bad Checks

There are several major exceptions to the information on how to compute the amount of your contract claim set out just above. These involve situations where a statute (law) establishes your right to receive extra damages, over and above the amount of the financial loss. The most common of these involves a bad check (or a check on which the writer stops payment in bad faith) where the person giving it to you does not make it good within 30 days of your written demand mailed via certified mail to do so. Civil Code Sec. 1719 states that you are entitled to either recover the amount of your bad check plus a service charge (up to $25 for one bad check and $35 for subsequent ones from the same person) or if you make a written demand for payment (mailed by certified mail) and the person who wrote the bad check doesn't make it good (plus the amount of your service charge) within 30 days from the date your demand was mailed, you can sue for the amount of the bad check, minus any partial payments, plus damages of three times the check amount, but not less than $100 or more than $1,500. Because this is a little tricky, let's review the rules using an outline format.

Small bad checks: In addition to the amount of the check (less any partial payments), you can sue for $100 in damages, no matter how small the bad check. Thus, if you get a $25 bad check, you can sue for $125.

Medium-sized bad checks: For bad checks between $34 and $500, you can sue for the amount of the check plus damages of three times that amount. Thus if you receive a $300 bad check, you can sue for the amount of the check plus $900 in damages, or a total of $1,200.

Big bad checks: In addition to the amount of the check, you can only sue for $1,500 in damages—no matter how large the check. Thus, for a $700 bad check, you can sue for $700 plus the $1,500 damage maximum, or a total of $2,200.

In addition, if the defendant has stopped payment on a check, you must be prepared to show "by clear and convincing evidence" that there is no good faith dispute about whether you are owed the money. For example, if a person stops payment on the check because he has a good faith belief that he didn't *owe the money*—either because he didn't get what he was supposed to pay for, or because what he got was somehow faulty, or because he was overcharged—then you can't collect damages, even if it turns out that you are owed the money.

Don't forget to demand payment before you sue. If someone gives you a bum check or stops payment on a check and you want to try and collect damages first, send her a letter by certified mail demanding payment of the amount of your bad check plus any applicable service charge, plus your mailing costs. Wait at least 30 days before filing suit, thereby giving the maker time to pay.

Example: BC Enterprises receives three bad checks—one for $20, one for $200 and one for $600. In each instance, BC makes a written demand for payment of the amount of the check plus a $25 service charge plus the cost of certified mail to the person writing the bad check, and sends it certified mail. After the requests for payment are ignored for 30 days, BC sues in Small Claims Court. For the first check, BC asks for $120 (the amount of the check plus $100). For the second, it asks for the amount of the check plus damages of three times the amount of the check, or $800. For the third check it asks for the $1,500 maximum damage amount plus the amount of the check, or a total of $2,100.

 Further Reading:
- *Money Troubles: Legal Strategies to Cope with Your Debts,* by Robin Leonard (Nolo). Contains the details of every state's bad check law.

 Defendants should document the existence of a good faith dispute. If you write a check and then stop payment because you believe the service or goods you purchased were substandard (or never provided), write a letter to the other party stating in detail why you were dissatisfied. If you are later sued in Small Claims Court, bring your letter to court and show it to the judge as part of your defense.

Here is a sample letter:

NOTICE

To: _____(name of check writer)_____

_____(your name)_____ is the payee of a check you wrote for
$ ____(amount)____. The check was not paid either because there were
insufficient funds in your account or because you stopped payment. If you do
not have a good faith dispute with (your name) and fail to pay (your name) the
full amount of the check in cash and the amount of (your name)'s bad check fee
of $_____ within 30 days after this notice was mailed, you could be sued and
held responsible to pay $ (enter amount of check plus damages) as well as the
cost of mailing this notice.

If the court determines that you do have a good faith dispute with (your name),
you will not have to pay the damages and mailing cost mentioned above. If you
stopped payment because you have a good faith dispute with (your name), you
should try to work out your dispute with (your name). You can contact me at:

_____(your name)_____
_____(street address)_____
_____(telephone number)_____

---

2. Computing the Exact Amount—Property Damage Cases

When your property has been damaged by the negligent or intentional act of someone
else, you usually have a right to recover the amount of money it would take to fix the
damaged item.

Example: *John Quickstop plows into Melissa Caretaker's new Dodge, smashing the left rear fender. How much can Melissa recover? Melissa is entitled to recover the amount it would cost to fix, or if necessary, replace, the damaged part of her car if John won't pay voluntarily. Melissa should get several estimates from responsible body and fender shops and sue for the amount of the lowest one. (See Chapter 19.)*

There is, however, a big exception to this rule. This occurs when the cost to fix the item exceeds its market value. You are not entitled to a new or better object—only to have your loss made good. Had Melissa Caretaker been driving a ten-year-old Dodge, the cost to fix the fender might well have exceeded the value of the car. In this situation, she would be entitled to the value of the Dodge, not what it would cost to repair it. In short, the most you can recover is the fair market value of a damaged item (the amount you could have sold it for) figured one minute before the damage occurred. From this amount, you have to subtract the item's scrap value, if any.

Give yourself the benefit of the doubt when putting a value on property. No one knows exactly how much any piece of used property is worth. Recognizing that reasonable minds can differ, it makes sense to place a fairly aggressive value on property that has been destroyed. But don't demand a ridiculous amount, or you'll likely offend the judge and perhaps even weaken your case.

Example: *Let's return to Melissa from our last example. If several used car price guides indicated her old Dodge was worth $1,800 and the fender would cost $2,000 to repair, she would be limited to an $1,800 recovery, less what the car could be sold for in its damaged state. If this was $100 for scrap, she would be entitled to $1,700. However, if Melissa had installed an expensive rebuilt engine a few weeks before the accident, she might legitimately argue that the car was worth $2,800. Assuming the judge agreed, Melissa would legally be entitled to recover the entire $2,000 to replace the fender.*

Unfortunately, knowing what something is worth and proving it are quite different. A car that you are sure is worth $4,000 may look like it's only worth $3,000 to someone else. In court, you will want to be prepared to show that your piece of property is worth every bit of the $4,000. The best way to do this is to get some estimates (opinions) from experts in the field (a used car dealer if your car was totaled). One way to present this type of evidence is to have the expert come to court and testify, but in Small Claims Court it can also be efficiently accomplished by having the expert prepare a written estimate, which you then present to the judge. Depending on the type of property involved, you may also want to check newspaper and flea market ads for the prices asked for comparable goods and submit these to the judge. And of course, there may be other creative ways to establish the dollar amount of the damage you have suffered. We talk more about proving your case in court in Chapters 16–21.

3.   Computing the Exact Amount—Cases Involving Damage to Clothing

Clothing is property, so why do I treat it separately? Two reasons: First, disputes involving clothing are extremely common in Small Claims Court. More important, judges seem to apply a logic to them that they apply to no other property damage cases. The reason for this is that clothing is personal to its owner and often has little or no value to anyone else, even though it may be in good condition. It follows that if a judge strictly applied the rules we just learned (that you are limited to recovering no more than the current market value of a damaged item), plaintiffs would often achieve little or no recovery. Recognizing this, most judges are willing to bend the rules a little. This involves arriving at a value for damaged clothing based on the item's original cost and how long it had been worn.

When suing for damage to new or almost-new clothing, it follows that you should sue for the amount you paid. If the damaged item has already been worn for some time, sue for the percentage of its original cost that reflects how much of its useful life was used up when the damage occurred. For example, if your two-year-old suit that cost $900 new was destroyed, sue for $450 if you feel the suit would have lasted another two years.

To summarize, in clothing cases, most judges want answers to these questions:
*   How much did the clothing cost originally?
*   How much of its useful life was consumed at the time the damage occurred?
*   Does the damaged item still have some value to the owner, or has it been ruined?

Example 1: *Wendy took her new $250 coat to Rudolph, a tailor, to have alterations made. Rudolph cut part of the back of the coat in the wrong place and ruined it. How much should Wendy sue for? $250—as the coat was almost new. She could probably expect to recover close to this amount.*

Example 2: *The same facts as just above, but the coat was two years old and had been well worn, although it was still in good condition. Here Wendy would be wise to sue for $175 and hope to recover between $100 and $150.*

Example 3: *This time let's return Wendy's coat to its almost new condition, but have Rudolph only slightly deface the back. I would still advise Wendy to sue for the full $250. Whether she could recover that much would depend on the judge. Most would probably award her a little less on the theory that the coat retained some value. Were I Wendy, however, I would strongly argue that I didn't buy the coat with the expectation I could only wear it in a closet and that, as far as I was concerned, the coat was ruined.*

4. Computing the Exact Amount—Personal Injury Cases

Lawyers quickly take over the great majority of cases where someone is injured. These claims are routinely inflated (a painfully sprained neck might be worth $15,000–$25,000 or more), at least in part because it is in many people's selfish interest to place a high value on injuries. Perhaps surprisingly, the adjusters and lawyers who work for insurance companies can sometimes be as much a part of this "something-for-nothing" syndrome as are the plaintiff's attorneys, who customarily receive a hefty percentage of the total recovery. This makes sense if you consider that if there weren't lots of claims, lots of lawsuits and lots of depositions and negotiations, insurance companies would have little reason to keep so many adjusters and lawyers on their payrolls.

Try to settle or mediate your personal injury claims. If you are seriously injured, you'll almost always want to sue for more than the Small Claims maximum. But to gain a fair recovery, you may not need to sue at all. Many people successfully negotiate or mediate a satisfactory settlement with an insurance company. For information on how to do this without being skinned, see *How to Win Your Personal Injury Claim*, by Joseph Matthews (Nolo).

Despite the potential drawbacks, some small personal injury cases do end up in Small Claims Court. Dog bite cases are one common example. To determine how much to sue for, add up the dollar amount of the following losses:

- Out-of-pocket medical costs, including medical care providers   _____

- Loss of pay, or vacation time, for missing work   _____

- Pain and suffering   _____

- Damage to property   _____

TOTAL _____

Now let's look at each of these categories in a little more detail.

Medical/Hospital bills. The amount of your medical and hospital bills, including transportation to and from the doctor, is routinely recoverable as long as you have established that the person you are suing is at fault. However, if you are covered by health insurance and the insurance company has already paid your medical costs, you will find that your policy says that any money you recover for these costs must be turned over to the company. Often, insurance companies don't make much effort to keep track of, or recover, Small Claims Court judgments as the amounts of money involved don't make it worthwhile. Knowing this, many judges are reluctant to grant judgments for medical bills unless the individual can show he is personally out of pocket for the money.

Loss of pay. Loss of pay or vacation time as a result of an injury is viewed in a similar way. Assume the cocker spaniel down the block lies in wait for you behind a hedge and grabs a piece of your derriere for breakfast, and as a result you miss a day of work getting yourself patched up. You are entitled to recover any lost pay, commissions or vacation time. However, if your job offers unlimited paid sick time, so that you suffer no loss for missing work, you have nothing to recover.

Pain and suffering. The third area of recovery is for what is euphemistically called "pain and suffering." When you read about big dollar settlements, a good chunk of the recovery almost always falls into this category. No question, recovering from some injuries really is a painful, miserable ordeal for which compensation is reasonable. But it is also true that in the hands of an aggressive lawyer, "pain and suffering" often becomes an excuse for an inflated or occasionally even a fraudulent claim. For example, a lawyer might ask a jury, "How much is every single minute that my poor client hobbled around on her unbearably painful ankle worth—$1, $5, $10,000?" Again, I don't suggest that recovery for "pain and suffering" is always wrong—just that it is often abused.

Suppose now that you have suffered a minor, but painful, injury and you do want to attempt to recover compensation for your discomfort in Small Claims Court. How much should you ask for? There is no one right answer. When valuing a client's pain and suffering, a lawyer will typically sue for three to five times the amount of the out-of-pocket damages (medical bills and loss of work). Therefore, if you were out of pocket $500, you might wish to ask for $1,500, the overage being for "pain and suffering." However, to get this, you'll have to convince the judge that you have suffered real pain and inconvenience. The best way to do this is to present bills for medical treatment. If the judge concludes you suffered a real injury, she will be more likely to add an amount for "pain and suffering." This is why lawyers routinely encourage their clients to get as much medical attention as is reasonably possible.

Example 1: Mary Tendertummy is drinking a bottle of pop when a mouse foot floats to the surface. She is immediately nauseated, loses her lunch and goes to the doctor for medication. As a result, she incurs a medical bill of $150 and loses an afternoon's pay of an additional $150. She sues the soda pop company for $900, claiming that the extra amount is to compensate her for pain and suffering. This may well be considered to be reasonable and, depending on the judge, she will probably recover most of this amount.

Example 2: The same thing happens to Roy Toughguy. But instead of losing his lunch, he just tosses the soda pop away in disgust and goes back to work. A few weeks later he hears about Mary's recovery and decides to sue—after all, he could use $900. How much is Roy likely to recover? Probably not much more than the price of the soda pop—since he didn't see a doctor, the judge is likely to conclude he suffered little or no injury.

Don't forget to include your property damage. Often a personal injury is accompanied by injury to property. Thus, a dog bite might also ruin your pants. If so, include the value of your damaged clothing when you determine how much to sue for. For information on how to place a dollar value on your property, see Section C2, above.

Small Claims is rarely the right court in which to sue for punitive damage. Even though it is legally possible to recover punitive damages based on the defendant's bad conduct in Small Claims Court, the court's $5,000 limit largely rules them out. However, there are several common exceptions to this rule. One is California's bad check law, under which a person who gets stuck with a dud check may be entitled to modest punitive damages over and above the face amount of the check (see Section C1, above). In addition, punitive damages can be awarded when a landlord fails to either return a tenant's security deposit on time or give a good reason why not (see Chapter 20). But in most situations, if you believe you have been injured by conduct wretched enough to support a claim for hefty punitive damages, see a lawyer.

5. Computing the Exact Amount—Emotional or Mental Distress

As noted in Chapter 2, in our increasingly crowded urban environment, there are all sorts of ways we can cause one another real pain without even making physical contact. For example, if I live in the apartment above you and pound on my floor (your ceiling) for an hour at 6:00 a.m. every day, I will probably quickly reduce you to the status of a raving maniac. What can you do about it besides slashing my tires? One remedy is for you to sue me in Small Claims Court based on the fact that my actions constitute the intentional infliction of emotional distress. But how much should you sue for? Unfortunately, it's impossible to provide a formula. It depends on how obnoxious my behavior is, how long it has gone on, how clearly you have asked me to cease it (this should be done several times in writing). And if this isn't vague enough, it will also depend greatly on the personality of the judge, who may be very skeptical of all neighbor disputes, thinking they don't belong in court in the first place. At the very least, you'll need to convince the judge you are an extremely reasonable person and your neighbor is a true boor, before you will be eligible for any recovery.

One way to help try to convince the judge you aren't a hypersensitive complainer is to sue for a reasonable amount. Thus, I would normally advise against suing for $5,000, or anything close to it, unless the other person's behavior clearly makes her out to be first cousin to Attila the Hun.

Prefer mediation when neighbors are involved. As discussed in Chapter 6, the process of filing, preparing and arguing a lawsuit tends to make both sides even madder than they were previously. And, of course, the losing side is likely to stay mad for a long, long time. This may be fine if you are suing a large company, or someone you are never likely to interact with again, but given a neighbor's ability to make you miserable in the future, it's usually best to at least try to settle your case through mediation before going to court.

D. Computing an Exact Amount—Malpractice Cases

In theory, most malpractice cases are worth far more than can be sued for in Small Claims Court. But because legal rules (what it takes to prove liability, for example) are usually tilted to favor professionals and these cases are expensive to bring, it's often hard to find a lawyer to represent you on a contingency fee (the lawyer doesn't charge you upfront but takes a percentage of the settlement), so quite a few end up being scaled down to fit into Small Claims Court.

For most types of malpractice you simply need to prove that the dollar value of harm caused you is at least equal to the amount you have sued for (usually the Small Claims maximum). Thus, if a doctor negligently misdiagnosed an illness and as a result you experienced serious medical problems, you would present the court with

- all medical, hospital and drug bills you paid that occurred after the misdiagnosis which you claim could have been avoided;

- the opinion of a second doctor that the first doctor's handling of your problem did not measure up to accepted medical standards (or, in plain language, that the first doctor screwed up);

- an estimate for your pain and suffering; and

- loss of any pay or vacation time.

Special rules for legal malpractice: As discussed in Chapter 2, Section I, if your suit is based on a lawyer's having failed to handle your case properly, you have to be able to prove not only that the lawyer was a bungler but that you would likely have won a recovery in your original case if the lawyer had done a reasonably competent job. And you must also show that your recovery would have been for at least as much as you are suing for in Small Claims Court.

E. Equitable Relief (or Money Can't Always Solve the Problem)

California allows judges to grant relief (provided you ask for it) in ways that do not involve the payment of money, if equity (fairness) demands it. In California Small Claims Court, "equitable relief" is limited to one or more of four categories: "rescission," "restitution," "reformation" and "specific performance." (CCP Sec. 116.610.) Let's translate these into English.

Rescission: This is a remedy that is used to wipe out a grossly unfair or fraudulent contract under any of the following conditions:

- it was based on a mistake as to an important fact, or

- it was induced by duress or undue influence, or

- one party simply didn't receive what was promised, through the fault of the other.

Example: If a merchant sued you for failure to pay for aluminum siding you contended had been seriously misrepresented, you could ask that the contract be rescinded, and any money you paid be returned to you. (CC Secs. 1689(b)(1)–1689(b)(7).) Don't hesitate to ask for this remedy whenever you feel you have been unfairly treated in a contract dispute.

Restitution: This is an important remedy. It gives a judge the power to order that a particular piece of property be transferred to its original owner when fairness requires the contracting parties be restored to their original positions. It can be used in the common situation in which one person sells another a piece of property (say a motor scooter) and the other fails to pay. Instead of simply giving the seller a money judgment that might be hard to collect, the judge has the power to order the scooter restored to its original owner. Where money has been paid under a contract that is rescinded, the judge can order it to be returned, plus damages. Thus, if a used car purchase was rescinded based on the fraud of the seller, the buyer could get a judgment for the amount paid for the car, plus money spent for repairs and alternate transportation.

Reformation: This remedy is somewhat unusual. It has to do with changing (reforming) a contract to meet the original intent of the parties in a situation where some term or condition agreed to by the parties has been left out or misstated and where fairness dictates the contract be reformed. Reformation is commonly used when an oral agreement is written down incorrectly.

Example: Arthur the Author and Peter the Publisher orally agree that Peter will publish Arthur's 200-page book. They then write a contract, inadvertently leaving out the number of pages. If Arthur showed up with a 3,000-page manuscript and demanded that it be published in its entirety, a court would very likely "reform" the contract to include the 200-page provision, assuming the judge was convinced that it should have been included in the first place.

Specific Performance: This is an important remedy that comes into play where a contract involving an unusual or "one-of-a-kind" object has not been carried out. Say you agree to buy a unique antique jade ring for your mother's birthday that is exactly like the one she lost years before, and then the seller refuses to go through with the deal. A court could cite the doctrine of "specific performance" to order that the ring be turned over to you. "Specific performance" will only be ordered in situations where the payment of money will not adequately compensate the person bringing suit.

A very confusing aspect of California's equitable relief provision is that, in theory, you don't ask for it on your plaintiff's claim form. This is true, although the judge has the power to grant equitable relief when you ask for money damages. Obviously, however, you are not likely to get relief you don't ask for. So, if you want one of the equitable remedies set out above, sue for your monetary loss and ask for equitable relief in court as soon as possible. If your request is greeted with disbelief, refer the judge to Section 116.610 of the Code of Civil Procedure and state that you simply want to request what the judge has the power to grant.

The Small Claims dollar maximum applies to cases involving equitable relief. In filling out your court papers for a case in which you want one of the types of equitable relief discussed here, you are still required to indicate that the value of the item in question is under the Small Claims maximum. Thus, you might describe the nature of your claim (Chapter 10, Section B, Step 1) as follows: "I want the delivery of my 'one-of-a-kind' antique jade ring, worth approximately $4,000, according to my contract with defendant."

Conditional judgments and equitable relief. In California judges have the power to issue conditional judgments in cases involving equitable relief. That is, they can order a party to perform, or stop, a certain act or else pay a money judgment. For example, you agree to sell your baby grand piano for $1,000. The buyer fails to pay, and you sue. The judge orders the buyer to either return the piano or fork over the $1,000. If this doesn't occur within a short period, the money judgment may be enforced. (See Chapter 24.)

■

5

Is the Suit Brought Within the Proper Time Limits (Statute of Limitations)?

The legislature sets up time limits within which lawsuits must be filed. These are called statutes of limitations. Time limits are different for different types of cases. If you wait too long, your right to sue will be barred by these statutes. Why have a statute of limitations? Because it has been found that disputes are best settled relatively soon after they develop. Unlike wine, lawsuits don't improve with age. Memories fade, witnesses die or move away and once-clear details tend to become blurred. In California, with one big exception, you have at least one year from the date of the event that gave rise to your lawsuit in which to file suit. The exception to this rule is for personal injury and property damage suits against public entities, such as cities, counties and school districts, where a claim must be filed within six months (see Section A, below).

Defendants usually don't need to worry about whether a case was filed on time. Most disputes brought to Small Claims Court are brought fairly promptly, so the question of whether the person suing has waited too long usually doesn't come up. However, if your case is one of the rare ones in which more than a year or two has gone by before you are sued, you will want to check out the relevant statute of limitations period.

A. California Statute of Limitations Periods

Here are the statute of limitations periods most likely to affect you. This is not an exhaustive list. You will find the limitation periods for more obscure types of legal actions in CCP Secs. 312–363.

Personal Injury: One year from the injury, or, if the injury is not immediately discovered, one year from the date it is discovered. (CCP Sec 340.) But if your claim is for sexual harassment on the job, you must first file a claim with the federal or California Equal Employment Opportunity Commission and have it rejected.

Oral Contracts: Two years from the day the contract is broken. (CCP Sec. 339.)

Written Contracts: Four years from the day the contract is broken. (CCP Sec. 337.)

Fortunately, some contracts which you may at first assume are oral may actually be written. People often forget that they signed papers when they first arranged for goods or services. For example, your charge accounts, telephone service and insurance policies, as well as most major purchases of goods and services, involve a written contract, even though you haven't signed any papers for years. And another thing—to have a written contract you need not have signed a document full of "whereases" and "therefores." Any signed writing in which you promise to do something (for example, pay money, provide services) in exchange for someone else's promise to provide you something in return is a written contract, even if it's scrawled on toilet paper with lipstick. When you go to a car repair shop and they make out a work order and you sign it—that's a contract. (See Chapter 2, Section C, for more about the law of contracts.)

Damage to Personal or Real Property: Three years from the date the damage occurs. Except the statute of limitations is ten years for lawsuits stemming from property damage that results from latent defects in the planning, construction or improvement of real property. (CCP Sec. 337.15.)

Fraud: Three years from the date of the discovery of the fraud. (CCP Sec. 338.)

Professional Negligence Against Health Care Providers: Three years after the date of the injury or one year from its discovery by plaintiff—or the time that plaintiff should have discovered it through reasonable diligence—whichever comes first.

Suits Against Public Agencies: As noted on line 2 of the Plaintiff's Claim, before you can sue a city, county or the state government, you must file an administrative claim form. The time period in which this must be done is six months for cases involving a personal injury and/or damage to personal property, and one year for claims for breach of contract and damage to real property. (Govt. Code Sec. 911.2.) If the government entity rejects your claim, you have an additional six months in which to file suit. (Govt. Code Sec. 945.6.) If the government entity does not act on your claim, you have two years from when you first had the right to sue to file your case in Small Claims Court. (Govt. Code Sec. 945.6.) These time limits are not technically statutes of limitations, but have a similar effect. (See Chapter 8 for a more complete discussion of how to sue governments in Small Claims Court.)

B. Computing the Statute of Limitations

Okay, now let's assume you have found out what the relevant limitations period is. How do you know what date to start your counting from? That's easy. Start with the day the injury to your person or property occurred, or, if a contract is involved, start with the day that the failure to perform under the terms of the contract occurred. Where a contract to pay in installments is involved, start with the day each payment was missed. (See sidebar, "Tricky Rules for Installment Contracts.")

TRICKY RULES FOR INSTALLMENT CONTRACTS

When an installment contract is involved, the statute of limitations (four years on a written contract) normally applies separately to each installment. To understand how this works, assume you agree in writing to pay $5,000 in five installments commencing January 1, 1998, and continuing on January 1 of each succeeding year through 2002. It follows that if you do not make the first payment the creditor can sue (based on your nonpayment of that installment) until January 1, 2002. Or looked at from your point of view, if the creditor fails to sue you by that date, you can claim that any subsequent lawsuit has been filed too late (in legalese, you would say the lawsuit is "barred" by the statute of limitations). But since your second payment isn't due until January 1, 1999, your creditor's lawsuit for this installment will not be barred by the statute of limitations until January 2, 2003, and so on.

1. Voluntary Payment After Statute Has Run Out

I am frequently asked to explain the legal implications of the following situation: After the statute of limitations runs out (say two years on an oral contract to pay for having a fence painted), the debtor commences voluntarily to make payments. Does the voluntary payment have the effect of creating a new two-year statute of limitations period, allowing the person who is owed the money to sue if the debtor again stops paying? No. Simply starting to pay on an obligation barred by the statute of limitations doesn't create a new period for suit. (CCP Sec. 360.) All the creditor can do is to keep his toes crossed and hope that the debtor's belated streak of honesty continues. However, if the debtor signs a written agreement promising to make the payments, this does reinstate the contract and create a new statute of limitations period. In legal slang, this is called "reaffirming the debt."

Example: Doolittle borrows $1,000 from Crabapple in 1993 under the terms of a written promissory note. The next month he loses his job and never pays back a penny. In 1998, Doolittle experiences a burst of energy, gets a job and resolves to pay off all of his old debts. He sends Crabapple $50. A week later, suffering terrible strain from getting up before noon, Doolittle quits his job and reverts to his old ways of waking up a few minutes before race time. Is the four-year statute of limitations allowing Crabapple to sue reinstated by Doolittle's payment? No. As we learned above, once the four-year limitation period for written contracts runs out, it can't be revived by simply making a payment. However, if after Doolittle sent Crabapple the $50 Crabapple coaxed him into signing an agreement saying that he would pay the remainder of the debt, Crabapple would again be able to sue and get a judgment if Doolittle failed to pay. Why? Because a written promise to pay a debt barred by the statute of limitations has the legal effect of re-establishing the debt.

⚠ Debtors—Beware of waiving statutes of limitations. If a creditor and debtor discuss an unpaid bill and the debtor asks the creditor to give her more time to pay, to lower payments or to make some other accommodation, the creditor, assuming he is willing to agree, will almost always require that the debtor waive the statute of limitations in writing. This means that if the debtor fails to pay, she must wait another four years before the creditor is prevented from successfully suing. The statute of limitations on a written contract is four years. CCP Sec. 360.5 allows the statute to be waived for an additional four-year period by written agreement.

2. Suspending the Statute of Limitations

In a few situations, the statute of limitations is suspended for a period of time (lawyers say "tolled"). This occurs if the person sued is in prison, living out of the state, insane or a minor. If the statute of limitations is suspended (tolled) by one of these events, it means that it simply isn't counted until the event is over, at which point it starts up again. (See CCP Secs. 351, 352.)

Example: Jack borrows money from Tim under a written contract. Jack fails to pay the money back on the day required. Six months later, Jack is sentenced to a year in jail. The four-year statute of limitations would be tolled (suspended) during this period and Tim would still have three-and-one-half years after Jack gets out of jail to collect.

Example: Ed, age 12, stars in a TV series. An accountant for the show tells Ed's family that he hasn't been paid all moneys due under his contract. Neither Ed nor his family do anything about it. Eight years later, trying to figure out how to pay for college, Ed wonders if he can still sue the TV production company. The answer is yes. Ed's time to sue is measured from his 18th birthday (that is, the statute of limitations period would be suspended or tolled while he was a minor). And since California has a four-year statute of limitation for disputes based on written contracts, this means that Ed could file suit at least until his 22nd birthday.

C. Defendant Should Tell the Judge If the Statute of Limitations Has Run Out

What should a defendant do if he believes that the statute of limitations period on the plaintiff's lawsuit has run out? Tell the judge. Sometimes a judge will figure this out without a reminder, but often she won't. If you are a defendant, don't ever assume that because the clerk has filed the papers and you have been properly served, this means that the plaintiff has started her suit on time. Clerks rarely get involved in statute of limitations questions. They will most probably file a suit brought on by a breach of contract occurring in 1917. ■

6

How to Settle Your Dispute

Litigation should be a last, not a first, resort. In addition to being time-consuming and emotionally draining, lawsuits—even the Small Claims variety—tend to polarize disagreements into win-all or lose-all propositions where face (and pocketbook) saving compromise is difficult. It's not difficult to understand how this occurs. Most of us, after all, are terrified of making fools of ourselves in front of strangers. When forced to defend our actions in a public forum, we tend rather regularly to adopt a self-righteous view of our own conduct, and to attribute the vilest of motives to our opponents. Many of us are willing to admit that we have been a bit of a fool in private—especially if the other person does too—but in public, we tend to stonewall, even when it would be to our advantage to appear a little more fallible.

Although I am a strong advocate of resolving disputes in Small Claims Court, I have nevertheless witnessed many otherwise sensible people litigate cases that never should have been filed in the first place. In some instances, the amount of money was too small to bother with. In others, the problem should have been talked out over the back fence. And there were some situations in which the practical importance of maintaining civil personal or business relationships between the parties made it silly to go to court over a few hundred or even thousands of dollars.

Let me make this last point in a slightly different way: It is almost always wise to first look for a non-court solution when the other party is someone you'll have to deal with in the future. Typically, this would include a neighbor, a former friend or a relative. Similarly, a small business owner will almost always benefit by working out a compromise settlement with another established local business, long-term customer or client. For example, an orthodontist who depends on referrals for most new customers should think twice before suing a patient who has refused to pay a bill in a situation where the patient is genuinely upset (whether rightly or wrongly) about the services she has received. Even if the orthodontist wins in court, he is likely to turn the former patient into a vocal enemy—one who may literally badmouth him from one end of town to the other and in the end cost him a lot more than he won in court.

A. Try to Talk Your Dispute Out

It is rarely a waste of time to try to negotiate a compromise with the other party. Indeed, you are all but required to make the attempt. The law in California states that, "where possible, a demand for payment must be made" prior to filing a court action. (CCP Sec. 116.320(b)(3).) Indeed, the importance of making a "demand" is underlined by the fact that you are asked on line 3 of the Plaintiff's Claim if a demand has been made, and if not, why. Most judges prefer that your "demand" be in writing.

But first things first. Before you reach for pen and paper, try to talk to the person with whom you are having the dispute. The wisdom of trying to talk out a dispute may seem obvious. But apparently it isn't, since I am frequently consulted by someone with an "insurmountable dispute" who has never once tried to calmly discuss it with the other party. I suspect the reason for this is that many of us have a strong psychological barrier to contacting people we are mad at, especially if we have already exchanged heated words. If you fall into this category, perhaps it will be easier to pick up the phone if you remind yourself that a willingness to compromise is not a sign of weakness. After all, it was Winston Churchill, one of the twentieth century's greatest warriors, who said, "I would rather jaw, jaw, jaw than war, war, war."

A compromise offer is not binding. It's important to know that an offer of compromise— whether made orally or in writing—does not legally bind the person making it to sue for that amount if the compromise is not accepted. Thus, you can make an oral or written demand for $2,000, then offer to compromise for $1,500, and, if your compromise offer is turned down, still sue for $2,000. If the person you are suing tries to tell the judge you offered to settle for less, the judge will not consider this to be relevant in making her decision.

In an effort to help you arrive at a good compromise, here are a few of my personal negotiation rules, which, of course, I modify to fit the circumstances:

- If you are the potential plaintiff, start by offering to settle for about 20% less than your original written demand. Why 20%? If you offer a smaller discount, chances are you won't be taken seriously. Offer a bigger discount and you're giving away too much too soon.

- If you are the potential defendant and conclude that the plaintiff probably does have a decent case, start by offering to pay about 50% of the amount demanded. This should be enough to start negotiations without conceding too much too soon. Many plaintiffs will ultimately agree to knock as much as one-third off their original demand to save the time and trouble of going to court.

- Money isn't always at the root of the problem. If you pay close attention to the other party's concerns, you may find that the key to arriving at an agreement can be found elsewhere. For example, a print shop owner who refuses to repay you $2,000 for a screwed-up job might agree to do the disputed job over and give you a discount on the next one in exchange for an agreement to continue to work together and speak well of each other in the future.

- The patient negotiator has the edge. Many Americans are in such a big hurry to arrive at a solution that they agree to a bad one. Take your time. If you make a low ball offer and the other person gets mad and hangs up, you can always wait a few days and call back with a slightly sweetened one.

- Good negotiators rarely change their position quickly, even if the other side does. Instead, they raise or lower their offer in very small increments. For example, if your opponent counters your original offer of a 20% reduction in exchange for a settlement by offering to pay 50% of what you originally asked for, you'll do best by not jumping to accept or even agreeing to split the difference. Instead, counter by reducing your original demand by an additional 5%-10%. Often this will result in your opponent further improving her offer. And even if she doesn't, you haven't lost anything, since once she has made the 50% offer, she is unlikely to withdraw it.

Why it's rarely wise to split the difference. Often, an inexperienced negotiator will quickly agree to the other party's offer to split the difference between their positions. It's rarely wise to do this. After all, by proposing to split the difference your opponent has all but conceded she'll pay that amount. Better to counter by reducing your first offer by a smaller amount and leave the next move up to your opponent.

- Estimate how much money a compromise settlement is worth to you, given the fact that a settlement eliminates the time and aggravation of going to court. I do this by putting a dollar value on my time and then multiplying by the number of hours I estimate a court fight will take. Also, based on the facts of your case, take into consideration the chances that you might lose, or get less than you ask for. In a recent study of 996 Small Claims cases that actually went to trial, only 32% resulted in the plaintiff receiving 100% of the amount claimed; 22% resulted in the plaintiff getting between 50% and 100% of the amount claimed; 20% resulted in the plaintiff getting less than half; and in 26% of the cases, the plaintiff got nothing at all. ("Small Claims and Traffic Courts," by John Goerdt (National Center for State Courts).)

Example: In a recent dispute my business, Nolo, had with a phone company, Nolo originally asked for $5,000. The phone company admitted some liability and offered to compromise. After considering the value of the time and energy Nolo would invest bringing the dispute to court, we decided that it would make sense to compromise for $3,500. And although we were sure we had a strong case, we had to admit that there was some possibility the judge would not agree, so we decided to subtract another $500 and accept a settlement for $3,000. Unfortunately, after several conversations and letters, the phone company wouldn't offer a dime more than $2,000. Since this was too low, we decided to go to court. As it happened, the Small Claims judge awarded us the entire $5,000. But then the phone company appealed and received a new trial. After the case was presented over again, the second judge reduced our final award to $3,500. Considering that it was easier to prepare the case the second time, we still probably came out ahead of the game, as compared to accepting the $2,000, but in truth, given the time needed to prepare for two court presentations, we probably netted only about $500 more.

To learn more about negotiating: On several occasions when I have been involved in important negotiations I've gotten help by rereading *Getting to Yes: Negotiating Agreements Without Giving In*, by Roger Fisher and William Ury (Penguin). I also like *Getting Past No: Negotiating Your Way From Confrontation to Cooperation*, by William Ury (Bantam).

If you settle, sign a written agreement pronto. If you talk things out with your opponent, write down your agreement as soon as possible. Oral settlement agreements, especially between people who have small confidence in one another, are often not worth the breath used to express them. And writing down an agreement gives each party a chance to see if they really have arrived at a complete understanding. Often one or more details still must be hashed out. (In Section D of this chapter, I show you how to reduce a compromise agreement to writing.)

B. Mediate Your Dispute

Mediation, a procedure in which the disputants meet with a neutral third party who helps them arrive at their own solution, is available in most areas of California. (It is required in Yolo County before a case can be heard in Small Claims Court.) Depending on your location, trained mediators may be standing by at the Small Claims courthouse or, if not, can usually be found at a local community mediation service. Either way, mediation is voluntary (both parties must agree to participate) and available at no or very low cost.

A mediation session, which will typically last anywhere from 30 minutes to three hours, consists of you and all other parties to a dispute sitting down with a mediator whose role is to help you arrive at your own solution. Unlike a judge, a mediator has no power to impose a judgment, with the result that mediation sessions tend to be much more relaxed than a court proceeding.

Many people who find themselves in the middle of a dispute ask why they should waste time mediating with an opponent who they believe is unreasonable. My best answer is that, when the parties to a Small Claims Court case voluntarily agree to mediate, the overwhelming majority of disputes are settled. And even in courts where everyone is forced to mediate as a mandatory precondition to going to court, about 50%

of cases settle. Settlement is especially likely when, deep down, one or both parties realize they have an interest in arriving at a solution at least minimally acceptable to the other party. As noted above, this is particularly common in disputes between neighbors or small business people who live or work in the same geographical area and really don't want the dispute to fester.

It is also of interest that studies have shown that people who agreed to have their cases mediated were more likely to be satisfied with the outcome of the case than litigants who went to trial. Not surprisingly, one reason for this is that people who arrive at a mediated settlement are more likely to pay up than are people who have a judgment imposed on them after losing a contested trial.

Is mediation always a good idea? No. If you are determined to get the total amount you are asking for, and you will have no ongoing relationship with the other party (for example, your dispute is with a large corporation or government agency), bypassing mediation (except in Yolo County, where it is required) and going directly to court makes more sense.

Example: John rented an apartment from Frontier Arms, Inc. When he moved out and left the unit undamaged and spotless, the Frontier Arms manager made up a bogus reason to avoid refunding his deposit. John decided that proposing mediation was a waste of time, since he was pretty sure a judge would enter a judgment for his entire $1,500, plus $600 punitive damages, provided by California law when a landlord retains a tenant's deposit without a good reason. (See Chapter 20.)

Assuming you do want to mediate, how can you get a reluctant opponent to the table in most California counties, where mediation isn't mandatory? Often you can get help from your local court-sponsored or community mediation program. Typically, as soon as you notify the agency that you have a dispute and would like to try mediation (notification is often automatic with a court-sponsored program), an employee or volunteer with the mediation program will contact the other party or parties and try to arrange a mediation session.

Defendant's Note: Suppose now that you are a defendant in a Small Claims case or have received a letter threatening suit. Should you ask for mediation? The answer is almost always a resounding yes, assuming you have a defense to all or part of the plaintiff's claim or believe that, while the plaintiff may have a decent case, he is asking for too much. Mediation will give you a great opportunity to present your side of the dispute and, hopefully, with the help of the mediator, arrive at an acceptable compromise. It can also allow you to bring up other issues that may be poisoning your relationship with the plaintiff, which would not be considered relevant in court.

Learn to be a good mediator. People who are well prepared to engage in mediation are likely to achieve far better results than those who take a more casual approach. The best source of information on how to mediate successfully is *How to Mediate Your Dispute: Find a Solution Quickly and Cheaply Outside the Courtroom*, by Peter Lovenheim (Nolo). I can almost guarantee that if you read it before you mediate, you will achieve better results than would otherwise have been possible.

C. Write a Formal "Demand" Letter

If your efforts to talk your problems out fail (or despite my urging you refuse to try) and you decide not to propose or agree to mediation, your next step is to send your adversary a letter. As noted above, many courts all but require that a written "demand" be made. But even where this isn't required, there are two reasons why doing so makes sense. First, in as many as one-third of all disputes, your "demand" letter will serve as a catalyst to arriving at a settlement. Second, even if no settlement results, setting out your case in a formal letter affords you an excellent opportunity to lay your case before the judge in a carefully organized way. Or, put another way, it allows you to "manufacture" evidence that you will likely be permitted to use in court if your case isn't settled.

You can be sued without first being sent a formal letter stating that a lawsuit is imminent. Some people believe they can't be sued until they receive a formal letter asking for payment and saying that a lawsuit will be filed if it isn't forthcoming. This is not necessarily true. A simple past due notice form from a creditor, which states that if the account isn't paid promptly, court action will be pursued, is usually found to meet the California requirement that a formal demand for payment be made.

A personal note is in order here. In the 20 years since I wrote the first edition of *Everybody's Guide to Small Claims Court*, readers have sent in hundreds of Small Claims success stories. One thing has consistently delighted me: Many self-proclaimed winners never had to file their Small Claims case in the first place. These readers took my advice and wrote the other party a clear, concise letter demanding payment. As a result of either the letter itself or conversations it engendered, they received all, or at least a significant part, of what they asked for.

That a simple letter can be so effective may at first seem paradoxical, especially if you have already unsuccessfully argued with your adversary in person or over the phone. To understand why the written word can be so much more effective, think about the times you have found yourself embroiled in a heated consumer dispute. After angry words were exchanged—maybe even including your threat of a lawsuit—what happened next? The answer is often "nothing." For all sorts of reasons, from a death in the family, to the chance to take a cool vacation, to simply not having enough time, you didn't follow up on your "I'll sue you" threat. And, of course, you aren't the only one who occasionally hasn't made good on a declaration of intent to file a lawsuit. In fact, so many people who verbally threaten to sue don't actually do it that many potential defendants don't take such threats seriously.

But things often change if you write a letter, laying out the reasons why the other party owes you money and stating that if you fail to get satisfaction, you plan to go to Small Claims Court. Now, instead of being just another cranky face on the other side of the counter or a voice on the phone, you and your dispute assume a slap-in-the-face realness.

Really for the first time, the other party must confront the likelihood that you won't simply go away, but plan to have your day in court. And they must face the fact that they will have to expend time and energy to publicly defend their position, and that you may win. In short, assuming your position has at least some merit, the chances that the other party will be willing to pay at least a portion of what you ask go way up when you make your case in writing.

1. How to Compose Your Letter

When writing your demand letter, here are some pointers to keep in mind:

1. Use a typewriter or computer.

2. Start by concisely reviewing the main facts of the dispute. At first it may seem a bit odd to outline these details; after all, your opponent knows the story. But remember—if you end up in court, the letter will be read by a judge, and you want her to understand what happened.

3. Be polite. Absolutely avoid personally attacking your adversary (even one who deserves it). The more annoying you are, the more you invite the other side to respond

in a similarly angry vein. This is obviously counterproductive to your goal of getting your opponent to make a business-like analysis of the dispute and ask herself such questions as:

- What are my risks of losing?
- How much time will a defense take?
- Do I want the dispute to be decided in public?

4. Ask for exactly what you want. For example, if you want $2,000, don't beat around the bush—ask for it (or possibly a little more to allow a little negotiating room). And be sure to set a deadline. One week (two weeks at the outside) is usually best; anything longer and your opponent has less motivation to deal with you right away.

5. Conclude by stating you will promptly file in Small Claims Court if your demand is not met.

6. Keep a copy of all correspondence in your file or folder.

2. A Real Small Claims Case

Now let's consider a real Small Claims case. The facts (with a little editorial license) were simple: Jennifer moved into Peter's house in August, agreeing to pay $550 per month rent. The house had four bedrooms, each occupied by one person. The kitchen and other common areas were shared. Things went well enough until one chilly evening in October when Jennifer turned on the heat. Peter was right behind her to turn it off, explaining that heat inflamed his allergies.

As the days passed and fall deepened, heat became more and more of an issue, until one cold, late November night when Jennifer returned home from her waitress job to find her room "about the same temperature as the inside of an icicle." After a short cry, she started packing and moved out the next morning. She refused to pay Peter any additional rent, claiming that she was within her rights to terminate her month-to-month tenancy without giving notice because the house was uninhabitable. It took Peter one month to find a suitable tenant and to have that person move in. Therefore, he lost rent in the amount of $550.

After calling Jennifer several times and asking her to make good the $550 only to have her slam down the phone in disgust, Peter wrote her the following letter:

61 Spring St.
Los Angeles, Calif.
January 1, 19__

Jennifer Tenant
111 Sacramento St.
Palos Verdes, California

Dear Jennifer:

You are a real idiot. Actually, you're worse than that: you're malicious—walking out on me before Christmas and leaving me with no tenant when you know that I needed the money to pay my child support. You know that I promised to get you an electric room heater. Don't think I don't know that the real reason you moved out was to live with your boyfriend.

Please send me the $550 I lost because it took me a month to re-rent the place. If you don't, I will sue you.

In aggravation,

Peter Landperson

To which Jennifer replied:

111 Sacramento St.
Palos Verdes, Calif.
January 4, 19__

Peter Landperson
61 Spring St.
Los Angeles, California

Dear Mr. Landperson:

You nearly froze me to death, you cheap bastard. I am surprised it only took a month to rent that iceberg of a room—you must have found a rich polar bear (ha ha). People like you should be locked up.

I hope you choke on an ice cube.

Jennifer Tenant

As you have no doubt guessed, both Peter and Jennifer made the same mistake. Instead of being business-like, each deliberately set out to annoy the other, reducing any possible chance of compromise. In addition, they each assumed that they were writing only to the other, forgetting that the judge would be privy to their sentiments. Thus, both lost a valuable chance to present the judge with a coherent summary of the facts as they saw them. As evidence in a subsequent court proceeding, both letters were worthless.

Now let's interrupt these proceedings and give Peter and Jennifer another chance to write sensible letters.

61 Spring St.
Los Angeles, Calif.
January 1, 19___

Jennifer Tenant
111 Sacramento St.
Palos Verdes, California

Dear Jennifer:

As you will recall, you moved into my house at 61 Spring St., Los Angeles, California, on August 1, 19___, agreeing to pay me $550 per month rent on the first of each month. On November 29, you suddenly moved out, having given me no advance notice whatsoever.

I realize that you were unhappy that the house was a little on the cool side, but I don't believe that this was a serious problem, as the temperature was at all times over 60 degrees and I had agreed to get you an electric heater for your room by December.

I was unable to get a tenant to replace you (although I tried every way I could and asked you for help) until January 1, 19___. This means that I am short $550 rent for the room you occupied. If necessary, I will take this dispute to court because, as you know, I am on a very tight budget. I hope that this isn't necessary and that we can arrive at a sensible compromise.

I am also willing to try to mediate this dispute using the local community mediation service, if you agree. I have tried to call you with no success. Perhaps you can give me a call in the next week to talk this over.

Sincerely,

Peter Landperson

To which our now enlightened Jennifer promptly replied:

January 4, 19___
111 Sacramento St.
Palos Verdes, Calif.

Peter Landperson
61 Spring St.
Los Angeles, California

Dear Peter:

I just received your letter concerning the rent at 61 Spring St. and am sorry to say that I don't agree either with the facts as you have presented them, or with your demand for back rent.

When I moved in August 1, 19___, you never told me that you had an allergy and that there would be a problem keeping the house at a normal temperature. I would not have moved in had you informed me of this.

From early October, when we had the first cool evenings, all through November (almost two months), I asked that you provide heat. You didn't. Finally, it became unbearable to return from work in the middle of the night to a cold house, which was often below 60 degrees. It is true that I moved out suddenly, but I felt that I was within my rights under California law, which states that a tenant need not pay rent for an uninhabitable space (see Moskovitz and Warner).

Since you mentioned the non-existent electric heater in your letter, let me respond to that. You first promised to get the heater over a month before I moved out and never did. Also, as I pointed out to you on several occasions, the heater was not a complete solution to the problem, as it would have heated only my room and not the kitchen, living room, dining areas. You repeatedly told me that it would be impossible to heat these areas.

Peter, I sincerely regret the fact that you feel wronged, but I believe that I have been very fair with you. I am sure that you would have been able to re-rent the room promptly if the house had been warm. Since I don't believe that any compromise is possible, mediation does not make sense. If you wish to go to court, I'll be there with several witnesses who will support my position.

Sincerely,

Jennifer Tenant

As you can see, while the second two letters are less fun to read, they are far more informative. In this instance, the goal of reaching an acceptable compromise or agreeing to mediation was not met, but both have prepared a good outline of their positions for the judge. Of course, in court, both Peter and Jennifer will testify, present witnesses and possibly other evidence that will tell much the same story as is set out in the letters. However, court proceedings are often rushed and confused and it's nice to have a written statement for the judge to fall back on. Be sure the judge is given a copy of your demand letter when your case is presented. The judge won't be able to guess that you have it; you will have to let her know and hand it to the clerk. (For more about how to conduct yourself in court, see Chapters 13–15.)

3. Sample Demand Letters

Below are letters a consumer might write to an auto repair shop after being victimized by a shoddy repair job and a contractor who botched a remodeling contract.

June 16, 199x
Tucker's Fix-It-Quick Garage
9938 Main St.
Fresno, CA

Dear Mr. Tucker,

On May 21, 199x, I took my car to your garage for servicing. Shortly after picking it up the next day, the engine caught fire because of your failure to properly connect the fuel line to the fuel injector. Fortunately, I was able to douse the fire without injury.

As a direct result of the engine fire, I paid the ABC garage $1,281 for necessary repair work. I enclose a copy of their invoice.

In addition, I was without the use of my car for three days and had to rent a car to get to work. I enclose a copy of an invoice showing the rental cost of $145.

In a recent phone conversation you claimed that the fire wasn't the result of your negligence and would have happened anyway. And even if it was your fault, I should have brought my car back to your garage so you could have fixed it at a lower cost.

As to the first issue, Peter Klein of the ABC Garage is prepared to testify in court that the fire occurred because the fuel line was not properly connected to the fuel injector, the exact part of the car you were working on.

Second, I had no obligation to return the car to you for further repair. I had the damage you caused repaired at a commercially reasonable price and am prepared to prove this by presenting several higher estimates by other garages.

Please send me a check or money order for $1,426 on or before July 15. If I don't receive payment by that date, I'll promptly file this case in Small Claims Court.

You may reach me during the day at 555-2857 or in the evenings until 10 p.m. at 555-8967.

Sincerely,

Marsha Rizzoli

June 20, 199x
Beyond Repair Construction
10 Delaney Avenue
Menlo Park, CA

Dear Sirs:

You recently did replacement tile work and other remodeling on my downstairs bathroom at 142 West Pine St., here in Menlo Park. As per our written agreement, I paid you $4,175 upon completion of the job on May 17, 199x.

Only two weeks later, on June 1, I noticed that the tile in the north portion of the shower had sunk almost half an inch, with the result that our shower floor was uneven and water pooled in the downhill corner before eventually going down the drain.

In our telephone conversations, you variously claimed that the problem:

- was in my imagination
- was my fault, because the floor was uneven to begin with
- was too minor to bother with.

Sorry, but I paid for a first-class remodeling job and I expect to receive it. Please contact me within 10 days to arrange to pay me $1,200 (the cost of redoing the work per the enclosed invoice from ABC Tile) or to arrange to redo the work yourself. If I don't hear from you by June 15, I will promptly file in Small Claims Court.

Sincerely,

Ben Price

D. Write Down the Terms of Any Settlement

If you and the other party agree to a settlement, either on your own or with the help of a mediator, it's important to promptly write it down. When a mediator is involved, preparing a written agreement is usually the last step in the mediation process. If you and your opponent negotiate your own settlement, you'll need to cooperate to reduce it to writing. Lawyers call a contract settling a dispute a "release," because in exchange for some act (often the payment of money), one person gives up or releases her claim against another. For instance, if the paint on John's building is damaged when Joan, a neighboring property owner, spray paints her building on a windy day, John might agree to release Joan from liability (that is, not sue Joan) if Joan agrees to pay $2,000 to have the damaged area of John's building repainted.

As long as a written release is signed by both parties, is fair—in the sense that neither party was tricked into signing on the basis of a misrepresentation—and provides each party with some benefit (if you pay me $500, I won't sue you and I'll keep my dog out of your yard), it is a valid contract. If either party later violates it, the other can file a lawsuit and receive a court judgment for appropriate damages.

It's important to understand that releases are powerful legal documents. If you completely release someone who damaged your car for $500, only to later find out that the damage was more extensive, you'll be stuck with the $500 unless you can convincingly claim the other party was guilty of misrepresentation or fraud. Of course, in most situations, where the details of a dispute are all well known, a release can be comfortably signed with the knowledge that the dispute will finally be laid to rest.

Assuming a Small Claims case has actually been filed, you may have a choice as to whether your agreement is presented to a judge and made part of a court order or is simply written as a binding contract between you and the other party. Especially if it's less trouble (sometimes getting a court order involves an extra trip to court), you may be tempted to accept a contract. Generally, I recommend against this unless you are sure the other party really will honor their agreement. A court order (judgment) is far easier to enforce than a contract. Especially if you suspect that the other side may not do what they promise, it is definitely worth a little extra effort to have your settlement contract incorporated into a judgment of a court. (However, this obviously won't be possible if the dispute is settled before a Small Claims lawsuit is even filed.).

Below we provide a sample release adopted from Nolo's book, *101 Law Forms for Personal Use*, by Attorney Robin Leonard and Marcia Stewart. That book contains a number of more specialized releases adapted to auto accidents, property damage and personal injuries that I don't have space to reprint here. It also contains mutual release forms for use when both parties are giving up claims. In addition, release forms are often available from office supply stores that carry legal documents and in lawyers' form books, available at law libraries.

No matter where you get your release, it should contain the following information:

1. The names and addresses of the party being released and the party granting the release.

2. A brief description of the "what," "when" and "where" of the dispute or issue to which the release pertains. (The release below provides several blank lines for you to briefly describe the events giving rise to the need for the release.)

3. A statement of what the person giving up a claim is getting in return. As mentioned, for a release to be a valid contract (which it must be to be enforceable), the person signing the release (releasor) must receive something of benefit (called "consideration" by lawyers) in exchange for her agreement to give up her right to sue. The release below provides a space for this "consideration" to be described. Typically, it is money. If so, simply enter the amount. If it is an agreement by the releasee to perform or not perform some act (for example, stop his dog from barking at night), describe the act.

4. A statement that the release applies to all claims arising from the dispute or issue, both those known at the time the release is signed and those that may come along later. This provision is very common in releases; without it they wouldn't be worth much.

5. A statement that the release binds all persons who might otherwise have a legal right to file a claim on behalf of the releasor (for example, the releasor's spouse or heirs).

Although I have included this provision in my releases for caution's sake, it is rare that it will ever prove relevant. In fact, such persons are usually bound by the release anyway.

6. The date the release is signed.

7. The signatures of the parties. Legally, only the person granting a release needs to sign it, but we think it is better practice for both parties to do so—after all, this important document contains statements that affect both their rights. In the case of mutual releases, which occur when both parties give up a claim against the other, both must sign.

8. The release below contains a place for the signatures of witnesses. There is no legal requirement for a release to be witnessed, but if you don't trust the other person and think he may later claim "it's not my signature," a witness can be a good idea. If a release involves a lot of money or a potentially large claim, you may want to bolster the chances of its being upheld (should it ever be challenged later) by signing it in front of a witness or two who can later testify, if the issue arises, that the other party was under no duress and appeared to know what he was doing. If your release involves a small claim, it is not necessary to do this. To encourage you to have your release witnessed where appropriate, I have included two lines on each release for witnesses to sign. If you decide to dispense with witnesses, put "N.A." on each of the lines.

GENERAL RELEASE

1. _____(person signing release)_____, Releasor, voluntarily and knowingly executes this release with the express intention of eliminating Releasee's liabilities and obligations as described below.

2. Releasor hereby releases _____(person being released)_____, Releasee, from all claims, known or unknown that have arisen or may arise from the following occurrence: (description of events giving rise to release, including location and date if appropriate—see box for sample language) _____ .

Sample Language:

> a. "Repair work incompletely done to Releasor's boat at the Fixemup ship-yards on 5/6/87."
>
> b. "Agreement by Releasee made during the week of June 6, 19_ to deliver the fully laid out and pasted-up manuscript for the book Do Your Own Brain Surgery to Releasor's address no later than July 6, 19_, which Releasee failed to keep."
>
> c. " A tree growing on Releasee's property at 1011 Oak St. fell into Releasor's backyard at 1013 Oak St. on August 7, 19_. It damaged Releasor's fence, which had to be replaced. The tree itself had to be removed by ABC Tree Terminators."

3. In exchange for granting this release Releasor has received the following consideration: ___(amount of money, or description of something else of value which person signing release received from other party—see box for sample language) ___ .

Sample Language:

> a. "$150 cash."
>
> b. "a used RCA television set."
>
> c. "an agreement by (Releasee's name) to desist from further activities as described in Clause 3 of this release."
>
> d. "an agreement by (Releasee's name) to repair Releasor's Apple Macintosh computer by January, 19_."

GENERAL RELEASE (continued)

4. In executing this release Releasor additionally intends to bind his or her spouse, heirs, legal representatives, assigns and anyone else claiming under him or her. Releasor has not assigned any claim covered by this release to any other party. Releasor also intends that this release apply to the heirs, personal representatives, assigns, insurers and successors of Releasee as well as to the Releasee.

This release was executed on _____, 199_, at _____(city and state)____

_____
Releasor's Signature

_____
Address

_____

_____
Releasor's Spouse's Signature

Witnesses:

_____
Name

_____
Name

_____
Releasee's Signature

_____
Address

E. Agreement Just Before Court

Occasionally, disputes are settled while you are waiting for your case to be heard. Even on court day, it is proper to ask the other person if he or she wishes to step into the hall for a moment to talk the matter over. If you can agree on a last-minute compromise, wait until your case is called by name by the courtroom clerk and then tell the judge the amount you have agreed upon and whether the amount is to be paid all at once, or over time. Typically, the judge will order that the case be dismissed if one person pays the other the agreed-upon amount on the spot, or, if payment is to be made later, she will enter a judgment for the amount that you have agreed on.

Another possibility is that you and your opponent will agree to a last-minute attempt to mediate. If so, you will want to explain this to the judge, who in turn will normally delay ("continue," in legalese) your case until the mediation session takes place. If mediation works and your case settles, you and the other party should jointly notify the court clerk. Again, unless the agreed amount is immediately paid, the debtor will normally want to return to court and have the settlement amount made part of an official court order (judgment). ■

7

Who Can Sue?

Who can sue in Small Claims Court? The answer is easy. You can—as long as you are 18 years of age (or an emancipated minor), have not been declared mentally incompetent in a judicial proceeding and are suing on your own claim.

Depending on whether you are an individual or business, here is how to list yourself on court papers:

Individuals: If you are the only person suing, simply list your full name where it says "Plaintiff" on the "Plaintiff's Statement" and sign the "declaration under penalty of perjury" on the "Claim of Plaintiff" form. (See sample forms in Chapter 10.)

Married couples: If both people are suing, list both names. Only one person need sign the "declaration under penalty of perjury" stating that all the information given is true and correct. (See Chapter 10.) It is okay for one spouse to appear for both as long as the claim is joint, the represented spouse has given consent and the court determines the interests of justice would be served.

Individually owned businesses and sole proprietorships: The owner must file a claim on behalf of an individually owned business. (However, you may be able to send someone else to court. See Section F, below.) List your name and the business name as plaintiff on the "Plaintiff's Statement," such as, "Jane Poe doing business as ABC Printing." The "declaration under penalty of perjury" should also be signed in your name (see Chapter 10). If the business uses a fictitious name (such as Tasty Donut Shop), you must file a declaration (available from the Small Claims clerk) stating that you have properly executed, filed and published a fictitious business name statement as required by Bus. & Prof. Code Sec. 17913. If this declaration is not filed with the Small Claims clerk, your case will be dismissed.

WHAT IF YOU WANT TO SUE, BUT CAN'T APPEAR IN COURT

People who are out of state or otherwise can't physically show up in Small Claims Court to present their case sometimes ask if there is another way to proceed. For people in certain categories—prisoners, business owners, landlords, certain military personnel stationed outside California—the answer is clearly yes (see the rest of this chapter for the specifics).

But even if you don't fit into an approved category, a Small Claims judge may agree to hear your case if you send a witness to court who is familiar with what happened and present the rest of your case in writing (by declaration). To see if this procedure will work in your area, talk to your county's Small Claims court advisor.

Partnerships: If you are filing a claim on behalf of a partnership, list the partnership name as plaintiff. Only one of the partners need sign the "declaration under penalty of perjury" (see Chapter 10). If your partnership uses a fictitious name, list it along with the partners' real names. (For example, "ABC Printing, a partnership, and Jane Poe and Phil Roe individually.") If your partnership uses a fictitious name—as opposed to the partners' real names—you must file a declaration stating that you have properly executed, filed and published a fictitious business name statement as required by Bus. & Prof. Code Sec. 17913. If this statement has not been filed, your case will be dismissed.

Corporations: If you are filing a claim on behalf of a corporation, whether profit or nonprofit, list the corporation as plaintiff. The "declaration under penalty of perjury" must be signed by either:

a. an officer of the corporation, or

b. a person authorized to file claims on behalf of the corporation by the corporation's Board of Directors who is not employed for the sole purpose of representing the corporation in Small Claims Court. In this instance, the person must state under penalty of perjury that she is properly authorized to represent the corporation.

Limited liability companies: List the limited liability company as plaintiff. The declaration under penalty of perjury may be signed by an officer of the limited liability company.

Unincorporated associations: If you are filing on behalf of an unincorporated association, do so by listing the name of the association and the name of an officer who will appear in court (such as, "ABC Canine Happiness Society, by Philip Pup, President").

Motor vehicle claims: When a claim arises out of damage to a motor vehicle, the registered owner(s) of the vehicle must file in Small Claims Court. So, if you are driving someone else's car and get hit by a third party, you can't sue for damage done to the car. The registered owner must do the suing.

Public entities: If you are suing on behalf of a public entity such as a public library, city tax assessor's office or county hospital, list your organization's official name (City of Fruitdale Public Library) and be prepared to show the court clerk proper authorization to sue.

⚠ Remember, you can file only two cases per calendar year over $2,500. If you are suing for an amount over $2,500, you must indicate on your Plaintiff's Claim that you haven't previously filed more than two Small Claims Court suits for more than this amount in the current calendar year (unless you are acting on behalf of a public agency, in which case you can file as many cases as you wish up to $5,000).

⚠ Additional pre-suit requirements for some occupations: In certain situations, to qualify to sue in Small Claims Court, other legal requirements must be met. For example, contractors, car repair dealers, structural pest control operators and TV repair people must be registered with or licensed by the relevant state agency as a condition of using Small Claims Court. Additionally, to be eligible to bring suit car repair outfits must give their customers a written estimate of costs. If you are being sued by someone who you feel may not meet one of these (or a similar) occupational requirements, tell the judge of your concern.

A. Participation by Attorneys

Attorneys, or other people acting as representatives, including bill collectors, cannot normally appear in Small Claims Court. This means you can't hire a lawyer or collection agency to go to Small Claims Court on your behalf. However, there are several exceptions to the "no lawyers or bill collectors in Small Claims Court" rule. The major one allows attorneys to appear to sue or defend their own claims. Attorneys can also testify, as witnesses, to what they've seen, such as a car accident or a properly cleaned apartment, but they cannot appear as experts to talk about the law. Attorneys are also allowed to use Small Claims Court to sue or defend on behalf of a partnership when all other partners are also attorneys, and on behalf of a professional corporation of which the attorney is an officer or director and all other officers and directors are attorneys. (CCP Sec. 116.530.)

Sometimes it's wise to get the advice of a lawyer before going to Small Claims Court. Consulting a private lawyer is normally not necessary to sensibly handle a Small Claims case. After all, free advice is available from your county's Small Claims advisor. (See Chapter 13.) However, in more complicated situations it may occasionally make sense to arrange for additional expert coaching. Hiring a lawyer to advise—but not represent you in the Small Claims courtroom—is legal. Make sure you work out a fee agreement in advance.

B. Suits by Prisoners

Before a prisoner can bring suit in Small Claims Court based on a claim against the correctional system, the prisoner must exhaust all administrative remedies established within the prison system (including compliance with Sections 905.2 and 905.4 of the Government Code). One way to show that this has been done is to attach the final administrative determination of the prisoner's claim to the Small Claims complaint (CCP Sec. 116.220(e)).

A prisoner is not required to personally appear in court. Instead, he may use the mail to file suit and submit written statements (declarations) under penalty of perjury to serve as evidence supporting his claim. In addition, he may (but doesn't have to) authorize another individual to appear in court as long as this person has not been paid and has not appeared in Small Claims Court for others more than four times during the calendar year. (CCP Sec. 116.540(f).)

C. Suits by Minors

If you are a minor (in other words, you have not yet reached your 18th birthday), your parent or legal guardian must sue for you, unless you are emancipated under Sections 60-70 of the California Civil Code. For a minor to sue, a form must be filled out and signed by the judge appointing a parent or legal guardian as the minor's "Guardian Ad Litem." This translates as "guardian for the purposes of the lawsuit." Ask the court clerk for a "Petition for Appointment of Guardian Ad Litem" form. It must be signed by both minor and guardian. When you have filled it out, take it to the Small Claims Court clerk and arrange to have the judge add his signature at the bottom, under "ORDER."

D. Special Rules for Military Personnel Transferred Out of State

A member of the U.S. military on active duty who is assigned to a duty station outside of California after her claim has occurred (except when the out-of-state assignment is for less than six months) can file in Small Claims Court by mail. Evidence can then be submitted in the form of a written declaration or by having another person appear in Small Claims Court on her behalf. This person would also have to fill out a declaration at the hearing to show that he is not a lawyer, not receiving compensation to appear on behalf of the absent plaintiff and that he has not presented more than four other similar claims in the past 12 months. (CCP Sec. 116.540(e).) This code section was adopted primarily to deal with the problem of members of the military who move out of state without being refunded their security deposits on rental housing.

E. Class Actions (Group Lawsuits)

In Small Claims Court there is no such thing as a true class action lawsuit, where a number of people in a similar situation ask a court's permission to join together in one lawsuit. However, as many community and advocacy groups have discovered, if a large number of people with a particular grievance (pollution, noise, drug sales) sue the same defendant at the same time in Small Claims Courts, something remarkably like a class action is created. This technique was pioneered in the early 1980s by a group of determined homeowners who lived near the San Francisco Airport. Several times the group won over 100 Small Claims Court judgments against the City of San Francisco based on excessive noise. They hired expert witnesses, did research, ran training workshops and paid for legal advice when needed as part of a coordinated effort to be sure they knew how to efficiently present their cases. The City of San Francisco tried to fend off these cases by arguing that the homeowners were, in effect, involved in a class action lawsuit and such suits are not permitted in Small Claims Court. A California Court of Appeals disagreed, saying that, "Numerous 'mass' actions against the City alleging that noise from the City airport constituted a continuing nuisance were neither too 'complex' nor had such 'broad social policy import' that they were outside the jurisdiction of Small Claims Court…." (*City and County of San Francisco v. Small Claims Div., San Mateo Co.* 190 Cal. Rptr. 340 (1983).)

A similar strategy has been widely used in a number of California cities to shut down drug houses. Neighbors organize to sue landlords who rent to drug-selling tenants, claiming the legal theory of nuisance (use of property so as to interfere with the rights of others (see Ch. 2, Section J). In these cases the nuisance claimed was the emotional and mental distress that accompanied living near a drug house. Typically, each neighbor sues for $5,000. Thus, 30 neighbors who coordinate their Small Claims filings can, together, bring what amounts to a $150,000 case. A number of drug house cases have resulted in large judgments, with the result that problems which had dragged on for months or years were quickly cleaned up.

Successful lawsuits based on legal nuisance have also been brought against polluting refineries and factories.

Losing defendants have the right to a new trial on appeal. People who sue and beat corporations, governmental entities and other defendants with deep pockets in Small Claims Court are likely to be faced with a tougher battle on appeal. That's because all losing Small Claims defendants have the right to appeal to Superior Court, where they have the right to be represented by a lawyer.

F. Business Owners Do Not Always Have to Personally Go to Court

There used to be a legal requirement that the owner of an individually owned small business personally show up in Small Claims Court. For example, the owner of an unincorporated shop who wished to sue on an overdue bill would have to be in court on the day the case was heard. Fortunately, California is now more understanding of business owners' time pressures. Today, if an unincorporated business wishes to sue on an unpaid bill, it can send an employee to court to testify about the debt if:

- the debt is reflected in the written records of the business,

- there is no other issue of fact (aside from the defendant's failure to pay the bill) present in the case, and

- the employee appearing in court is a regular employee of the business familiar with the company's books and able to testify about how this specific debt was recorded in them.

In addition (under Section 116.540 of the Code of Civil Procedure and Section 1271 of the Evidence Code) the business record evidencing the debt must have been made:

- in the normal course of business (that is, contained in the business's regular records);
- at or near the same time as the debt arose; and
- under conditions that indicate its reliability as evidence.

Note that this method is only allowed when the fact that the money is owed is cut and dried. If there is likely to be any dispute about how the debt arose or the amount at issue, the business owner must be present and, as a practical matter, should bring any employee with firsthand knowledge of the dispute. For example, if a TV repair business brings suit to collect an unpaid bill and sends a bookkeeper who knows nothing about what goes on in the repair shop to court, the suit will probably be lost if the defendant shows up and says the TV was not fixed properly. In this situation, some judges may postpone (continue) the case for a few days to allow the business owner to show up and present testimony about the quality of the repair, but don't count on it.

G. Special Rules for Owners of Rental Property

Under the terms of CCP Sec. 116.540(h), a person who owns apartments, houses or other rental real property can send a manager or other property agent to Small Claims Court on his behalf if these requirements are met:

1) The manager really does manage the property and is not just hired to go to Small Claims Court.

2) The manager has a contract to manage the property.

3) The claim relates to the rental property.   ■

Who Can Be Sued?

You can sue just about any defendant—person, partnership, corporation, LLC, government entity—in a California Small Claims Court, as long as they live or do business in California. And you can even sue out-of-staters in this state if the dispute stems from business they do here, property they own here or an accident on a California highway.

No suits against the federal government in California courts. To sue the United States Government, you must file in federal, not state, court. Contact the nearest Federal District Court clerk's office for information.

A. How to Sue an Individual

If you are suing an individual, simply name him or her, using the most complete name that you know for that person. If the person calls himself J.R. Smith and you don't know what the J.R. stands for, simply sue him as J.R. Smith. However, if with a little effort you can find out that J stands for James, it's better to sue him as James R. Smith.

What to do if a person uses several names. Lots of people use two or more names. Thus Jason Graboskawitz may also use J. T. Grab. When in doubt, list the name the person uses most often for business purposes first, followed by the words "also known as" (or "a.k.a.") and any other names. Thus you might sue Jason Graboskawitz, a.k.a. Jason Grab.

B. How to Sue Two or More People

If you are suing more than one person on a claim arising from the same incident or contract, list the names of all defendants. Then you must serve each of them. (See Chapter 11.) Listing both names is also required when your suit is against a husband and wife.

Example: J.R. and June Smith, who are married, borrow $1,200 from you to start an avocado pit polishing business. Unfortunately, in the middle of the polishing, the seeds begin to sprout. J.R. and June get so furious that they refuse to repay you. If you wish to sue them and get a judgment, you should list them as James R. Smith and June Smith—not Mr. and Mrs. Smith. But now suppose that J.R. borrowed $1,200 for the avocado pit business in January, June borrowed $1,000 to fix her motorcycle a month later and neither loan was repaid. In this situation, you would sue each in separate Small Claims actions.

Two defendants are better than one and three are better than two. If two or more people are responsible for your loss (three tenants damaged your apartment), sue them all. This will enable you to get judgments against several people. You'll be glad you did when you try to collect—if one defendant turns out to be an artful dodger, you can go after the others.

C. How to Sue an Individually Owned Business

Here you list the name of the owner and the name of the business (Ralph C. Jones—doing business as [d.b.a.] Jones's Texaco). But never just assume that the name of the business is really the same as the name of the owner. For all you know, Jim's Garage may be owned by Pablo Garcia Motors, Inc. (See Section E, "How to Sue a Corporation or Limited Liability Company (LLC)," below.) If you get a judgment against Jim's Garage and there is no Jim, it will be worthless unless you take steps to have the judgment changed to reflect the correct name. This can take extra time and trouble. Far better to be sure you sue the right person in the first place.

California requires that all people doing business using a name other than their own file a Fictitious Business Name Statement with the county clerk in the county or counties in which the business operates. This is public information, which you can get from the county clerk. Another way to figure out who owns a business is to check with the Business Tax and License Office in the city where the business is located. (If the business is not located in an incorporated city, try the county.) The tax and license office will have a list of the owners of all businesses paying taxes in the city. They should be able to tell you, for example, that the Garden of Exotic Delights is owned by Rufus Clod. Once you find this out, you sue Rufus Clod, d.b.a. The Garden of Exotic Delights.

If for some reason the tax and license office or the county clerk can't help, you may want to check with the state. Millions of people, from exterminators to embalmers, must register with one or another office in Sacramento. So, if your beef is with a teacher, architect, smog control device installer, holder of a beer or wine license or member of another group that must register, you will very likely be able to learn who and where he is with a letter or phone call. Check the Sacramento County phone book under the listing for the State of California. When you find an agency that looks like they should have jurisdiction over the type of business you wish to sue, call their public information number and explain your problem. It may take a little persistence, but eventually you should get the help you need.

How to fix an incorrect business name: If you sue the owner of a business using a fictitious name, but don't get the name right, CCP Sec. 116.560 allows you to substitute the correct name either at the court hearing or after judgment. Ask the Small Claims Court clerk for more information.

D. How to Sue a Partnership

All partners in a general partnership business are individually liable for all the acts of the business. It follows that you should list the names of all the business partners, even if your dispute is only with one (Patricia Sun and Farah Moon, d.b.a. Sacramento Gardens). See Section C, just above, for information on how to learn just who owns a particular business. As is true of businesses generally, out-of-state partnerships can't be successfully sued in California unless they engage in business in this state. (See Chapter 9, Section A, for more on what it means to do business in California.)

Example: You go to a local cleaners with your new sky blue suit. They put too much cleaning fluid on it, which results in a small gray cloud that settles on the right rear shoulder. After unsuccessfully trying to get the cleaners to take responsibility for improving the weather on the back of your suit, you start thinking about a different kind of suit. When you start filling out your court papers (see Chapter 10), you realize that you know only that the store says "Perfection Cleaners" on the front, and that the guy who has been so unpleasant to you is named Bob. You call the city business tax and license people and they tell you that Perfection Cleaners is owned by Robert Johnson and Sal De Benno. You should sue both and also list the name of the business.

⚠️ **Special procedures to sue limited partnerships:** Limited partnerships normally consist of one or a few general partners who are subject to being sued and a number of limited partners who, as investors, normally can't be sued. So if you are suing a limited partnership, list the name of the partnership itself and the general partner or partners. Do not list the limited partners. These partnerships must register with the California Secretary of State. For information on who to sue and serve with papers, contact the California Secretary of State's Limited Partnership Division, P.O. Box 944225, Sacramento, CA 94244-2250, 916-653-3365.

E. How to Sue a Corporation or Limited Liability Company (LLC)

Corporations and limited liability companies (LLCs) are legal people. This means that you can sue, and enforce a judgment against, the business entity itself. You should not sue the owners of the corporation or LLC, or its officers or managers as individuals, unless you have a personal claim against them that is separate from their role in the corporation or LLC. That's because in most situations, the real people who own or operate the corporation or LLC aren't themselves legally liable to pay the corporation's or LLC's debts. This concept is called "personal limited liability" and is one big reason why many people choose to incorporate or form an LLC in the first place.

Be sure to list the full name of the corporation or LLC when you file suit (John's Liquors, Inc., a Corporation). Here again, the name on the door or on the stationery may not be the organization's real name, as corporations and LLCs occasionally use fictitious names. Check with the city or county business license people where the corporation or LLC is headquartered. In addition, the California Secretary of State's Office, Corporate Status Unit, 1500 - 11th Street, Sacramento, CA 95814, 916-653-7315, maintains a complete list of all California corporations and all out-of-state corporations "qualified" to do business in California. You may sue a corporation or LLC in California even if its headquarters are in another state, as long as they do business here.

F. How to Sue On a Motor Vehicle Accident

Special rules apply when it comes to motor vehicle accidents. If your claim arises from an accident with an automobile, motorcycle, truck or R.V., you should name both the driver of the vehicle and the registered owner as part of your suit. Most of the time, you will obtain this information at the time of the accident. If a police accident report was made, it will also contain this information. You can get a copy of any police report from the police department for a modest fee. If there was no police report—and assuming you have the license number of the offending vehicle—contact the Department of Motor Vehicles. Tell them you want to find out who owns a vehicle and her address for purposes of filing and serving a lawsuit based on a motor vehicle accident. For a small fee, they will tell you who owns a vehicle for which you have a license number.

Remember, when you sue more than one person (in this case the driver and the owner, if they are different), serve papers on both. When a business owns a vehicle, sue both the driver and the owners of the business.

G. How to Sue Minors

It is very difficult to sue a minor for breach of contract because minors can disavow (back out of) any contract they sign as long as they do it before they turn 18, unless the contract was for a necessity of life—for example, food—in which case the minor's parents are probably responsible. The exception is for "emancipated minors," who are legally treated as adults. This includes minors who are on active duty in the armed services, are married or have been emancipated (freed from parental control) by court order.

You can sue minors for damage to your person or property. If you wish to do so, you must also list a parent or legal guardian on the court papers. Do it like this:

"John Jefferey, a minor, and William Jefferey, his father."

What about damage to property caused by minors? It is usually not worthwhile to sue children, since most, almost by definition, are broke (there are exceptions, of course). But what about suing the offending kid's parents? Normally a parent is not legally responsible to pay for damages negligently caused by his children. However, when a child is guilty of "malicious or willful misconduct," a California parent can be liable up to $10,000 per act (up to $60,000 if a gun is involved) and sometimes for personal injuries. Parents are also liable for damage done by their minor children in auto accidents when they authorized the child to drive.

Example 1: *John Johnson, age 17, trips over his shoelace while delivering your newspaper and crashes through your glass door. Can you recover from John's parents? Probably not, as John is not guilty of "willful misconduct."*

Example 2: *John shoots out the same glass door with a slingshot after you have repeatedly asked his parents to disarm him. Can you recover from the parents? Probably.*

H. How to Sue Government Agencies

Before you can sue a city because your car was illegally towed away or a city employee who caused you damage, or for any other reason involving personal injury or property damage, you must first file a claim with the city and have it denied. To do this, get a claim form from the city clerk. For cases involving a personal injury or damage to property, your claim must be filed within six months of the date of the incident. (Govt. Code Sec. 911.2.) For claims involving breach of contract or damage to real property, you have one year in which to file your claim. (Govt. Code Sec. 911.2.) The city attorney will review your claim and make a recommendation to the city council. Sometimes the recommendation will be to pay you—most often it will be to deny your claim, no matter how meritorious. Once the city council acts, you will receive a form letter. If it's a denial, you have six months in which to file your Small Claims case. (Govt. Code Sec. 945.6.) Take the denial with you when you file; the Small Claims clerk will want to see it.

The rules for suits against counties and districts (for example, school districts) are basically the same. Get your complaint form from the clerk of the Board of Supervisors (or the Board governing the district). Complete and file it promptly. Within a month or so after filing, you will be told whether your claim is approved or denied. If your claim is denied, you can then proceed to file in Small Claims Court within six months.

Claims against the State of California must also be filed within six months for personal injury and property damage, and one year for breach of contract or damages to real property. Claims should be filed with the State Board of Control, 630 K Street, 4th Floor, Sacramento, CA 95814; mailing address: P.O. Box 3035, Sacramento, CA 95812-3035; telephone: 916-322-4428.

Suits against the federal government, a federal agency or even against a federal employee for actions relating to his or her employment can't be brought in Small Claims

Court. The federal government may not be sued in any state court without its consent. Suits against the federal government normally must be filed in Federal District Court.

I. How to Sue Contractors and Their Bonding Companies

Whenever you sue a licensed contractor for anything relating to work she has done improperly (or not at all), you'll normally find that her business is "bonded" by a "surety" or "guaranty" company. This means that in addition to suing the contractor (who, after all, may have gone belly up), you can also sue and collect a judgment from the "bonding company," based on the contractor's poor workmanship or failure to abide by the agreement. However, to do this in Small Claims Court, you must also name the contractor as part of your lawsuit and succeed in serving your papers on her. None of this is difficult. List both the contractor and the bonding company as defendants on your court papers, (for example, "John Jones Construction, Inc. and BCA Contractors Indemnity Company" (See Chapter 11.)). If you don't sue the contractor—only the bonding company—or even if you do but can't serve your papers on her (perhaps because she has skipped town), your case against the surety company will be transferred to the formal court system, where lawyers and formal procedures are the norm. (CCP Sec. 116.340(g).) And, unfortunately, although you can sue most defendants for up to $5,000 in Small Claims Court, because of a nasty piece of self-interested legislation pushed through the California legislature by the insurance industry, you can only sue a guaranty (bonding) company for $2,500. (CCP Sec. 116.220(c).)

What to do if you can't resolve a dispute with a contractor: If a contractor failed to finish the job or otherwise left you in the lurch, it can be a good idea to file a complaint with the Contractor's State License Board, Box 26000, Sacramento, CA 95826. (Be sure to let the contractor know you are doing it.) This may get the contractor back to work.

J. How to Sue the Estates of Deceased People

Death does not prevent lawsuits from being brought and judgments collected against the deceased's estate. However, it does present a number of technical legal hurdles.

Assuming the defendant made a will (or died without a will or other estate planning device such as a living trust), a probate proceeding will be held. All claims against the estate should be made promptly, in writing, to the personal representative of the deceased person's estate and directly to the probate court. If the personal representative knows about the debt owed to you, you should receive a formal notice to file your claim—but this won't happen if your debt isn't known. If you don't receive notice promptly after a person who owes you money dies, and you don't know who the personal representative is (usually it's a surviving spouse, adult child or other close relative), check court probate filing records in the county where the defendant lived at the time of his death. If the personal representative doesn't honor your claim, you will need to file suit within three months.

It's possible that in some instances you may check for a probate filing and not find one. That's because these days, many people use living trusts and other devices to transfer the property of a deceased person directly to its inheritors. Your best bet is to present your claim to the deceased person's spouse, child or close relative. If it is denied or ignored, you have the right to file suit against anyone who inherits from the deceased. Do it as soon as possible. ■

Where Can You Sue?

Small Claims Courts are local. This makes sense, because the dollar amounts involved aren't large enough to require people to travel great distances. A Small Claims Court judicial district covers part of a city, an entire city, several cities or a county. The next city or county will have its own similar, but separate, Small Claims Court. Normally, your dispute will be with a person or business located nearby. If so, all you really need to know is that you can sue in the judicial district in which the defendant resides or, if a corporation or LLC is involved, where its main place of business is located.

Occasionally, however, the person or business you want to sue resides at a considerable distance from where you live. How you should proceed in this situation depends primarily on whether the defendant is located in California or a different state.

A. Where to Sue Out-of-State Defendants

Often, tricky rules govern whether you can sue a defendant who lives outside of California—or in the case of a business, has its headquarters elsewhere—in a California Small Claims Court. Here they are.

1.   Suits Against Out-of-State Individuals

The basic rule is that California courts—including Small Claims Courts—only have the power (lawyers call this jurisdiction) to hear cases involving individuals who reside in this state. If you want to sue someone who lives in Nevada and doesn't travel to California, you will have to sue in Nevada, not here in California. Rules governing how a Californian can bring a Small Claims case in another state vary from one state to the next. Often you can file papers by mail, but normally you'll need to show up in person on court day. But some states allow people on active duty in the military and occasionally others to present their case entirely in writing.

There are two big exceptions to the rule that out-of-state residents can't usually be sued in California.

1)   Out-of-state residents can successfully be sued here if they are served with court papers while in California.

2)   People who are involved in a vehicle accident on a California road (and the owner of the vehicle) may be sued in a California court no matter where they live. To accomplish this, papers must be served on both the out-of-state defendant and the California Department of Motor Vehicles.

2.   Suits Against Out-of-State Businesses

When it comes to suing a business in Small Claims Court, a California-based plaintiff may sue any business that is organized (incorporated or established as an LLC) in California. In addition, suit may be brought against any business which has an office, warehouse, retail establishment, restaurant or other physical facility here, even if that business is headquartered or organized elsewhere. For example, if an airline lands its planes at a California airport and has a ticketing office here, you can bring suit against the airline company in a California Small Claims Court, even though the airline is incorporated in Texas. Similarly, an out-of-state property owner such as a landlord who owns property in California, can be sued here.

And even if a business does not maintain a physical facility in California, you can still sue here if the business has what lawyers refer to as "minimum contacts" with California. This is a tricky and often litigated legal abstraction, but usually courts will find that "minimum contacts" exist if:

- The business actively sells its goods or services in California.
- The business has a franchise or dealership in California. For example, you can sue Ford in any state where they have an authorized dealer.

- The business employs a sales rep who calls on you personally or by phone to solicit your business.

- The business solicits business in California—by sending you a catalogue, for example.

- The business solicits your business online, as would be the case with an online store. (But just your accessing an out-of-state business informational site is not enough to give the courts of California power to hear a lawsuit against that business.)

- The business places advertising in California's media.

What this amounts to is that most large national businesses can be sued in all 50 states, but smaller businesses which operate in one or a few states and don't solicit business elsewhere can only be sued in the states where they operate.

Example 1: On vacation in Vermont, you are injured at a small local restaurant. When you return to California, you file suit in Small Claims Court. Your case will be tossed out because California courts do not have power (jurisdiction) to hear a case involving a defendant which doesn't operate, advertise or solicit business in this state. The only place you can sue is in Vermont.

Example 2: Same vacation, but this time you are injured at a discount store with branches in all fifty states. Now when you return to California you can sue in Small Claims Court. The fact that the store does business in California gives California's courts jurisdiction to hear your case.

B. Where to Sue California Defendants

Assume now that the person or business you have a claim against lives or does business in California. It follows that you are eligible to sue in a Small Claims Courts in this state. The next question you must answer—and document in your plaintiff's claim—is, which one? Because California is such a huge state, rules (lawyers call them "venue rules") have been developed so that a defendant won't be unnecessarily inconvenienced by having to appear in a court hundreds of miles from where she lives or works. (For example, venue rules say you can always sue a San Francisco resident in San Francisco, but in most instances not in Los Angeles.)

Figure out which judicial district the defendant lives or does business in. The most basic venue rule states that a defendant can always be sued in the judicial district where she lives or operates a business. (As you'll see, in many circumstances suit can also be filed in other judicial districts.) In any case, figuring out where to sue means you'll need to understand how the boundaries of judicial districts are drawn. Sometimes districts have the same boundaries as a city or county, but this isn't always true. Especially in urban areas, it's not always easy to figure out where the judicial district stops and the next one starts. If you need information as to the boundaries of a judicial district, call the Small Claims clerk in the city that seems most likely, and ask.

SUMMARY OF CALIFORNIA RULES ON WHERE YOU CAN SUE

You can sue in any judicial district where:

- an individual defendant resides;

- a corporation or limited liability company (LLC) does business;

- injury to persons or personal property occurred;

- the defendant entered into a contract (does not apply to retail installment or auto sales contracts);

- an obligation (contract) was to be performed (does not apply to retail installment or auto sales contracts or those to furnish goods, services or loans intended for personal or household use);

- the individual defendant resided or a corporation or limited liability company defendant did business at the time the contract was entered into (does not apply to retail installment or auto finance sales contracts).

SPECIAL RULES FOR
RETAIL INSTALLMENT CONTRACTS

The rules set out below apply to most retail installment sales of goods and services for personal, family or household use (not for business use), but not including motor vehicles. They do not cover the services of physicians and dentists or services regulated by the federal government.

For the great majority of retail installment sales, you can sue in the judicial district where:

- the buyer signed the contract;

- the buyer resided at the time the contract was signed;

- the buyer resides at time of suit;

- the goods are attached to real property (for example, a portable storage shed).

SPECIAL RULES FOR AUTOS SUBJECT TO THE
AUTOMOBILE SALES FINANCE ACT

The rules set out below apply to the installment sale and long-term lease of new and used motor vehicles (but not trailers or mobile homes) purchased primarily for personal (not business) use.

On these auto purchase contracts you can sue in the judicial district where:

- the buyer signed the contract;

- the buyer resided at the time the contract was signed;

- the vehicle is permanently garaged.

1. You Can Sue a Person Where He Resides or a Corporation or LLC Where It Does Business

It makes good sense that a person can be sued where he or she resides, or a corporation where it does business, doesn't it? If a suit is brought where the defendant is located, she can't complain that it is unduly burdensome to appear in court. Unfortunately, books have been written about the technical legal definition of residence. Indeed, I remember with horror trying to sort out a law school exam in which a person with numerous homes and businesses arguably had "contact" with six different judicial districts. The point of the examination was for us students to figure out where he could be sued. Thankfully, you don't have to worry about this sort of nonsense. If you believe a business or individual to be sufficiently present within a particular judicial district so that it would not be a hardship for them to appear in court there, go ahead and file your suit there. The worst that can happen is that the judge or clerk will tell you to refile your case someplace else. This will not be a big problem if you have filed fairly promptly after the date of the incident that gave rise to your lawsuit, since you will have plenty of time to refile before the statute of limitations runs out (see Chapter 5).

Example: Downhill Skier lives in the city, but also owns a mountain cabin where he spends several months a year. Late one snowy afternoon, Downhill drives his new Porsche from the ski slopes to his ultra-modern, rustic cabin. Turning into his driveway, he executes a bad slalom skid right into Woodsey Carpenter's 1957 International Harvester Pickup. Where can Woodsey properly sue? Obviously, in the city where Downhill has his permanent address, and probably also in the county where the cabin is located, on the theory that Downhill also lives there. But read on—as you will see under Section B3, below—Woodsey is also eligible to sue Downhill in the mountain county on the theory that the damage occurred there.

You have a choice of locations when suing more than one defendant. You can sue multiple defendants in any judicial district in which one resides even though the other(s) live in another part of the state.

2. You Can Sue in the Judicial District Where the Contract Upon Which Your Suit Was Based Was Entered Into

In addition to suing where the defendant resides, you can also sue at the place where an obligation (contract) was signed. This is good common sense, as the law assumes that if people enter into a contract to perform something at a certain location, it is probably reasonably convenient to both. If, for example, Downhill gets a telephone installed in his cabin, or has the fender on his Porsche fixed, or has a cesspool put in, or agrees to sit for a portrait in the mountain county, he can be sued there if he fails to keep his part of the bargain. Of course, as we learned above, Downhill can also be sued in the city (judicial district) where he resides permanently, or where the contract was entered into.

Example: *John Gravenstein lives in Sonoma County, California, where he owns an apple orchard. He signs a contract with Acme Mechanical Apple Picker Co., an international corporation with offices in San Francisco, New York, Paris and Guatemala City. John signs the contract in Sonoma County. The parts are sent to John from San Francisco via UPS. They turn out to be defective. After trying and failing to reach a settlement with Acme, John wants to know if he can sue them in Sonoma County. Yes. Even though Acme doesn't have a business office in Sonoma County and they performed no action there in connection with their agreement to sell John the spare parts, the contract was signed there.*

If you have a choice of judicial districts, it's fine to pick the most convenient one. As you should now understand, there may be two, three or more judicial districts in which you can file your case. In this situation, simply choose the one most convenient to you. But check your local rules to make sure which places are appropriate in your case. If you choose the wrong one, chances are your action will be dismissed. If it is dismissed, you can refile in the correct district, as long as the statute of limitations hasn't run out in the meantime.

Unfortunately, it isn't always easy to determine the location where a contract has been "entered into." This is particularly likely to be true when the people making the contract are at different locations. If you enter a contract over the phone or online, for example, there could be an argument that the contract was entered into either where you are or where the other party is. Rather than trying to learn and apply all the intricacies of contract law, your best bet is probably to sue in the place most convenient to you, claiming that the contract was made there. On the other hand, if someone sues you at the wrong end of the state and you believe there is a good argument that the contract was formed where you live (that's where you accepted the other party's offer), write the court as soon as you have been served and ask that the case be dismissed.

3.   You Can Sue Where the Injury to a Person or to His/Her Property Occurred

If you are in a car accident, a dog bites you, a tree falls on your noggin or a neighbor floods your cactus garden, you can sue in the judicial district where the event or injury occurred, even if this is a different district from the one in which the defendant resides.

Example: Downhill is returning to his home in San Francisco. He is driving his Porsche carefully, thankful that no one was injured when he hit Woodsey. At the same time, John Gravenstein is rushing to the city to try and get spare parts for his still-broken apple picker. John jumps a red light and crumples Downhill's other fender. The accident occurs in Marin County, a county in which neither John nor Downhill live. After parking his car and taking a taxi home, Downhill tries to figure out where he can sue if he can't work out a fair settlement with John. Unfortunately for him, he can't sue in San Francisco, as John doesn't reside there and the accident occurred in Marin. Downhill would have to sue either in Marin County, where his property was damaged, or in Sonoma County, where John lives. Luckily for Downhill, Marin County adjoins San Francisco. Had the accident occurred in Los Angeles County, however, Downhill would have been put to a lot more trouble if he wished to sue (presumably he would have chosen Sonoma County, which is much closer to his home than is L.A.).

Allowing a plaintiff to sue where the damage happens helps in the situation where you're injured on another's property, but the owner lives out of state. You can sue the owner if the suit relates to that property, though collecting may not be so easy. More on this in Chapter 11, Serving Your Papers.

4.   Retail Installment Sales Contracts and Motor Vehicles Finance Sales

If your case involves a motor vehicle or a major piece of property such as a television or appliance that you bought on time, you may file suit where you presently live, where the vehicle or goods are permanently kept, where you lived when you entered into the contract or where you signed the contract.

Example: Downhill buys a major appliance on time subject to the Retail Installment Sales Act while he lives in San Francisco. Later he moves to Fresno and stops paying his bill. Can he be sued for the unpaid balance in San Francisco? Yes, he can.

C. What Happens If Suit Is Filed in the Wrong California Small Claims Court?

The sometimes complicated rules as to where you can sue and be sued, discussed earlier in this chapter, result in much confusion. Every day, individual Californians and businesses are sued in the wrong court. If this happens to you, you have two choices (CCP Sec. 116.370):

1. Show up and go ahead with the case. Although the court has independent authority to transfer a case to a correct court, the judge is likely to go ahead with your trial if both parties show up ready to proceed. Doing this may not be a bad choice if the court you are sued in isn't too inconvenient.

2. Challenge the judicial district in which the case is filed (called "challenging venue"). Venue can be challenged by promptly writing a letter to the court with a copy to the other party explaining why the case has been filed in the wrong place, or by showing up on the court date and doing it in person.

If a court determines that suit has been filed in the wrong court (venue is improper), it will dismiss the case, with the result that the plaintiff will have to refile in a correct court. But what happens if a defendant writes to protest venue but the court finds that, in fact, suit was brought in the correct court? The court must delay (continue) the trial for at least 15 days and notify all parties of the new date.

2100 Coast Drive
Laguna Beach, CA
December 12, 19__

Oakland-Piedmont-Emeryville
Small Claims Court
600 Washington
Oakland, CA

Re: *Upton vs. Downey*
      # 987 321

Dear Judge:

I am the defendant in this case. Based on the fact that I have been sued in the wrong judicial district and would be highly inconvenienced if I have to defend myself there, I request that you please dismiss this court action.

My request is based on the fact I live in Laguna Beach, California, and the car accident that gave rise to this case occurred in Orange County. The fact that plaintiff later moved to Oakland and chose to file suit in your court does not amount to a valid legal reason to have it heard there.

Sincerely,

Fred Downey

■

10

Plaintiff's and Defendant's Filing Fees, Court Papers and Court Dates

A. How Much Does It Cost?

The Small Claims filing fee in California is $20 for people who have filed 12 or fewer claims in any given Small Claims Court over the past 12 months. It costs the same amount to file a Defendant's Claim. For more frequent filers, the fee is $35. There is an additional fee for serving papers by certified mail on each defendant. You can recover your filing and service costs if you win. (See Chapter 15.)

If you cannot afford these fees, the court may waive them. You must fill out an Application for Waiver of Court Fees and Costs. The clerk will have this form and will help you complete it.

B. Filling Out Your Court Papers and Getting Your Court Date

Now let's look at the initial court papers themselves to be sure that you don't trip over a detail. Official forms are the same throughout California, but occasionally individual judicial districts adopt additional local forms. You should have little trouble filling out your papers by following the examples printed here, but if you do, simply ask the clerk for help. Small Claims clerks are required by law to give you as much form preparation help as possible, and refer you to your county's Small Claims Advisor if you need additional advice (see Chapter 13, Section B). It should go without saying that adopting a friendly, courteous approach towards the clerk will usually produce the best results.

Step 1. Fill Out the Plaintiff's Statement

To start your case in Small Claims Court, go to the Small Claims clerk's office and fill out a simple form. In some counties, this form is called a Plaintiff's Statement. In others, you will use the Plaintiff's Claim and Order to Defendant form mentioned in Step 2, just below. All you need to do is properly name the defendant(s), as discussed in Chapter 8, and briefly state what happened, as outlined in Chapter 2, Section A.

Be sure you sue the correct defendant in the right place. In Chapter 8, we discuss how to properly name the defendant. In Chapter 9, you'll find the rules which establish the proper judicial district or districts in which to file your Small Claims case.

Step 2. Plaintiff's Claim and Order to Defendant

When you have completed your Plaintiff's Statement form—or if your court skips that step, the form entitled Plaintiff's Claim and Order to Defendant—give it to the clerk and pay the filing fee. Your case will be assigned a number and you will be asked to sign your Claim form under penalty of perjury. You will keep one copy of the Claim of Plaintiff, another copy must be served on the defendant and a third will stay in the clerk's file to go to the judge on your trial day. (See Chapter 11.) Following are samples of the Plaintiff's Statement and Plaintiff's Claim and Order to Defendant.

PLAINTIFF'S STATEMENT

Form No. 211-127 (REV. 11/97)   **PLAINTIFF'S STATEMENT**

State your name and residence address, and the name and address of any other person joining with you in this action. If this claim arises from a business transaction, give the name and address of your business and complete a fictitious business name declaration on back of this form if applicable.

A.   Name   Andrew Printer

      Address   1800 Marilee St.   Phone No.   (510) 827-7000)
                           Street
               Fremont,   CA   94602
                  City   State   Zip

B.   Name

      Address   Phone No.
                           Street
                  City   State   Zip

State the name and address of each person or business firm you are suing. See "Information to Plaintiff."
    If you are suing one or more individuals, give full name of each.
    IF YOU ARE SUING A BUSINESS OWNED BY AN INDIVIDUAL, GIVE THE NAME OF THE OWNER AND THE NAME OF THE BUSINESS HE/SHE OWNS. YOU MUST STATE IF YOU WANT TO SUE THE INDIVIDUAL AS WELL AS THE BUSINESS.
    If you are suing a partnership, give the name of the partners and the name of the partnership.
    If you are suing a corporation, give the corporations full name, and the name and title of an officer.
    If your claim arises out of a vehicle accident, the driver and the registered owner of the other vehicle must be named.

A.   Name   Acme Illusions, Inc.

      Address   100 Primrose Path   Phone No.   (510) 654-1201
                           Street
               Oakland   CA   94602
                  City   State   Zip

B.   Name

      Address   Phone No.
                           Street
                  City   State   Zip

C.   Name

      Address   Phone No.
                           Street
                  City   State   Zip

1. a. Defendant owes me $ 950.00 __ not including court costs, because (**BRIEFLY** describe claim and date):
       Failure to pay for printing and typesetting

    b. ☐ I have had an **arbitration of an attorney-client fee dispute.** (Attach form Attorney-Client Fee Dispute Attachment).
2. ☐ This claim is against a government agency, and I filed a claim with the agency. My claim was denied by the agency, or the agency did not act on my claim before the legal deadline. (See "Information to Plaintiff")
3. a. ☒ I have asked defendant to pay this money, but it has not been paid.
    b. ☐ I have NOT asked defendant to pay this money, because (**explain briefly**):
4. a. From "Venue Table" on reverse side select the reason why this is the proper court for your case.
      ☐A Place appropriate letter in box at left. If you select D, E, or F, specify additional facts below:

    b. Give the address where contract was signed; OR, where the service was to be rendered; OR where the damage occurred:
       100 Primrose Path,   Oakland,   California
           (Street Address)   (City or locality)
5. I (have/have not) _____ filed more than one other small claims action anywhere in California during this calendar year in which the amount demanded is more than $2500.00.
6. I (have/have not) _____ filed more than 12 small claims, including this claim, during the previous 12 months.
7. I understand that
    a. I may talk to an attorney about this claim, but I cannot be represented by an attorney at the trial in the small claims court.
    b. I must appear at the time and place of trial and **bring all witnesses, books, receipts, and other papers or things** to prove my case.
    c. **I have no right of appeal on my claim,** but I may appeal a claim filed by the defendant in this case.
    d. If I cannot afford to pay the fees for filing or service by a sheriff, marshal, or constable, I may ask that the fees be waived.
8. I have received and read the information sheet explaining some important rights of plaintiffs in the small claims court.
I DECLARE UNDER PENALTY OF PERJURY UNDER THE LAWS OF THE STATE OF CALIFORNIA THAT THE FOREGOING IS TRUE AND CORRECT.

Date:
    April 27, 19   ►   Andrew Printer
       (TYPE OR PRINT NAME)   (SIGNATURE OF PLAINTIFF)

PLAINTIFF'S STATEMENT SMALL CLAIMS
(SEE REVERSE)

PLAINTIFF'S CLAIM

Name and Address of Court:	Alameda County Municipal Court Oakland-Piedmont 600 Washington Street Oakland, CA 94614

SC-100

SMALL CLAIMS CASE NO.: 002001

— NOTICE TO DEFENDANT — YOU ARE BEING SUED BY PLAINTIFF	— AVISO AL DEMANDADO — A USTED LO ESTAN DEMANDANDO
To protect your rights, you must appear in this court on the trial date shown in the table below. You may lose the case if you do not appear. The court may award the plaintiff the amount of the claim and the costs. Your wages, money, and property may be taken without further warning from the court.	Para proteger sus derechos, usted debe presentarse ante esta corte en la fecha del juicio indicada en el cuadro que aparece a continuación. Si no se presenta, puede perder el caso. La corte puede decidir en favor del demandante por la cantidad del reclamo y los costos. A usted le pueden quitar su salario, su dinero, y otras cosas de su propiedad, sin aviso adicional por parte de esta corte.

PLAINTIFF/DEMANDANTE (Name, street address, and telephone number of each):	DEFENDANT/DEMANDADO (Name, street address, and telephone number of each):
Andrew Printer 1000 Marilee St. Fremont, CA 94536 Telephone No.: (510) 555-5555	Acme Illusions, Inc, 100 Primrose Path Oakland, CA 94602 Telephone No.: (510) 555-1212

Telephone No.:	Telephone No.:
Fict. Bus. Name Stmt. No. Expires:	☐ See attached sheet for additional plaintiffs and defendants.

PLAINTIFF'S CLAIM

1. a. ☐ Defendant owes me the sum of: $ 950.00   , not including court costs, because *(describe claim and date)*:
   He failed to pay for a printing and typesetting job which was
   completed on March 15, 19___.

   b. ☐ I have had an **arbitration of an attorney-client fee dispute.** *(Attach Attorney-Client Fee Dispute form (see form SC-101).)*

2. ☐ This claim is against a government agency, and I filed a claim with the agency. My claim was denied by the agency, or the agency did not act on my claim before the legal deadline. *(See form SC-150.)*

3. a. ☒ I have asked defendant to pay this money, but it has not been paid.

   b. ☐ I have NOT asked defendant to pay this money because *(explain)*:

4. This court is the proper court for the trial because   [A] *(In the box at the left, insert one of the letters from the list called "Venue Table" on the back of this sheet. If you select D, E, or F, specify additional facts in this space):*

5. I ☐ have ☒ have not   filed more than one other small claims action anywhere in California during this calendar year in which the amount demanded is more than $2,500.

6. I ☐ have ☒ have not   filed more than 12 small claims, including this claim, during the previous 12 months.

7. I understand that
   a. I may talk to an attorney about this claim, but I cannot be represented by an attorney at the trial in the small claims court.
   b. I must appear at the time and place of trial and bring all witnesses, books, receipts, and other papers or things to prove my case.
   c. **I have no right of appeal on my claim,** but I may appeal a claim filed by the defendant in this case.
   d. If I cannot afford to pay the fees for filing or service by a sheriff, marshal, or constable, I may ask that the fees be waived.

8. I have received and read the information sheet explaining some important rights of plaintiffs in the small claims court.

I declare under penalty of perjury under the laws of the State of California that the foregoing is true and correct.

Date: April 27, 19___

.....Andrew.Printer......................   ▶ *Andrew Printer*
          (TYPE OR PRINT NAME)   (SIGNATURE OF PLAINTIFF)

ORDER TO DEFENDANT

You must appear in this court on the trial date and at the time LAST SHOWN IN THE BOX BELOW if you do not agree with the plaintiff's claim. Bring all witnesses, books, receipts, and other papers or things with you to support your case.

TRIAL DATE FECHA DEL JUICIO	DATE	DAY	TIME	PLACE	COURT USE
1.					
2.					
3.					

Filed on *(date)*:   Clerk, by_____ , Deputy

— The county provides small claims advisor services free of charge. Read the information on the reverse. —

| Form Adopted by the
Judicial Council of California
SC-100 [Rev. January 1, 1998] | **PLAINTIFF'S CLAIM AND ORDER TO DEFENDANT**
(Small Claims) | **WEST GROUP**
Official Publisher | Cal. Rules of Court, rule 982.7;
Code of Civil Procedure,
§ 116.110 et seq. |

Step 3. Getting Your Hearing Date

One of the great advantages of Small Claims Court is that disputes are settled quickly. This is important. Many people avoid lawyers and the regular courts primarily because they can take seemingly forever to get a dispute settled. Business people, for example, increasingly rely on private mediation or arbitration, caring more about resolving a dispute promptly than winning a complete victory. Anyone who has had to wait more than a year for a case to be heard in one or another constipated formal trial court knows, through bitter experience, the truth of the old cliché, "Justice delayed is justice denied."

Section 116.330(c) of the Code of Civil Procedure requires that, if the defendant resides in the same county in which the action is brought, the hearing should be held no sooner than 15 days and not longer than 40 days from the time the papers are filed. If the defendant lives outside of the county where you bring suit, the case will be heard not less than 30 nor more than 70 days from the date you file your complaint. If there is more than one defendant, and one or more lives in the county where you file and one or more in another county, the case will be treated as if all defendants live within your county: that is, the case will be heard within 40 days of the time the papers are filed.

When you file your papers, you should also arrange with the clerk for a court date. Select a date that is convenient for you. You need not take the first date the clerk suggests. Be sure to leave yourself enough time to get a copy of the "Claim of Plaintiff" form served on the defendant(s). (This is ten days if the defendant resides in the county where you bring suit and 15 days if she resides in another county—see Chapter 11 for instructions on how to serve your court papers on the defendant.) If you fail to properly serve your papers on the defendant in time, there is no big hassle—just notify the clerk, get a new court date and try again.

Small Claims Court cases are most often heard beginning at 9:00 a.m., Monday–Friday. Larger courts are also required to hold evening or Saturday sessions.

Filing papers by mail is possible, but not recommended. Small Claims clerks will accept cases filed by U.S. mail. Although some Small Claims Courts encourage this practice, I recommend it only if you are a long distance from the court in which you must sue. The problem with filing by mail is that there is no one on the spot to answer questions. Since the details of getting a small claim properly filed can be confusing, it often helps to review them with a real live person. (See Chapter 13, Section B.) However, if you do wish to file by mail, send a large self-addressed envelope with triple first class postage to the court clerk with your request for the necessary forms. The clerk will return the Plaintiff's Statement and Claim of Plaintiff forms. Fill out the former and sign the latter. Return both to the clerk with your filing fee, a self-addressed, stamped envelope and money for certified mail service if you wish to follow this service approach.

C. The Defendant's Forms

No papers need be filed to defend a case in a California Small Claims Court. You just show up on the date and at the time indicated, ready to tell your side of the story. (If you need to get the hearing delayed, see Section D, "Changing a Court Date," below.) It is proper, and advisable, for a defendant to call or write the plaintiff and see if a fair settlement can be reached without going to court or to propose mediation. (See Chapter 6.)

Sometimes, a party you planned to sue sues you first (for example, over a traffic accident where you each believe the other is at fault). No problem. You can—but do not have to—file your own Claim of Defendant against that person for up to $5,000 in Small

Claims Court and have it heard by a judge at the same time that the plaintiff's claim against you is considered. When you file a Claim of Defendant, you become a plaintiff as far as this claim is concerned. This means that, if you lose, you can't appeal, because California law clearly states that plaintiffs can't appeal. Of course, if you lose on the original plaintiff's claim, where you are the defendant, you can appeal that portion of the judgment. (See Chapter 23 for more on appeal rules.)

Another alternative is not to file your claim as part of the plaintiff's case, but to exercise your right (CCP Sec. 426.60) to wait and file a separate lawsuit later, either in Small Claims Court or the appropriate formal court.

Lots of people believe that a claim filed by a defendant must arise out of the same incident or fact situation as the plaintiff's claim. Although it's true that this is usually the case, it's not a requirement. You can file a Defendant's Claim even if you contend that the plaintiff owes you money for something completely different. (For example, the plaintiff sues you for a car accident, but you file a Defendant's Claim based on her failure to repay a loan.)

But what happens if you wish to make a claim against the plaintiff (on facts arising out of the same incident) for more than $5,000? First reread Chapter 4 and decide whether you want to scale down your claim to fit into Small Claims. If you don't, you must file your claim in either Justice or Municipal Court (up to $25,000) or Superior Court (over $25,000) and pay all necessary filing fees. Then you must file a form called a "Declaration" with the Small Claims Court clerk notifying the court that you have filed the higher court action. This must be done prior to the hearing date for the Small Claims Court case and costs $1. In addition, a copy of this affidavit and a copy of the Complaint filed in Municipal or Superior Court must be served on the plaintiff in person. The next step is up to the Small Claims judge. Under CCP Sec. 116.380, she has the power to:

1) render judgment on the plaintiff's Small Claims case prior to transfer (this means the defendant's case in Justice, Municipal or Superior Court will still go forward, but the two cases won't be decided together),

2) not render judgment and transfer the Small Claims case to the other court (this is the most likely result), or

3) refuse to transfer the Small Claims case on the grounds that the ends of justice would not be served (this is only likely if the defendant's case in formal court seems to be without merit).

DEFENDANT'S CLAIM

Name and Address of Court:	Alameda County Municipal Oakland-Piedmont 600 Washington St. Oakland, CA	SC-120

SMALL CLAIMS CASE NO.

— NOTICE TO PLAINTIFF — **YOU ARE BEING SUED BY DEFENDANT**	— AVISO AL DEMANDANTE — *A USTED LO ESTA DEMANDANDO EL*
To protect your rights, you must appear in this court on the trial date shown in the table below. You may lose the case if you do not appear. The court may award the defendant the amount of the claim and the costs. Your wages, money, and property may be taken without further warning from the court.	Para proteger sus derechos, usted debe presentarse ante esta corte en la fecha del juicio indicada en el cuadro que aparece a continuación. Si no se presenta, puede perder el caso. La corte puede decidir en favor del deman- dado por la cantidad del reclamo y los costos. A usted le pueden quitar su salario, su dinero, y otras cosas de su propiedad, sin aviso adicional por parte de esta corte.

PLAINTIFF/DEMANDANTE (Name, address, and telephone number of each):

Andrew Printer
1800 Marilee St.
Fremont, California 94536

Telephone No.(510) 555-5555

DEFENDANT/DEMANDADO (Name. address. and telephone number of each):

Acme Illusions, Inc.
100 Primrose Path
Oakland, California 94602

Telephone No.: (510) 555-1212

Telephone No :

Fict. Bus. Name Stmt. No.   Expires:

Telephone No :

☐ See attached sheet for additional plaintiffs and defendants.

DEFENDANT'S CLAIM

1. Plaintiff owes me the sum of: $ 300.00   , not including court costs, because (*describe claim and date*):
   of delays and poor workmanship in a printing job he performed for me on March 15, 19__.

2. a. ☐ I have asked plaintiff to pay this money, but it has not been paid.
   b. ☐ I have NOT asked plaintiff to pay this money because (explain):

3. I ☒ have ☐ have not filed more than one other small claims action anywhere in California during this calendar year in which the amount demanded is more than $2,500.

4. I understand that
   a. I may talk to an attorney about this claim, but I cannot be represented by an attorney at the trial in the small claims court.
   b. I must appear at the time and place of trial and bring all witnesses, books, receipts, and other papers or things to prove my case.
   c. **I have no right of appeal on my claim,** but I may appeal a claim filed by the plaintiff in this case.
   d. If I cannot afford to pay the fees for filing or service by a sheriff, marshal, or constable, I may ask that the fees be waived.

5. I have received and read the information sheet explaining some important rights of defendants in the small claims court.

I declare under penalty of perjury under the laws of the State of California that the foregoing is true and correct.

Date: (May 9, 19__)
...... Waldo Fergus ......
(TYPE OR PRINT NAME)

▶ *Waldo Fergus, President*
(SIGNATURE OF DEFENDANT)

ORDER TO PLAINTIFF

You must appear in this court on the trial date and at the time LAST SHOWN IN THE BOX BELOW if you do not agree with the defendant's claim. Bring all witnesses, books, receipts, and other papers or things with you to support your case.

		DATE	DAY	TIME	PLACE	COURT USE
TRIAL DATE	1.					
FECHA DEL JUICIO	2.					
	3.					
	4.					

Filed on (date):   Clerk, by _____, Deputy

—The county provides small claims advisor services free of charge. (Advisor phone number:) —

Form Approved by the
Judicial Council of California
SC-120 [Rev. January 1, 1990]

DEFENDANT'S CLAIM AND ORDER TO PLAINTIFF
(Small Claims)

Cal. Rules of Court. rule 982.7;
Code of Civil Procedure, § 116.110 et seq.

D. Changing a Court Date

It is sometimes impossible for a defendant to be present on the day ordered by the court for the hearing. It can also happen that the plaintiff will select a court date and get the defendant served only to find that an unexpected emergency makes it impossible for him to be present.

It is normally not difficult to get a case delayed. To arrange this, it's best to call the other party and see if you can agree on a mutually convenient date. Yes, sometimes it is difficult to face talking to someone with whom you are involved in a lawsuit, but if possible swallow your pride and just treat this as a routine business transaction. Once all parties have agreed to a new date, send the court clerk a letter or memo signed by both parties. Normally the court will postpone the hearing and set another court date. (If the papers have already been served on the defendant, a $10 fee will be charged.) Here is a sample:

---

11 South Street
San Diego, CA
January 10, 19__

Clerk of the Small Claims Court
San Diego, California

Re: SC 4117 *Rodriguez v. McNally*

Mr. Rodriguez and I agree to request that you postpone this case to a date after March 1, 19__. If possible, we would prefer that it not be scheduled on March 27 or 28.

_____
John McNally

_____
John Rodriguez

If you speak to the other party and find that he is completely uncooperative—or you can't get through to her—put your request for a delay (continuance) in writing, along with the circumstances that make it impossible for you to keep the first date. Send your letter to the clerk of the Small Claims Court.

Here is a sample:

---

37 Birdwalk Blvd.
Occidental, Calif.
January 10, 19__

Clerk
Small Claims Court
City Hall

Re: Small Claims No. 374-628

Dear Clerk:

I have been served with a complaint (No. 374-628) by John's Laundry, Inc. The date set for a hearing, February 15, falls on the day of my son's graduation from Nursing School in Oscaloosa, Oklahoma, which my husband and I plan to attend.

I called John's Laundry and asked to have the case delayed one week. They just laughed and said that they would not give me any cooperation.

I feel that I have a good defense to this suit. Please delay this case until any date after February 22, except March 13, which is my day for a medical check-up.

I understand that there is a fee of $10.00 to request a postponement. Please find my check enclosed.

Thank you,

Sally Wren

E. If One Party Doesn't Show Up

If one party to a case doesn't appear in court on the proper day at the proper time, the case is normally decided in favor of the other. Depending on whether it is the plaintiff or defendant who fails to show up, the terms used by the judge to make his decision are different. If the plaintiff appears, but the defendant doesn't, a "default judgment" is normally entered in favor of the plaintiff. (See Chapters 12 and 15 for more information on defaults.) Occasionally, although it happens far less frequently, it is the plaintiff who fails to show up. In this situation, the judge will normally either dismiss the case or decide it on the basis of the defendant's evidence. The defendant will usually prefer this second result, especially if a Claim of Defendant has been made. That's because if the case is simply dismissed (called a dismissal without prejudice to the case being refiled), the plaintiff can refile it. If you find yourself in this situation, check with the court clerk.

1. Setting Aside a Default (Defendant's Remedy)

Under CCP Sec. 116.730, a defendant has 30 days to move to set aside (vacate) a default judgment (180 days from discovering that a judgment has been entered if the defendant wasn't properly served. (CCP Sec. 116.740(a).) To do this, get a Notice of Motion to Vacate Judgment form from the clerk, file it and serve it on the plaintiff. The clerk will then schedule a hearing, to be held at least ten days later, and will notify the parties of the time, date and place. The defendant then must appear at the hearing and explain (or submit written justification for) why there was "good cause" for her original failure to appear. The judge will decide whether or not there is good cause to vacate the default and grant a new trial. Some judges will routinely vacate defaults on the basis of almost any hard luck story ("I overslept," "I forgot what day it was," "My sister was sick"), while others are extremely unsympathetic to the idea of vacating a default judgment unless the defendant can show an extremely good cause for missing the original court date, such as that the original papers were not properly served on her and that she didn't know about the hearing.

As the judge has great legal discretion as to whether or not to vacate a default, it's obviously impossible to predict what any particular judge will do. For this reason, defendants should quickly move to set aside as soon as they realize they missed the original trial. It's often a bad mistake to wait until the end of the 30-day period established by CCP Sec. 116.730, as this may be considered a negative factor by the judge. The defendant should also be prepared to convince the judge he had a very good reason to miss the original hearing.

Plaintiffs who are the beneficiaries of a default judgment—and who understandably would prefer that it not be set aside—should emphasize the fact that they played by the rules and showed up on the original court date, while the defendant failed to do so. If the plaintiff had witnesses ready to testify at the original trial at which the default was entered, and these people will be difficult to produce a second time, this too should be emphasized.

There is no appeal from a default judgment unless you first try and get the default set aside. Even if you have a great case, if you fail to show up in court and a default judgment is entered, you have no right to file an appeal until you first try to have the default set aside in Small Claims Court. If the Small Claims judge denies your motion to vacate the default judgment after you have appeared in court or submitted a written justification, you may appeal this denial (but not the decision on the underlying case) within ten days. While it is fairly unlikely that this type of appeal will be granted, if it is and the default is vacated, the Superior Court has the authority to go ahead and hear the merits of your case on the spot. (CCP Sec. 116.730(f).) This means both sides should be prepared to argue the facts of the case in Superior Court should the default be set aside.

2. Vacating a Judgment of Dismissal (Plaintiff's Remedy)

If a plaintiff does not show up in court at the appointed time to pursue her own case, the judge will dismiss it. Normally this means the plaintiff can refile it as long as the statute of limitations has not run out in the meantime (see Chapter 5). However, there is an exception to this rule. If the judge dismisses the case "with prejudice," it means it can't be refiled unless the dismissal is vacated. In my view, it is improper to dismiss a case "with prejudice" just because a plaintiff doesn't show up, but occasionally a judge will do it.

If the plaintiff doesn't show up in a situation where the defendant has filed a Defendant's Claim—and the plaintiff has been served—the judge will very likely enter a default judgment on behalf of the defendant. (See Chapter 15, Section A.) If this is done, the judgment must be vacated before the plaintiff can have the dispute considered on its merits. To vacate a default judgment entered against a plaintiff who does not appear, the plaintiff must file a motion to vacate the judgment within 30 days after the clerk has mailed a notice of entry of judgment. However, in practice it's best to file this notice as soon as possible. Normally, what will happen next is that the clerk will set a hearing before the judge as to whether the default judgment on the defendant's claim should be vacated. (The plaintiff must serve a notice on any defendant(s) who received a judgment in their favor.) At the hearing, the judge will inquire as to why the plaintiff missed the original hearing. If the plaintiff can't make this hearing as to whether the default should be set aside, she may submit her excuse in the form of a written affidavit. But I don't advise following this approach. Since the judge will only set aside the default if she finds "good cause" for the original failure to appear, it's always best to tell your story in person. Remember, the plaintiff is the one who initiated the case and established the court date, so no one is going to have a great deal of sympathy for her failure to show up.

NOTICE OF MOTION TO VACATE JUDGMENT

Name and Address of Court:

SMALL CLAIMS CASE NO.:

PLAINTIFF/DEMANDANTE (Name, street address, and telephone number of each):

DEFENDANT/DEMANDADO (Name, street address, and telephone number of each):

Telephone No.:

Telephone No.:

Telephone No.:

Telephone No.:

☐ See attached sheet for additional plaintiffs and defendants.

NOTICE TO (Name):

One of the parties has asked the court to CANCEL the small claims judgment in your case. If you disagree with this request, you should appear in this court on the hearing date shown below. If the request is granted, ANOTHER TRIAL may immediately be held. Bring all witnesses, books, receipts, and other papers or things with you to support your case.	Una de las partes en el caso le ha solicitado a la corte que DEJE SIN EFECTO la decisión tomada en su caso por la corte para reclamos judiciales menores. Si usted est en desacuerdo con esta solicitud, debe presentarse en esta corte en la fecha de la audiencia indicada a continuación. Si se concede esta solicitud, es posible que se efectœe otro juicio inmediatamente. Traiga a todos sus testigos, libros, recibos, y otros documentos o cosas para presentarlos en apoyo de su caso.

NOTICE OF MOTION TO VACATE (CANCEL) JUDGMENT

1. A hearing will be held in this court at which I will ask the court to **cancel** the judgment entered against me in this case. If you wish to oppose the motion you should appear at the court on

HEARING DATE FECHA DEL JUICIO		DATE	DAY	TIME	PLACE	COURT USE
	1.					
	2.					
	3.					

2. I am asking the court to cancel the judgment for the reasons stated in item 5 below. My request is based on this notice of motion and declaration, the records on file with the court, and any evidence that may be presented at the hearing.

DECLARATION FOR MOTION TO VACATE (CANCEL) JUDGMENT

3. Judgment was entered against me in this case on (date):
4. I first learned of the entry of judgment against me on (date):
5. I am asking the court to cancel the judgment for the following reason:
   a. ☐ I did not appear at the trial of this claim because (specify facts):

   b. ☐ Other (specify facts):

6. I understand that I must bring with me to the hearing on this motion all witnesses, books, receipts, and other papers or things to support my case.

I declare under penalty of perjury under the laws of the State of California that the foregoing is true and correct.

Date:

_____   ▶ _____
(TYPE OR PRINT NAME)   (SIGNATURE)

CLERK'S CERTIFICATE OF MAILING

I certify that I am not a party to this action. This Notice of Motion to Vacate Judgment and Declaration was mailed first class, postage prepaid, in a sealed envelope to the responding party at the address shown above. The mailing and this certification occurred

at (place): _____ . California,
on (date): _____

Clerk, by _____ , Deputy

—The county provides small claims advisor services free of charge. —

Form Approved by the Judicial Council of California SC-135 [Rev. January 1, 1997*]	* NOTE: Continued use of form SC-135 (Rev. January 1, 1992) is authorized through December 31, 1997. **NOTICE OF MOTION TO VACATE JUDGMENT AND DECLARATION** (Small Claims)	Cal. Rules of Court, rule 982.7 Code of Civil Procedure, §§ 116.720, 116.730, 116.740

If the motion to vacate the judgment is granted, and all parties are present and agree, the case may be heard on the spot. If the judgment is vacated, but the defendant is not present, or it is otherwise inconvenient to proceed, the clerk will establish a new hearing date.

If your motion to set aside the default is denied, you may appeal to the Superior Court within ten days, but only as to the decision not to grant the motion.   ■

11

Serving Your Papers

After the plaintiff files her Claim of Plaintiff form with the Small Claims clerk—following the instructions in Chapter 10 under "Filling Out Your Court Papers and Getting
Your Court Date"—a copy must be served on the defendant(s). This is called "service of
process," and your lawsuit is not complete without it. The reason that you must serve

the other side is obvious—the defendant(s) are entitled to be notified of the nature of your claim and the day, time and place that they can show up to defend themselves. Normally your court papers must be served within California, since California courts don't have power (jurisdiction) over out-of-staters. However, there are three exceptions to the rule that a person or business must be served within California, as follows:

- A nonresident who owns real estate in California and has no agent in California for service of process may be served out of state, if, and only if, the claim relates to that property. The defendant doesn't have to personally appear in court. She can submit a written declaration, or allow another person (other than an attorney) to appear on her behalf. (CCP Sec. 116.340(e).)

- A nonresident owner or operator of a motor vehicle involved in a traffic accident on a California highway can be served by serving Small Claims papers on the California Director of Motor Vehicles with notice sent to the defendant (ask your Small Claims clerk for rules).

- A business which doesn't have a physical location in California, but nevertheless does business here, can be served out of state. (See Chapter 9, Section A.)

A. Who Must Be Served

All defendants that you list on your Claim of Plaintiff should be served. It is not enough to serve one defendant and assume that he will tell the other(s). This is true even if the defendants are married or living together. If you sue more than one person and can serve only one, a judge can only enter a judgment against the person served, in effect dismissing your action against the other defendant(s). You can refile against these defendants if you wish.

B. How to Serve Your Papers on an Individual

There are several approved ways to serve papers on individual defendants. (See Section C below, for information on serving a business.) All depend on your knowing where the defendant is. If you can't find the defendant personally and do not know where she lives or works, you can't serve her, and it probably makes little sense to file a lawsuit.

SERVING SOMEONE WITH A POST OFFICE BOX

If you only know an individual defendant's post office box, you'll need to get her street address in order to serve her. To do this, you must give the post office a written statement saying that you need the address solely to serve legal papers in a pending lawsuit. This should work, but if it doesn't, refer the post office employee to Administrative Support Manual Sec. 352.44e(2).

Method 1: Personal Service

Any person who is 18 years of age or older, except the person bringing the suit, may serve the defendant by handing him the Claim of Plaintiff anyplace in California. Any person means just that—in some counties, you can hire the county sheriff or marshal (often good for its sobering effect) or a private process server (listed in the Yellow Pages), or you can have a friend or relative do the service. Again, the only person 18 years or older who can't serve the papers in your lawsuit is you.

Using this method, the Claim of Plaintiff must be handed to the defendant personally. The person making a service who doesn't know the individual to be served should make sure that he is serving the right person. If a defendant refuses to take the paper, acts hostile or attempts to run away, the process server should simply put the paper down and leave. Valid service has been accomplished. The process server should never try to use force to get a defendant to take any papers.

Method 2: By Certified Mail

You can also attempt to serve your Claim of Plaintiff by certified mail with a return receipt. This approach is extremely easy since the clerk of the court does the mailing for you. There is a modest fee in California for each defendant, which is recoverable if you win. (See Chapter 15.) Unfortunately, the mail depends for its success on the defendant signing for the letter. Most businesses and many individuals routinely sign to accept mail. However, some people never do, knowing instinctively, or perhaps from past experience, that nothing good ever comes to them by certified mail. I have asked several court clerks for an estimate as to the percentage of certified mail services that are accepted. The consensus is 50%. If you try using the mail to serve your papers and fail, and end up paying a process server, tell the judge about it as part of your presentation and your out-of-pocket costs should be added to the judgment.

Check to be sure your papers were served. Never show up in court on the day of the court hearing on the assumption that your certified mail service has been accomplished. If the defendant didn't sign for the paper, you will be wasting your time. Call the court clerk a couple of days in advance and find out if the service of process has been completed. This means the certified letter has been signed for by the defendant, not by someone else at the address.

Method 3: Substituted Service (or "Nail and Mail")

Because it can be a pain in the neck to find a person for the purposes of serving her personally, and lots of people won't sign to accept certified mail, it is fortunate that there is an alternate service procedure called "substituted service" which provides an easier way to serve most defendants. It works like this: Small Claims papers (Claim and Order to Defendant) may be served by an adult who is not named in the lawsuit by leaving a copy at the defendant's dwelling place in the presence of a competent member of the household who is at least age 18 (and who must be told what the papers are about) or at the defendant's place of business during normal office hours with the person in charge. In either case, a copy of the papers must also be mailed to the defendant by first class mail. Service is complete ten days after mailing. Be sure that all steps, including mailing the extra copy, are carried out by an adult who is not named in the lawsuit.

Method 4: Department of Motor Vehicles (for Out-of-State Motorists Only)

As noted at the beginning of this chapter, there is a special procedure you may be able to use to serve an out-of-state defendant if your claim is based on an automobile accident which occurred in California. In this case, you can treat the Director of the Department of Motor Vehicles as the defendant's in-state agent for service of process. After checking the rules carefully with your Small Claims clerk, mail one copy of the Plaintiff's Claim to the Director (return receipt requested), along with a fee for each defendant to be served. Also, you must notify the defendant of your action by presenting her, through registered mail or personal service, with notice of service and a copy of the claim. (Vehicle Code Secs. 17454, 17455.)

Once you have completed service, you must give the court the receipt you received from the DMV, a declaration that you mailed the notice of service and a copy of the claim to the defendant, and a return mail receipt from the defendant. Also note that because of the potential inconvenience to an out-of-state defendant of defending a case in California, there are special rules when process is served through the DMV. Specifically, the defendant has 60 days to appear, and the court will normally grant any requested continuances to make sure the defendant has a chance to defend herself.

C. How to Serve Papers on a Business

When you sue a business, the same methods of service discussed just above can be used. However, if you use the personal service or certified mail service methods, the person who you must serve will depend on how the business is legally organized. (See Method 2, below.) And if you only know a business defendant's post office box, you'll normally want to get its street address. For businesses, the post office will release the street address upon written request and payment of a small fee.

Method 1: Substituted Service

The substituted service method is usually the easiest and best way to serve a business which has an office, store or other physical location. Simply have an adult (other than you) leave the papers at the defendant's business during usual business hours with the person in charge and then mail a copy of the summons and complaint to the person to be served at the same address. Service is complete ten days after mailing. It's that easy.

Method 2.   Personal and Certified Mail Service

Personal service or certified mail service (carried out by the Small Claims clerk) can be used to serve a business and will probably be your best choice if the business doesn't operate an office, store or other physical location.

Certified mail service will only work with reputable businesses. If a business has no physical location and you are having trouble locating its principals, serving your papers by certified mail probably won't work. Even if you find an address for an owner, chances are good she won't sign to accept the court papers.

Who you must serve depends on how the business is organized.

Sole proprietorship: Serve the owner.

Partnership: Serve at least one partner.

Limited partnership: Serve the partner who runs the business (the general partner).

Corporation (profit or nonprofit): Serve an officer (president, vice-president, secretary or treasurer).

Limited liability company: Serve an officer (president, vice-president, secretary or treasurer).

Sometimes it can be difficult to figure out who the officers of a corporation or limited liability company are. One simple approach is to call the business and ask who, and where, they are. If they won't tell you, the city or county business tax and license people where the business is located should be able to do so. (See Chapter 8.) Or for corporations or LLCs organized in this state, you can contact the California Secretary of State and ask for a "Last Statement of Officers" (there is a small fee). If you have trouble getting someone at a large national corporation to accept service, call or write the California Secretary of State, Corporate Status Unit, 1500 11th Street, Sacramento, CA 95814, 916-653-7315. They will be able to tell you who is authorized to accept service for the company in California. If a corporation has no authorized agent and you can find no corporate officer authorized to accept service in California, you may still be able to accomplish valid service by serving papers on the California Secretary of State. To do this you must get a court order from the Small Claims Court clerk. Send this paper to the Secretary of State with a fee. Unfortunately, while this accomplishes legal service, it is rarely warranted. Why? Because if you can't find anyone to serve, it's unlikely you can find assets to collect from.

D. How to Serve a Contractor or Anyone Else With a Surety Bond

If an action is filed against a contractor or other defendant who is bonded and the company issuing the bond (usually called a guaranty or surety company) is also sued, a reasonable attempt should be made to complete service on the contractor or other principal defendant, as well as the company issuing the bond. If the contractor or other principal cannot be served, the case is not eligible to be heard in Small Claims Court and must be transferred to Municipal Court.

E. How to Serve a Public Agency

As discussed in Chapter 8, Section H, before you can sue a city, county or other government body, you must first file a claim against that agency within six months of the incident that gives rise to your claim. (The fact that you did this must be stated in your Plaintiff's Claim.) After your claim is denied—or if it is ignored—you can go ahead and sue in Small Claims Court. To serve your papers, call the governmental body in question and ask them who should be served. Then proceed, following the rules set out in Section B, Method 1, 2 or 3, above.

F. Notify the Court That Service Has Been Accomplished ("Proof of Service")

If you have asked the court clerk to serve your papers by certified mail, you need do nothing. The court clerk sends out the certified mail for you, and the signed post office receipt comes back directly to the clerk if service is accomplished. It's as simple as that.

However, a court has no way of knowing whether or not papers have been successfully filed by personal or substituted service unless you tell them. This is done by filing a piece of paper known as a Proof of Service with the court clerk after the service has been made. The Proof of Service must be signed by the person actually making the service. A Proof of Service is used both by the plaintiff and by the defendant if he files a Claim of Defendant. It must be returned to the clerk's office not less than 48 hours before the trial. A Proof of Service is used when any legal documents are served by personal service.

Frequently there isn't time after a defendant is served for her to properly complete service of a Claim of Defendant. In this situation, the defendant should simply file her Claim of Defendant and bring up the service problem in court. The plaintiff may well waive the time of service requirement and agree to proceed. Or, the plaintiff may request that the judge continue the case to a later date. The judge will normally grant the continuance if there is a good reason.

PROOF OF SERVICE

PARTY ☒ PLAINTIFF ☐ DEFENDANT *(Name and Address)*:	TELEPHONE NO.:	FOR COURT USE ONLY

PARTY ☒ PLAINTIFF ☐ DEFENDANT *(Name and Address)*:   TELEPHONE NO.:

Debbie Nakamura
200 W. Hedding St.
San Jose, CA 95110

NAME AND ADDRESS OF COURT:
Santa Clara Small Claims Court
1095 Homestead Rd.
Santa Clara, CA 95050

PLAINTIFF(S):
     Debbie Nakamura
DEFENDANT(S):
     Sam Blue

PROOF OF SERVICE **(Small Claims)**	HEARING DATE: 12/22/__	DAY: Wed.	TIME: 9:00AM	DEPT./DIVISION: 1	CASE NUMBER: 002001

1. At the time of service I was at least 18 years of age and not a party to this action, and **I served copies** of the following:

☐ Plaintiff's Claim   ☐ Order of Examination   ☒ Other *(specify)*:   Notice of Motion to Vacate
☐ Defendant's Claim   ☐ Subpena Duces Tecum   Judgment

2. a. Party served *(specify name of party as shown on the documents served)*:
      Sam Blue

   b. Person served: ☒ party in item 2.a.   ☐ other *(specify name and title or relationship to the party named in item 2.a.)*

3. By delivery   ☒ at home   ☐ at business
   a. date: December 3, 19__
   b. time:
   c. address: 191 North First St., San Jose, CA 95113

4. **Manner of service** *(check proper box)*:
   a. ☐ **Personal service.** I personally delivered to and left copies with the party served. **(C.C.P. 415.10)**
   b. ☐ **Substituted service on corporation, unincorporated association (including partnership), or public entity.** By leaving, during usual office hours, copies in the office of the person served with the person who apparently was in charge and thereafter mailing (by first-class mail, postage prepaid) copies to the person to be served at the place where the copies were left. **(C.C.P. 415.20(a))**
   c. ☐ **Substituted service on natural person, minor, incompetent, or candidate.** By leaving copies at the dwelling house, usual place of abode, usual place of business, or usual mailing address other than a U. S. Postal Service post office box of the person served in the presence of a competent member of the household or a person apparently in charge of the office or place of business, at least 18 years of age, who was informed of the general nature of the papers, and thereafter mailing (by first-class mail, postage prepaid) copies to the person to be served at the place where the copies were left. **(C.C.P. 415.20(b))**
   d. ☒ Date of mailing: December 4, 19__   **From** *(city)*:   Santa Clara, CA 95050

> **Information regarding date and place of mailing is required for services effected in manner 4.b. and 4.c. above. Certified mail service may be performed only by the Clerk of the Court in small claims matters.**

5. **Person serving** *(name, address, and telephone number)*:

   Barbara Durant
   200 W. Hedding St.
   San Jose, CA 95110

   a. **Fee** for service: $
   b. ☒ Not a registered California process server
   c. ☐ **Exempt** from registration under B&P Section 22350(b)
   d. ☐ **Registered** California process server
      1. ☐ Employee or independent contractor
      2. **Registration Number:**
      3. **County:**

6. ☒ I declare under penalty of perjury under the laws of the State of California that the foregoing is true and correct.
7. ☐ I am a California sheriff, marshal, or constable and I certify that the foregoing is true and correct.

Date: December 3, 19__   ▶ *Barbara Durant*
                                                      (SIGNATURE OF SERVER)

Form Approved by the
Judicial Council of California
SC-104 [New January 1, 1992]

PROOF OF SERVICE
(Small Claims)

Code of Civil Procedure
§§ 415.10, 415.20

G. How to Serve Subpoenas

In Chapter 14, we discuss subpoenaing witnesses and documents. Subpoenas can't be served by mail. They must be served by personal service. The rules as to who can do the serving are the same as those set forth in Section B1, above, with one important difference: Any person, including the person bringing the suit, can serve the subpoena. In addition, the person making the service must be ready to pay the person subpoenaed a witness fee on the spot if it is requested. If you hire a sheriff or marshal to do the service, he or she will ask you to pay this fee, plus the service fee, in advance. (See Chapter 14, Section B, for details.)

H. How to Serve a Claim of Defendant

As you will remember from our discussion in Chapter 10, a Claim of Defendant is the form that the defendant files when he wishes to sue the plaintiff for money damages arising out of the same incident that forms the basis for the plaintiff's suit. A Claim of Defendant should be filed with the clerk and served on the plaintiff at least five days prior to the time that the court has set for the hearing on the plaintiff's claim, unless the plaintiff has served the defendant less than ten days before the date of the court hearing. In this event, the Claim of Defendant need only be served on the plaintiff one day prior to the hearing. (CCP Sec. 116.360(c).)

There will not be time to serve the Claim of Defendant by mail, so you will have to use personal service or substituted service, returning a Proof of Service form to the court clerk. If you are a defendant who has filed a claim and you are unable to serve the plaintiff, simply show up at the court hearing date with your papers and serve the plaintiff in the hallway (not the courtroom). Then explain to the judge why it was impossible to locate the plaintiff earlier. The judge will either put the whole case over (delay the case) for a few days, or allow you to proceed with your claim that day. Either way, she will accept your Claim of Defendant as validly served.

I. How to Serve Someone in the Military— Declaration of Non-Military Service

It is proper to serve someone who is on active duty in the armed forces. If she shows up, fine. If she doesn't, you have a problem. We learned in Chapter 10 that as a general rule, if a properly served defendant doesn't show up, you can get a "default judgment" against her. This is not true if the person you are suing is in the military (there is no problem suing someone in the reserves).

Default judgments cannot normally be taken against people on active duty in the armed forces because Congress has given our military personnel special protections. To get a default judgment, a statement must be filed under penalty of perjury that he or she is not in the military. The "Declaration of Non-Military Service" is part of your Claim of Plaintiff package and is routinely filled out and signed as part of every case, unless, of course, the defendant is on active duty in the military. Fortunately, if a defendant is on active duty all is not lost. A California Attorney General's Opinion (34 Ops. Att. Gen. 60 (1959)) has been interpreted in many counties to mean that if a soldier/sailor would not be unduly prejudiced by having to appear, she must do so. The plaintiff can accomplish this by contacting an officer who has knowledge of the military person's duty schedule and, assuming it's true, getting a statement that no military necessity prevents them from appearing in court. Then, if the military person doesn't appear, a default judgment will probably be granted. In fact, contacting the superior officer often results in the person agreeing to show up.

J. Costs of Personal Service

Professional process servers commonly charge from $20–$50 per service depending on how far they must travel. You can usually get these costs of service added to your judgment if you win, but be sure to remind the judge to do this when you conclude your court presentation. However, a few courts will not give the successful party an award to cover a process server's costs unless she first tried to have the papers served by the cheaper certified mail approach (Section B, Method 2, above). Other judicial districts prefer that you don't use the mail approach at all, because they feel that it wastes time, since too often the mail isn't accepted. Ask the Small Claims clerk in your district how she prefers that you accomplish service and how much the judge will allow as a service of process fee.

K. Time Limits in Which the Claim of Plaintiff Must Be Served

The defendant is entitled to receive service of the Claim of Plaintiff form at least ten days before the date of the court hearing, if she lives within the county in which the courthouse is located. If the defendant lives outside the county where the trial is to take place, he must be served at least 15 days before the trial date.

If the defendant is served fewer than the required number of days before the trial date, he can either go ahead with the trial anyway, or request that the case be delayed (continued) for 15 to 30 days. If it is impossible to show up in person to ask for a delay, call the court clerk and point out that you weren't served in the proper time and that you want the case put over (postponed). The clerk should see to it that a default judgment is not entered against you. (See Chapter 10, Section D, Changing a Court Date.) But just to be sure, get the clerk's name.

To count the days to see if service has been accomplished in the correct time, do not count the day the service is made, but do count the day of the court appearance. Also count weekends and holidays, unless the last day falls on a weekend or holiday. If so, the period extends to the next day that is not a holiday. (CCP Sec. 12.) Thus, if Jack served Julie on July 12 in Los Angeles County with a "Declaration and Order" listing a July 22 court date in the same county, service would be proper. This is true even if Saturday and Sunday fell on July 13 and 14. To count the days you would not count July 12, the day of service, but you would count July 13, 14, 15, 16, 17, 18, 19, 20, 21 and 22, for a total of ten days. If you are unable to serve the defendant(s) within the proper time, simply ask the court clerk for a new court date and try again.   ■

12

The Defendant's Options

This chapter is devoted to a review of the concerns of Small Claims defendants. Most of this material has already been discussed in the first eleven chapters, but since the plaintiff, as the initiator of a lawsuit, has so far gotten more than half the attention, let's now look at a Small Claims case exclusively from the point of view of the person being sued.

How should a defendant approach a Small Claims case? Start by understanding that there is no one correct course of action—it all depends on the facts of the dispute and your personal desires.

A. Claim That You Weren't Properly Served with Court Papers

You may conclude that you were not properly (legally) served with the plaintiff's court papers. (See Chapter 11.) Perhaps the Claim of Plaintiff was left with your neighbors, or maybe you weren't given the correct number of days in which to respond. Figuring that since there is one or more procedural defects in the plaintiff's case, you may even be tempted to not show up in court. This would be a mistake. The judge may be unaware of or overlook the problem and issue a default judgment against you. If this happens, you will have to go to the trouble of requesting that the default be vacated. (See Chapter 10.)

When the plaintiff fails to have court papers properly served on you or makes some other procedural error, the proper procedure is to contact the court in writing, explain the problem and ask that the case be dismissed. If the court can't or won't help, show up on the day in question and make your request in person. If the problem involves a failure to properly serve papers on you, chances are the plaintiff will re-serve you at this time, but at least the case should be delayed (continued) to give you a chance to prepare your defense.

B. Claim You Were Sued in the Wrong Small Claims Court

If you think the plaintiff has filed suit in the wrong California Small Claims Court or, in legal lingo, "in the wrong venue" (see Chapter 9), you can challenge the court's right to hear the case (challenge the venue).

As discussed in Chapter 9, you can do this in two ways. First, you can go to court on the day your case is scheduled and request that the case be dismissed. If the judge disagrees with you, she will simply go ahead and hear the case. However, if the judge agrees that the location (venue) is improper, she will dismiss the case, unless for some reason you volunteer to have it heard right then—perhaps just to get it over with.

Your second, and probably easier, option is to write directly to the court, explaining why you think the claim was brought in the wrong place. (CCP Sec. 116.370(b).) If the judge agrees that the suit was brought in the wrong place, she will dismiss it. If she disagrees, she will postpone the hearing for at least 15 days to give you an opportunity to appear. You will receive notification of the court's decision by mail.

Out-of-state defendants should ask for a dismissal. As discussed in Chapter 9, Section A, if you don't live—or do business—in California, a California Small Claims Court normally doesn't have power ("jurisdiction,") to enter a valid judgment against you, unless court papers are served on you while you happen to be in California. Exceptions to this rule exist for out-of-staters sued because of a dispute involving their real property located in California or because of a traffic accident that occurred in this state. If you are an out-of-state resident and receive Small Claims papers via the mail, promptly write a letter to the court explaining that you do not believe you are subject to the court's jurisdiction. Stay in touch with the court until you are sure the case has been dismissed.

C. You Have a Partial Defense—Try to Compromise

If you feel that perhaps the plaintiff has some right on his side, but that you are being sued for too much, your best bet is to try to work out a compromise settlement. (See Chapter 6, Section A, for more on how to negotiate.) One good approach is to call or write the plaintiff and make a settlement offer. How much depends on the relative merits of your case as compared to that of the plaintiff's, and whether the plaintiff is asking for a reasonable or inflated amount. Assuming the plaintiff has a pretty strong legal position (you probably are legally liable) and is asking the court for an amount that's, broadly speaking, reasonable, I recommend that you make an initial offer to pay about half of his request. Remember, even with a strong case, the plaintiff may be motivated to accept your lowball offer, if for no other reason than to save the time and trouble it takes to prepare for and appear in court. More likely, your initial offer will set in motion a little dance of offer and counteroffer, ending with the plaintiff accepting a compromise of somewhere between 65% and 80% of her original demand. Obviously, if the plaintiff is asking for way too much, or you are not sure that a judge would find that you are liable in the first place, you'll want to offer less or fight the case.

Any settlement you make should be set down in writing along the lines outlined in Chapter 6, Section D.

Don't rely on being judgment-proof. Some defendants who have at least a partial defense to the plaintiff's claim are tempted not to show up and defend a case in Small Claims Court because they have no money and figure that, even if they lose, the plaintiff can't collect. If you have a decent defense, this is just plain dumb. Judgments are good for ten years and can be renewed, if necessary. Hopefully, you'll get a job or otherwise put a few dollars together sometime in the future and, if so, you probably won't want them immediately taken away to satisfy a Small Claims judgment that you believe shouldn't have been entered in the first place. So wake up and defend yourself while you can. One possible exception to this "always fight back if you have a decent case" advice occurs when you plan to declare Chapter 7 bankruptcy. Bankruptcy wipes out most debts, including those that have been turned into a Small Claims judgment.

For more information as to whether personal bankruptcy makes sense, see *Bankruptcy: Is It the Right solution to Your Debt Problems,* by Robin Leonard (Nolo).

D. You Want to Avoid Conflict—Try to Mediate

In Chapter 6, Section B, I discuss mediation in some detail. Please reread this material. As you do, consider that engaging in mediation is frequently beneficial to the defendant, because mediation tends to encourage a compromise settlement for a lower amount than the plaintiff has demanded. In addition, mediation gives the defendant a chance to raise issues that would not be considered relevant by a Small Claims Court judge. For example, in a dispute between neighbors, small business people or relatives, mediation affords an opportunity for both legal and emotional (human) concerns to be raised and dealt with.

 Ask the Small Claims clerk for help setting up mediation. Mediation of all Small Claims cases can be set up in various ways in different California counties. In some it can take place in the courthouse itself. In others it's available at a nearby community mediation project. Ask the Small Claims Court clerk where mediation is available in your area. Then contact the mediation project and enlist their help in bringing the plaintiff to the table.

E. You Have Absolutely No Defense

Now let's assume that you were properly served with plaintiff's papers in a proper court and that you have no valid defense on the merits of the case. Perhaps you borrowed money under the terms of a written contract and haven't been able to pay it back. Since you know you'll lose, you may conclude that it makes little sense to defend yourself in court. Your decision not to show up will very likely result in a default judgment being entered against you. This judgment will most probably be for the dollar amount demanded by the plaintiff, plus the amount of his filing fee and any reasonable costs to serve the papers on you. (In Chapters 10 and 15 I discuss default judgments and how you can probably get one vacated if you act immediately.)

Even if you owe 100% of the plaintiff's demand, it never hurts to make an offer. Especially if you have the money, why not offer to pay 75%-90% of what the plaintiff requests. To save the trouble of going to court—or for some other reason you may never guess—the defendant may accept even though if he went to court he would almost surely win a judgment for the whole amount.

F. You Want to Pay the Plaintiff in Installments

If you do not dispute the amount of the plaintiff's claim, but want to make payments in installments rather than all at once, your best bet is to show up on the day your case is scheduled and explain your situation to the judge. Tell the judge how much you can afford to pay each month.

Or you can wait until the judgment is entered and promptly file a form entitled Request to Pay Judgment in Installments, along with a Financial Declaration Form (both are available from the court clerk) explaining why it would be difficult or impossible to pay any judgment all at once. For example, if you are on a fixed income, have recently been unemployed and have a lot of debts or have a low or moderate income and a large family, just state these facts—there is no need to tell a long sob story. The plaintiff (now called the judgment creditor) has ten days in which to accept or oppose your proposed payment schedule. (See Chapter 23 for more on paying a judgment in installments.)

G. Fight Back

Suppose now you feel you don't owe the plaintiff a dime and you want to actively fight the case filed against you. To do this, simply show up in court on the date stated in the papers served on you, ready to present your side of the story. (See Chapter 10.) A defendant need not file any papers with the court clerk unless she wants to countersue the plaintiff by filing a Claim of Defendant. Although it is unusual, a few types of defendants don't even need to appear in court themselves, but are legally authorized to send someone else to Small Claims Court on their behalf or, if they prefer, present their case in writing. These include prisoners and nonresident real property owners. In addition, landlords may send their property managers to court to represent their interests. (See Ch. 20 for more on landlords' rights.)

Before you even think about the merits of the plaintiff's case, your first job is to check to be sure the plaintiff has brought it within the time allowed by the statute of limitations (Chapter 5). If not, tell the judge at the beginning of your presentation and request that the plaintiff's case be dismissed.

To successfully present your defense, you'll want to be prepared to make a well-organized, convincing oral statement, backed up with as much evidence as possible. Good case presentation strategies, including how to present witnesses, estimates, diagrams and other evidence, are discussed in Chapters 13–22 and apply both to defendants and plaintiffs. If the plaintiff has asked for too much money, you'll also want to be sure you tell the judge exactly why (see Chapter 4).

Here are some tips that should help you mount a powerful defense:

- *Take apart your opponent's case.* To do this, you will normally want to focus on any facts that show you are not legally liable. (As part of doing this, reread Chapter 2 to see what the plaintiff must prove for all the common types of Small Claims cases). If after doing this you reluctantly conclude the plaintiff arguably does have a winning case, next consider whether he has asked for the right dollar amount. Obviously, if you can convince a judge that you only owe a couple of hundred, not several thousand, dollars, you will have won a substantial victory (see Chapter 4).

  Example: The plaintiff sues you for a breach of contract. You reread Chapter 2, Section C, to understand what the plaintiff must prove to win her case. Then, assuming the facts support your position, you might claim that no contract existed in the first place. Or that even if a contract did exist, the plaintiff violated its terms so thoroughly that you were justified in considering it to be void. And even if you have to admit that you broke a valid contract, you might claim the plaintiff is asking for far too much money.

Example: *You are sued by someone claiming your negligent conduct resulted in their property being damaged (as would be the case in a fender-bender). To prevail, you would want to convince the court that you were not negligent (careless), or, if you were, the plaintiff was more at fault. And even if the judge decides that the case was your fault, you might want to claim that the plaintiff paid far more than was necessary to have his car fixed.*

- *Gather evidence.* As emphasized in Chapters 13 and 14, the key to winning in Small Claims Court is very often to convince the judge that your version of the facts is correct. To do this, you'll normally need to back up your oral presentation with convincing evidence. One good approach is to present the testimony of an eyewitness (if you are lucky enough to have one) or an expert witness who agrees with your position (a mechanic who can explain how the plaintiff damaged your engine). In addition, if it's available you will want to show the judge any documentary evidence such as letters, photos and opinions of experts—or sometimes even damaged property—that back up your version of events. For example, if you are a computer repair person sued by someone who claims you ruined her PC, you may want to get a written opinion from another repair shop that the current problem with the computer has nothing to do with the defect you fixed. In addition, it would make sense to present any advertisements or trade pricing data that tend to show that the plaintiff is placing an inflated value on her used computer.

- *Be prepared to make a convincing courtroom presentation.* The plaintiff gets to talk first. Patiently and quietly wait until it's your turn.

  When the plaintiff is done, be prepared to make an incisive and logical presentation of why the plaintiff should receive little or nothing. As mentioned several times in this book, once you have your arguments thought out, it is an extremely good idea to practice exactly what you plan to say in front of a friend or family member until it is letter perfect. One trick to getting and keeping the judge's attention is not to repeat uncontested facts presented by the plaintiff, but to immediately focus on why the plaintiff's case is misguided.

Example: *Tom, the landlord, listens patiently as Evie, the tenant, spends five minutes presenting a rambling, sometimes incorrect history of their landlord–tenant relationship as an introduction to her main point that she should have gotten her security deposit back because she left the rental unit clean and undamaged. When it's finally*

Tom's turn, he ignores Evie's inconsequential mistakes. Instead, he focuses on the exact point of the dispute by saying, "Your Honor, the key to my defense is that the plaintiff left the rental at 127 Spring Street in a dirty and damaged condition. I have pictures to demonstrate this and a reliable witness to back it up. But first I would like to briefly list the three worst problems."

H. If You, Not the Plaintiff, Were Wronged—File a Claim of Defendant

Finally, some defendants will not only want to dispute the plaintiff's claim, but will also want to sue him. Perhaps you are outraged that the plaintiff sued first, since you are the person who was wronged. To assert your own claim against the plaintiff, promptly file a Claim of Defendant for up to $5,000 in Small Claims Court, or for a larger amount in Municipal or Superior Court. (For more on what to do if you wish to sue the plaintiff, see Chapter 10, Section C, and Chapter 11, Section H.)

Assuming your case stays in Small Claims Court, both your claim and the plaintiff's will be heard together. You should prepare and present your case just as you would if you had filed first—that is, understand the legal basics that underlie your case, make a practical and convincing oral presentation and back it up with as much hard evidence as you can find.

A defendant's counterclaim can be based on different facts than the plaintiff's claim. Most of the time any claim a defendant asserts against the plaintiff will arise from the same fact situation that gave rise to the plaintiff's lawsuit. But this isn't required. If you have a valid claim against the plaintiff which arises out of a different event from the one that forms the basis of her suit, you can nevertheless assert it as the basis for a defendant's claim. (See Chapter 10, Section C.)

Example: Amy sues Beth for $1,000 for an unpaid loan. Beth countersues Amy for $1,500, based on her claim that Amy failed to return a valuable ring she borrowed. Both disputes should be heard by the same Small Claims judge on the same day. ■

Getting Ready for Court

Once your papers have been filed with the Small Claims clerk and the defendant(s) have been properly served, the preliminaries are over and you are ready for the main event— your day in court. Movies, and especially TV (yes, even "Court TV"), have done much to create false impressions of court proceedings. Ask yourself what a trial might have been like before every lawyer fancied himself Raymond Burr, Charles Laughton or even Johnnie Cochran, and judges acted "parental" or "stern" or "indignantly outraged" in the fashion of Judge Judy.

I mention this "movie-itis" because it is a particularly common ailment in Small Claims Court. Cases that should be easily won are sometimes lost because one party or the other goes marching around the courtroom antagonizing everyone with comic opera imitations of Marcia Clark. And don't assume you are immune. Movie-itis can often be a stealth disease, with many people never realizing they have it. To find out if you are likely to be infected, ask yourself a few self-diagnostic questions:

- Have you frequently watched courtroom scenes on TV or in the movies?

- Have you ever imagined that you were one of the lawyers?

- How many times have you watched a court case in person as compared to watching a made, or staged, for the media trial?

I'm sure you get the idea. Chances are good that, like most of us, your idea of what a court proceeding is like comes mostly from Hollywood. If so, the best advice I can give you is to put aside everything you think you have learned watching the media and just be yourself. To succeed in Small Claims Court, you don't need fancy clothes, words or attitudes. Just use plain English to tell the judge what happened and why you are in the right. If you feel a little anxious about a first court appearance, drop by the court a few days before your case is heard and watch several hearings. You may not learn a great deal that will be directly helpful in your case, but you will almost surely be a lot more relaxed and comfortable when your turn comes.

Movie-itis aside, most people I have watched present or defend Small Claims cases have done pretty well. But it's also true that only a few made outstanding presentations. It's fair to ask, what set this elite group apart? I bet you know what I'm going to say. That's right—practice and preparation. The people who did best had clearly prepared carefully enough that they were able to make a clear, concise verbal presentation, backed up by the orderly introduction of convincing evidence.

The rest of this chapter contains basic information about how Small Claims Court works. I'll discuss how to prepare and present different types of cases in the next chapters.

A. Interpreter Services

The Small Claims Court clerk is required to make a reasonable effort to maintain and make available a list of interpreters in as many languages as possible who are willing to aid parties for no fee or a reasonable fee. However, failure to have an interpreter for a particular language on the list, or even failure to provide a list at all, does not invalidate any proceedings. But if for any reason a competent interpreter isn't available at the first hearing, the court must postpone the hearing (one time only) to allow the party to get an interpreter. Future postponements are at the judge's discretion. (CCP Sec. 116.550.)

Language problems? Look for help from community organizations. Many ethnic and cultural organizations offer interpreter services to low-income persons free of charge. Be sure to contact the appropriate organization well in advance of your court date to ask for help.

B. Free Small Claims Advice

Every county must provide a program of free advice to Small Claims litigants on how to present their claims or defenses in Small Claims Court. (CCP Sec. 116.940.) Many counties take this mandate very seriously, providing excellent counseling services run by competent advisors available at convenient hours. Smaller counties often provide help by phone. Ask the clerk about times and places for your local advisory programs. Advisors can be particularly helpful if you can't answer any of the following questions:

1. Do I have a good case?

2. Is the legal theory on which my case is based sound? (I discuss this in detail in Chapter 2.)

3. How can I organize my testimony and that of my witnesses in order to have the best chance to convince the judge to rule in my favor?

Several areas offer a free 24-hour phone service, featuring a menu of pre-recorded advice on various aspects of Small Claims Court. No matter where you live, these services may provide just the information you need.

- Berkeley/Oakland, call 510-644-6303

- San Francisco, call 415-292-2124

- Los Angeles, call 213-974-6135

- the San Diego area, call 619-694-2066

Be ready to do some of your own research. No matter how much help you receive and how good it is, there will be times when you'll need to do some of your own legal research. I discuss how to do this in Chapter 1, Section D.

C. Getting Help From a Private Lawyer

Lawyers cannot represent you in a California Small Claims Court. However, it's legal and occasionally cost-effective to hire a lawyer to give you advice only. If you are worried about some legal aspect of your case and can't get an answer from a free Small Claims advisor (see Section B, above) or by doing your own research (see Chapter 1, Section D), it can be sensible to discuss the problem with a lawyer. This should not cost more than $100-$150 for a short consultation. Make sure you negotiate the fee in advance.

D. Mediation

As discussed in considerable detail in Chapter 6, free or low-cost mediation services are available in many California communities on a voluntary basis (except in Yolo County, where an attempt to mediate is required before going to court). Ask any Small Claims clerk or advisor for information on how to contact local mediation programs. These programs are designed to help people settle their own disputes—not to impose a decision, as is done in Small Claims Court. Especially if you will inevitably have a continuing relationship with the person with whom you have a dispute—as is the case with a neighbor or family member—trying to achieve a compromise settlement is almost always wiser than fighting it out in court. Even if your opponent has previously been reluctant to engage in mediation, you can again raise this possibility with the judge just before your case is heard. The judge, who has the power to continue (postpone) the case to allow the parties to try to settle it, may attempt to talk the other party into giving mediation a try.

E. Practice Your Court Presentation

As mentioned, once you are pretty sure your case can't be settled and you will need to go to court, your best approach is to practice presenting it. Line up an objective, tough-minded friend and run through your entire case just as you plan to on court day. Ask your friend for suggestions, not compliments. For example, he may tell you that you need a witness or written documentation, a better grasp of the legal technicalities involved or a better-organized presentation. Take his advice to heart and make all possible improvements. Then practice again.

F. Getting to the Courthouse

Before you locate the right courtroom, you obviously have to get to the right building. Sometimes, doing this can be tricky, because Small Claims courts are often not in the main courthouse. Like a half-forgotten stepsister, many are housed wherever the city or county has an empty room. In short, don't assume that you know where your Small Claims Court is unless you've been there before. Plaintiffs have already had to find the clerk's office to file their papers, so they probably know where the courtroom is, but defendants should check this out in advance. Be sure, too, that your witnesses know exactly where and when to show up. And do plan to be a few minutes early—people who rush in flustered and late start with a strike against them.

G. Court Times

Small Claims cases are most often scheduled either at 9:00 a.m or early in the afternoon. Usually a number of cases are set for the same time and heard in turn. In larger judicial districts, Saturday or evening sessions must also be held. If it is not convenient for you to go to court during business hours, request that your case be scheduled at one of these other sessions.

H. Understanding the Courtroom and Basic Procedure

Most Small Claims proceedings are conducted in standard courtrooms also used for other types of court proceedings. Indeed, sometimes you will have to sit through a few minutes of Municipal or Superior Court before the Small Claims calendar is called.

Most judges still sit on little elevated wooden throne boxes and wear depressing black dresses (called robes). Both of these affectations trace their history back through a thousand years of English history to a time when courts were controlled by king, nobility and clergy, all of whom were entitled to dispense justice from on high. In addition to the judge, a clerk and a bailiff will normally be present. They usually sit at tables immediately in front of the judge. The clerk's job is to keep the judge supplied with necessary files and papers, and to make sure that proceedings flow smoothly. The bailiff is there to keep order in the courtroom if tempers get out of hand.

No written record of court proceedings is kept. A Small Claims clerk is not the same as a court reporter, who keeps a word-by-word record of proceedings. In California, no such record is kept in Small Claims Court, and no court reporter is present, although in a few areas, tape recordings are made and may be reviewed if a case is appealed.

Courtrooms are divided about two-thirds of the way toward the front by a little fence (known to initiates as the "bar"). The public must stay on the opposite side of the bar from the judge, clerk, bailiff and attorneys, unless asked to come forward. This invitation occurs when your case is called by name (*Smith vs. Jones Ford* or *Abercrombie vs. Lee*) by the clerk. At this point you, and any witnesses, will normally be asked to step to the front of the room and sit at a table (known as the "counsel table"). At this point, you will face the judge with your back to the spectator section of the courtroom. In a few courtrooms, judges try to hurry things along by asking everyone to stand in front of the judge's bench. The idea seems to be that if people can't sit down, they will present their cases faster. This might be okay if the judge would stand, too, but since they never do, I feel it's insulting.

In Small Claims Courts, you must swear (or affirm, if you wish) to tell the truth. Often this oath is administered before the first case is heard to everyone who will testify at that session. However, occasionally the oath will be administered to participants separately as each case is called.

In the great majority of Small Claims Courts, you, your opponent and your witnesses will present the entire case from the long counsel table. This means that neither you nor your witnesses sit in the witness box next to the judge. Many people (and judges) feel that it is polite to stand when addressing the judge, but you should do what feels most comfortable.

Normally, the plaintiff will be asked to present her case first and introduce any witnesses, who will also get a chance to have their say. When the plaintiff is done, it will be the defendant's turn to speak and present witnesses. Both sides should have any papers or other evidence that backs up their story carefully organized to present to the judge. This can include bills, receipts, estimates, photographs, contracts, letters to or from your opponent and other types of documentation or physical evidence. At the appropriate place in your presentation, tell the judge you have evidence you want her to see, and then hand it to the clerk, who in turn will give it to the judge. As I emphasize often in this book, appropriate documentation can be a huge aid to winning your case. But don't go overboard: Judges are a little like donkeys—load them too heavily and they are likely to become uncooperative and possibly even ornery.

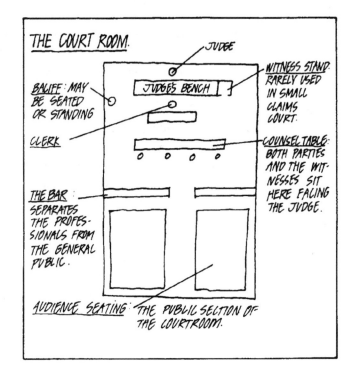

I. Dealing With Your Opponent

As you plan your courtroom strategy, give thought to your opponent. What sort of presentation will she make? And even more important, how can you best counter her arguments? Incidentally, spending time figuring out how to cope with your opponent's best points is not only an effective way to flesh out your case, but it can be a good way to turn the negative energy you probably feel (frustration, annoyance, anger) into something creative.

Once in court, always be polite when presenting or defending your case. If you are hostile or sarcastic, you run the considerable risk of losing the respect of the judge. Never interrupt your opponent when she is speaking—you will get your chance. When you do, lay out the key facts that support your position directly to the judge; don't conduct an argument with the other side.

How to cope with the big lie: I am sometimes asked what to do if your opponent tells the judge a huge fib. Although not an everyday occurrence, big lies definitely are told in Small Claims Court and can sometimes strongly influence the judge in your opponent's favor if you aren't prepared to poke holes in them. If your adversary tells a whopper, your best approach will be to wait calmly for your turn to speak and then say something like this: "Your honor, almost everything defendant (or plaintiff) has said about __ X __ is simply not true. Please let me prove this to you with facts." Then present your testimony and evidence—or if you have already shown the judge key evidence, remind him of why it demonstrates that your opponent's story is totally false. For example, if your former landlord who failed to return your security deposit swears you left the apartment filthy, you should totally destroy his credibility if you can show the judge photos or a video which demonstrates how clean it really was. Fortunately, if you can demonstrate that your opponent has told one big lie, the judge will distrust and hopefully disbelieve the rest of what he says.

J. Dealing With the Judge or Commissioner

The person who hears your case may be a regular Municipal Court judge who also presides over many other types of cases. But, increasingly, full-time commissioners are being hired to handle Small Claims cases. This is an administrative category designed to allow lawyers to be paid lower salaries and benefits than are paid to judges (a bit like colleges hiring non-tenured instructors instead of full professors). By and large, commissioners—who usually hear Small Claims cases on a daily basis—do a very competent job, sometimes better than judges, who have other duties and have occasionally been known to act as if they are too important to hear such small disputes.

In addition to commissioners and regular judges, volunteer lawyers are also routinely appointed when a judge or commissioner is ill or on vacation. The legal slang for a temporary judge is "judge, pro tem." If your case comes up on a day when only a pro tem judge is present, you will be given a choice as to whether you want to go ahead or have it rescheduled on a day when a regular judge or commissioner will be present. Especially if your case is contested and you feel it involves fairly complicated legal issues, I recommend that you do not accept a pro tem judge. Pro tem judges are not paid, rarely trained and often do not have much practical experience in the legal areas that are commonly heard in Small Claims Court. While some are excellent, too many are seriously substandard, meaning that as a group they are best avoided. Perhaps it will really bring this point home if I tell you that in the 20 years I have authored this book, I've received more complaints about lousy pro tem judges than for any other aspect of Small Claims Court.

⚠ Sometimes an attempt is made to hide your right to reject a temporary judge. In some court-rooms, before court begins for the day, a clerk will ask you to sign a form accepting a particular judge, without clearly explaining that she is a local lawyer serving on a temporary (pro tem) basis and that you have the right to say no. Don't fall for this. Whenever you are asked to approve a judge, you can be sure the person is a substitute for the real judge, and that you do have the right to have your case heard before a real judge or commissioner. Again, based on the dozens of complaints I've received about pro tems, I advise you to insist on having your case heard by a full-time professional, not an amateur.

What if your case will be heard by a regular judge or commissioner who you don't like, either because you know the person or because you have been put off by the way she has handled other cases? For example, you might live in a small town or city and be convinced a particular judge, whose reputation you know, is likely to be hard on you (for example, you are a landlord and the judge is known to be pro-tenant). Fortunately, a little-known law (CCP Sec. 170.6) allows you to "disqualify" a regular judge simply on your honest belief that he is "prejudiced" against you. No one will ask you to prove it. To disqualify a judge, you can simply say, when your case is called (after you've been "sworn in"), something like this: "Your Honor, I believe you are prejudiced against my interest, and I request a trial before another judge."

Especially for cases where a lot is at stake—for example, a number of people file nuisance cases based on drug dealing or noise (see Chapter 7, Section E)—it often makes sense to do some research on the judge who is likely to be assigned your case. Start by asking the Small Claims Court clerk for a list of the judges who may be assigned to your case. One good way to check them out is to have someone in your group (or perhaps a friend or relative) who has the necessary contacts talk to several local lawyers who have practiced before them. Many lawyers will readily share their opinions, especially if they consider a particular judge to be obnoxious or incompetent. If you discover reliable information about a particular judge that makes you doubt her ability to be fair, be prepared to challenge her.

Assuming you go ahead and present your case to a particular judge, the next question is, how can you convince him you are right? Answer this question by imagining yourself to be in the judge's shoes. What would you value most from the people appearing before you? Before I spent a few weeks sitting as a temporary judge, my answer was "politeness, a well-organized factual presentation and reasonable brevity." After experiencing Small Claims Court from the judge's chair, I would only add one word—"evidence." By this, I mean a presentation that consists of more than just your oral statement as to what happened. Witnesses, written statements, police accident reports and photographs all give a judge the opportunity to make a decision based on something more reliable than who tells the better story. And two more points. First, remember that the person who is deciding your case has heard thousands of stories very much like yours, and will either cease paying attention or get annoyed if you are needlessly repetitive. Second, don't let the robe and other trappings of judicial office obscure the fact that you are dealing with a human being who, like anyone else, is far more likely to be sympathetic to your point of view if you can convince him that you occupy the moral high ground (for example, you are honest, kind and pay your debts) and that your opponent is the bad guy (tricky, hard-hearted and fails to keep his promises).

K. Organizing Your Testimony and Evidence

As mentioned frequently in this text, it's essential that you organize what you have to say and the physical evidence you wish to show the judge. Do this by dividing your testimony into a list of the several main points you want to make. Under each heading, note any items of physical or documentary evidence you wish to show the judge. If your evidence consists of a number of items, make sure that you put them in order and can find each item quickly.

Example (from the plaintiff's point of view): Let's assume your case is based on a hotel's failure to return your deposit when you canceled a wedding reception three months before the event was to be held. Your list of key points—and the evidence to back them up—might look like this:

- *Valley View Hotel refused to return my $500 deposit when I canceled my wedding reception.*
- *This was true even though I canceled 83 days before the event.*
- *The contract I signed with the hotel allowed a full refund if cancellation occurred more than 60 days before the event. (Show contract to the judge.)*

- *When I canceled, Valley View told me (and claims they sent me a letter stating) that their cancellation policy had been changed the previous month to require 90 days notice in order to get a refund.*
- *I never received a letter and had no idea of the policy change until I canceled and asked for my money back.*
- *Even if Valley View did send me a letter, the change should not affect my contract, which was signed prior to the policy change. The key point here is, since I never signed a new contract, the existing contract was still valid.*
- *In any event, the hotel has a duty to try and re-rent the banquet room to minimize (mitigate) any damages they suffered. And they had plenty of time (83 days) to do so. (See Chapter 4, Section C1, for a discussion of the mitigation of damages point.)*
- *Ninety days is an unreasonably long cancellation policy.*
- *Here is a list of the cancellation policies of five other hotels in the area, all of which allow a full refund on much shorter notice than 83 days. (Give list to the judge.)*

Example (from the defendant's point of view): *Since Valley View goes second, their representative can't know in advance what the plaintiff will say and what evidence it will present. It follows that Valley View will need to adopt a little more flexible approach. Still, since chances are that Valley View reps have talked to the plaintiff or exchanged letters, they probably have a pretty good idea of what to expect. Accordingly, Valley View's list might look something like this.*

- *True, we didn't refund the $500. The reason was we turned down two other receptions for that same day before plaintiff canceled. Since we ended up with no other function, we lost at least $500.*
- *Although it is true that the written contract allowed cancellation prior to 60 days before the event, plaintiff was notified that this policy had been changed to 90 days before the contract was signed in two ways:*
    - √ *A sign on the reservations desk where the plaintiff sat to sign the contract. (Show sign to judge.)*
    - √ *Testimony of Angie Ells, who booked the reservation. Angie will testify that she included written notice of the change with the contract package. (Show judge a copy of the notice.)*

 Chapters 14–22 contain an extensive discussion about how to prepare for court and what to do once you get there.   ■

Witnesses

For many types of cases it is extremely helpful to have someone in court with you who has a firsthand knowledge of the facts of your case and who can support your point of view. Witnesses are particularly valuable for cases where key facts are in dispute, such as is common with a car accident or landlord–tenant security deposit fight. However, in some fact situations, witnesses aren't as necessary. For example, if a friend borrowed $500 and didn't pay it back, you don't need a witness to prove that your now ex-friend's signature on the promissory note is genuine, unless you expect him to base his defense on the theory that it was forged.

A. Who Makes a Good Witness

A good witness should have firsthand knowledge of the facts in dispute. This means either she saw something that helps establish your case (for example, the car accident, or dog bite, or dirty apartment) or is an expert you have consulted about an important aspect of your case (for example, a car mechanic who testifies that your engine wasn't fixed properly). The judge will not be interested in the testimony of a person who is repeating secondhand or generalized information such as "I know Joe is a good, safe driver and would never have done anything reckless," or "I didn't see Joe's apartment before he moved out, but both Joe and his mother, who couldn't be here today, told me that they worked for two days cleaning it up."

Above all, a good witness is believable. This isn't always an easy quality to define. For example, a police officer may be a symbol of integrity to some people, while others will automatically discount much of what she says. But remember, it's the judge you are trying to convince, and judges tend to be fairly establishment folk. They make comfortable salaries, own their own homes and generally tend to like the existing order of things. Most judges I know would tend to believe a police officer.

In many types of cases, such as a car accident, you won't have much choice as to witnesses. You will be lucky to have one person who saw what happened. Often this will be a close friend or family member. There is no rule that says you can't have these people testify for you. Indeed, I have often seen a person's spouse, roommate or close friend give very convincing testimony. But given a choice, it is usually better to have a witness who is neither buddy nor kin. That's because a judge may discount testimony of people to whom you are close on the theory that they would naturally be biased in your favor. One little trick to dispel this judicial cynicism is to have a closely related witness bend over backwards to treat the other side as fairly as possible. Thus, if your brother is your only witness to the fact that ABC Painting splashed paint on your boat, he might point out to the judge not only that he saw ABC employees screw up, but that it was a very windy day and the painter was understandably having a hard time keeping the paint where it belonged.

In some types of disputes, such as whether your house was properly painted or the work on the car engine competently completed, you have an opportunity to plan ahead to locate witnesses. That's because the type of witness you need is usually not an eyewitness who saw the work in progress, but instead an expert in the field who can convincingly explain what went wrong. Obviously this type of witness is only valuable if she really does have good credentials so that a judge is likely to believe what she says. Thus, in a dispute over whether or not car repairs were properly done, it's preferable to bring a letter from a car mechanic with 20 years' experience who has completed a load of training courses rather than one from your neighbor "who knows a lot about cars."

I will talk more about witnesses as I go through the various case examples (Chapters 16–21). Here let's outline the basic techniques most predictive of success:

- Prepare your witness thoroughly as to what your legal and factual position is and what your opponent is likely to say. In court, the witness will be on her own, and you want to be sure that the story comes out right. It is completely legal to thoroughly discuss the case with your witness beforehand, as long as you do not coach or encourage the witness to lie or exaggerate.

- Never ask a witness to testify in court unless you know exactly what he will say. This sounds basic, but I have seen people lose cases because their witnesses got mixed up, and in one instance, where the witness actually supported the other side.

- Never use a subpoena to require a witness to be present unless you make sure that it is okay with the witness, as might be the case if she needs a good reason to take off a few hours from her job (more about subpoenas in Section B, below). Otherwise you may end up making the person so mad he will testify against you.

- Do not offer to pay an eyewitness to testify on your behalf (except for the small witness fee he is legally entitled to by law (see Section B, below)). If discovered, your payment will likely be seen as a bribe.

- It's proper and perfectly legal to pay an expert witness—say a car mechanic who has examined your engine—a reasonable fee for her time. But it is usually not necessary to pay such a witness to actually come to court. That's because under Small Claims Court's informal rules, the expert can simply write a letter to the judge explaining her findings, which you can then present as part of your case.

Don't act like a lawyer when asking your witnesses to testify. In the courtroom, your witness will normally sit next to you at the table facing the judge and tell what he knows about the dispute from there (in some courtrooms, the judge may ask all parties and witnesses to approach the judge's bench and stand there in a little group). In Small Claims Court, it is fairly rare for the judge to ask a witness to take the witness stand, but it happens in a few courts. Assuming your witness is seated at the counsel table, it is best for her to stand when it's her turn to speak and simply explain what happened. There is no need for you to pretend to be a lawyer and ask your witness a lot of leading questions. The judge is likely to ask the witness questions and may even interrupt her presentation and cause her to lose her train of thought. When the witness is done, if you feel she has left something out, simply ask a question designed to produce the information you want.

B. Subpoenaing Witnesses

In California, you can require that a witness with firsthand knowledge of what happened be present if that person resides within the state. To do this, go to the clerk's office and get a "subpoena" form. Fill it out and have it served on the person you wish to have present. But remember, you never want to subpoena a person unless you have talked to her first and gotten an okay. The very act of dragging someone into court who doesn't want to come may set her against you. A subpoenaed witness is entitled to a fee of $35, plus 20¢ per mile each way from home to court. If you win your case, you will probably be able to recover your witness fees from the other side. The judge has discretion as to whether or not to grant you your witness fees. Most judges are strict about this, making the loser pay the winner's witness fees only if they find that the subpoenaed witness was essential to the preparation of the case. This means that if your case is so strong that you don't need a witness to appear in person but you subpoena one anyway, you may well have to pay the witness fee even though you win the case.

Here is the standard California subpoena form, available at the Small Claims Court clerk's office. You will need to prepare an original and two copies. Once prepared, take the subpoena form to the clerk, who will issue it. Service must be made personally and the Proof of Service, which is on the back of the subpoena, returned to the clerk's office. Rules for service are discussed in Chapter 11.

CIVIL SUBPOENA

ATTORNEY OR PARTY WITHOUT ATTORNEY (Name and Address):	TELEPHONE NO.:	FOR COURT USE ONLY
John O'Gara 15 Scenic St. Albany, CA		

ATTORNEY FOR (Name): In Pro Per

NAME OF COURT: Municipal Court, County of Alameda
STREET ADDRESS: 2000 Center St.
MAILING ADDRESS:
CITY AND ZIP CODE: Berkeley, CA 94704
BRANCH NAME: Berkeley-Albany Judicial District
PLAINTIFF/PETITIONER: Public Library

DEFENDANT/RESPONDENT: John O'Gara

CIVIL SUBPENA	CASE NUMBER:
☐ Duces Tecum	(fill in number)

THE PEOPLE OF THE STATE OF CALIFORNIA, TO (NAME): Jane Doe

1. **YOU ARE ORDERED TO APPEAR AS A WITNESS** in this action at the date, time, and place shown in the box below UNLESS you make a special agreement with the person named in item 3:

   a. Date: Time: ☐ Dept.:   ☐ Div.:   ☐ Room:
   b. Address:

2. **AND YOU ARE**
   a. ☒ ordered to appear in person.
   b. ☐ not required to appear in person if you produce the records described in the accompanying affidavit and a completed declaration of custodian of records in compliance with Evidence Code sections 1560, 1561, 1562, and 1271. (1) Place a copy of the records in an envelope (or other wrapper). Enclose your original declaration with the records. Seal them. (2) Attach a copy of this subpena to the envelope or write on the envelope the case name and number, your name and date, time, and place from item 1 (the box above). (3) Place this first envelope in an outer envelope, seal it, and mail it to the clerk of the court at the address in item 1. (4) Mail a copy of your declaration to the attorney or party shown at the top of this form.
   c. ☐ ordered to appear in person and to produce the records described in the accompanying affidavit. The personal attendance of the custodian or other qualified witness and the production of the original records is required by this subpena. The procedure authorized by subdivision (b) of section 1560, and sections 1561 and 1562, of the Evidence Code will not be deemed sufficient compliance with this subpena.

3. **IF YOU HAVE ANY QUESTIONS ABOUT THE TIME OR DATE FOR YOU TO APPEAR, OR IF YOU WANT TO BE CERTAIN THAT YOUR PRESENCE IS REQUIRED, CONTACT THE FOLLOWING PERSON BEFORE THE DATE ON WHICH YOU ARE TO APPEAR:**
   a. Name: John O'Gara   b. Telephone number: (510) 555-1212

4. **Witness Fees:** You are entitled to witness fees and mileage actually traveled both ways, as provided by law, if you request them at the time of service. You may request them before your scheduled appearance from the person named in item 3.

> DISOBEDIENCE OF THIS SUBPENA MAY BE PUNISHED AS CONTEMPT BY THIS COURT. YOU WILL ALSO BE LIABLE FOR THE SUM OF FIVE HUNDRED DOLLARS AND ALL DAMAGES RESULTING FROM YOUR FAILURE TO OBEY.

Date issued:

▶

....
(TYPE OR PRINT NAME)

_____
(SIGNATURE OF PERSON ISSUING SUBPENA)

(TITLE)

(See reverse for proof of service)

Form Adopted by Rule 982
Judicial Council of California
982(a)(15) [Rev. January 1, 1991]

CIVIL SUBPENA

Code of Civil Procedure, §§ 1985, 1986, 1987

C. Subpoenaing Police Officers

If you wish to subpoena a police officer, fire fighter or other peace officer to testify to anything observed or investigated in the course of duty, you will have to pay that person's salary for the time he or she takes off work to appear. You must pay this in advance in the form of a $150 deposit, payable to the agency employing the officer. The subpoena may be served on the officer personally or on his or her superior.

D. Subpoenaing Documents

In addition to witnesses, you can also subpoena documents. This is rarely done in Small Claims Court, but it may occasionally be helpful. An organization such as a police department, phone company, hospital or business may have books, ledgers, papers or other documents that can help your case. To get them brought to court, you must prepare a form entitled "Subpoena Duces Tecum." This is very similar to the standard subpoena form, except that there is a space to describe the papers or other documents that you want brought to court. To get a "Subpoena Duces Tecum" issued, you must attach a declaration under penalty of perjury stating why you need the written material. Prepare three copies of all papers and, after you get the clerk to issue the subpoena, serve it on the witness using personal service, as described in Chapter 11. As with a regular subpoena, the witness is entitled to ask for a fee. The Proof of Service is on the back of the subpoena form and must be filled out and returned to the clerk. To comply with the subpoena, the custodian of the records may mail them to court unless you demand the custodian show up personally. (See CCP Sec. 1985; Evidence Code Secs. 1560-1566.)

A Subpoena Duces Tecum must be directed to the person who is in charge of the documents, books or records you want produced in court. It may take a few phone calls to find out who this is. Be sure you get this information accurately. If you list someone on the Subpoena Duces Tecum who has nothing to do with the documents, you won't get them. When dealing with a large corporation, public utility or municipal government, it is wise to list the person who is in overall charge of the department where the records are kept. Thus, if you want records having to do with library fines from a public library, or having to do with business license fees from the city tax and license department, you should not list the city manager or the mayor, but should list the head librarian or the director of the tax and license office.

Example: Let's take a hypothetical case. You are being sued by the city on behalf of the public library for $800 for eight rare books which they state you failed to return. You know that you did return the books, but can't seem to get that across to the library, which insists on treating you like a thief. You learn that each April the library takes a yearly inventory of all books on their shelves. You believe that if you can get access to that inventory, you may be able to figure out where the library misplaced the books, or at least show that a significant percentage of the library's other books are not accounted for, raising the implication that they, not you, lost the books.

Your first step is to ask the library to voluntarily open the inventory to you. If they refuse, you may well want to subpoena it. Here's how:

1. Check the "Duces Tecum" box on the Subpoena form.

2. Prepare a Declaration under penalty of perjury using the form available from the court. Briefly describe the documents you need and why they are necessary to prove issues involved in the case. If you want the custodian of the records to show up in person, give a reason. Don't argue the merits of your case.

3. Have a subpoena issued by the Small Claims clerk. Then have the subpoena served, being sure that the Proof of Service (see Chapter 11, Section F) is properly filled out and returned to the clerk.

DECLARATION FOR SUBPOENA DUCES TECUM

Name and Address of Court:	Municipal Court, County of Alameda Berkeley-Albany Judicial District 2000 Center Street Berkeley, CA 94704

SMALL CLAIMS CASE NO. (123456)

PLAINTIFF/DEMANDANTE (Name, address, and telephone number of each):	DEFENDANT/DEMANDADO (Name, address, and telephone number of each):
Public Library 100 Allston Way Berkeley, CA 94704	John O'Gara 100 Scenic Drive Berkeley, CA 94702
Telephone No.:	Telephone No.:
Telephone No.:	Telephone No.:

☐ See attached sheet for additional plaintiffs and defendants.

DECLARATION FOR SUBPENA DUCES TECUM

1. I, the undersigned, declare I am the ☐ plaintiff ☒ defendant ☐ judgment creditor ☐ other (specify):
in the above entitled action.
2. This action has been set for hearing on (date): (Jan. 7, 2000) at (time): (9:00 A.M.) in the above named court.
3. (Name): Robert Riwyle has in his or her possession or under his or her control
the following documents relating to (name of party) library fines of John O'Gara
   a. ☐ Payroll receipts, stubs, and other records concerning employment of the party. Receipts, invoices, documents, and other papers or records concerning any and all accounts receivable of the party.
   b. ☐ Bank account statements, canceled checks, and check registers from any and all bank accounts in which the party has an interest.
   c. ☐ Savings account passbooks and statements, savings and loan account passbooks and statements, and credit union share account passbooks and statements of the party.
   d. ☐ Stock certificates, bonds, money market certificates, and any other records, documents, or papers concerning all investments of the party
   e. ☐ California registration certificates and ownership certificates for all vehicles registered to the party.
   f. ☐ Deeds to any and all real property owned or being purchased by the party.
   g. ☒ Other (specify):

   Book inventory information collected by the main branch of the
   public library during the calendar year 19__.

These documents are material to the issues involved in this case for the following reasons (specify):

   My contention is that I returned the books for which the
   library is suing me. The inventory should back me up on this.

I declare under penalty of perjury under the laws of the State of California that the foregoing is true and correct.

Date: (fill in)
........John O'Gara........................   ▶ *John O'Gara*
          (TYPE OR PRINT NAME)   (SIGNATURE OF JUDGMENT CREDITOR)

Form Approved by the Judicial Council of California SC-107 [New January 1, 1992]	**DECLARATION FOR SUBPENA DUCES TECUM** (Small Claims)	Code of Civil Procedure, §§ 1985-1987.5

💡 **Ask to examine documents prior to your court hearing.** The documents you have subpoenaed will be mailed or presented to the court—not to you. You will probably want an opportunity to examine them, and should request it from the judge. He may well let you look at them right there in the courtroom while other cases go ahead. Or, if necessary, he may continue the case for a few days and arrange to have you make your examination at the place of business of the owner of the records.

E. Written Evidence

In Small Claims Court, there are no formal rules of evidence requiring that a witness testify in person. While it is often preferable to have a witness appear in court, this isn't always possible, and a judge will accept written statements from both eyewitnesses ("I was there and saw the filthy apartment") and expert witnesses ("I examined the transmission and found that a rebuilt part was installed improperly"). (For a sample written statement in a security deposit case, see Chapter 20, Section A.) If you do present the written statement of a witness, make sure the witness states the following facts:

For an eyewitness:
- Who the witness is.
- The date of the event.
- What she saw, heard, smelled, felt or tasted, and where and how she did so.

For an expert witness:
- Who the witness is.
- The witness's work and education credentials, which demonstrate her expertise in the field she is commenting on. (If these are lengthy, it's a good idea to include the person's resume or vitae.)
- What he did to be able to render his opinion. ("I examined the paint on Mr. Jones's 35-foot Cabin Cruiser and subjected it to the following test....")
- When he did it.
- His conclusion (the paint used was not suitable for salt water immersion).
- If possible, an estimate of the cost to redo the work properly.
- Any other facts that have a bearing on the dispute.

Make sure you establish your expert's experience and training. It's a good idea to attach a separate list of the expert's credentials. If your expert has a resume or vitae listing educational and experiential credentials, attach it to the letter in which she states her findings. The more distinguished your expert, the more likely the judge is to respect her opinion.

Here is a sample letter by an eyewitness:

---

37 Ogden Court
Larchville, CA
September 30, 19__

Presiding Judge
Small Claims Court
Ukiah, California

Re: *John Swift vs. Peter Petrakos*
Small Claims Case No. 11478

Your Honor:

On September 15, 19__, at approximately 7:30 a.m, I was parked near the corner of South Dora and 7th Streets in Larchville. Just after 7:30, I witnessed an auto accident involving John Swift and Peter Petrakos.

I clearly saw Mr. Petrakos' Toyota, which was heading north on South Dora, go through a red light and hit Mr. Swift's blue van, which was proceeding west on 7th, well inside the 25 MPH speed limit. I noticed that the traffic light facing Mr. Petrakos did not turn to green for ten seconds or so after the accident, so it is clear to me that Mr. Petrakos really did go through the light while it was fully red. In short, this was not a situation where Mr. Petrakos was just a tiny bit early getting into the intersection at a light change.

Sincerely,

Victor Van Cleve

And a sample letter by an expert witness (see Chapter 17 for another letter by an expert witness):

Gail McClosky
47 Penrod Street
Helena, Montana
Sept. 30, 19__

Judge
Small Claims Court
San Diego, California

Re: *Ed Zilosky vs. Peter Jackson*
Small Claims Case No. 11478

Dear Judge:

I am a fully licensed contractor with 20 years' experience here in San Diego (Contractor's License (4021B)). For the last ten years I've run my own five-person contracting company specializing in building enclosures and buildings to house horses and other large animals. I enclose a resume outlining my specialized training and experience in this field.

On April 23, 19__, I was asked by James Dills to inspect several new stalls he had built in the main barn of his Lazy T Riding Stable by R&B Construction.

In my opinion these stalls are seriously below normal industry standards for three reasons.

1) They are too small for the animals intended to be kept in them. [Continue with details.]

2) Walls and doors are built of plywood too thin to safely contain an agitated animal. [Continue with details.]

3) Construction is so rough and unfinished in several places as to pose a danger of injury to an animal intended to be kept there. [Continue with details.]

In conclusion, I believe the stalls are so poorly constructed they can't reasonably be upgraded to provide safe habitable housing for horses. Were they mine, I would rip them out and start over.

Sincerely,

Gail McClosky

F. Judges as Witnesses

CCP Sec. 116.520 states, "The court may consult witnesses informally and otherwise investigate the controversy... ." In practice this means as much, or as little, as an individual judge wants it to. But it clearly does allow the conscientious Small Claims judge great discretion to climb down off the bench to check out an important fact.

Asking a judge to check out a key fact in your case can be a valuable technique in some situations. For example, in disputes involving damaged clothing it is routine to bring the damaged or defective garment into court for the judge's examination. Indeed, it normally makes sense to bring physical evidence that meets these three criteria:

- Showing it to the judge will help your case.

- It will fit through the door.

- Bringing it into the courtroom is not dangerous or inappropriate, as would be the case with an animal, firearm or extremely dirty or smelly items.

But what if your evidence is impossible to bring into the courtroom (a car with a poor paint job or a supposedly pedigreed puppy that grew up looking as if Lassie were the mother and Rin Tin Tin the father)? Simply ask the judge to accompany you outside the building to the parking lot to examine the car, or the dog, or whatever else is important to your case? Many (but not all) judges will cheerfully do so if you make a convincing argument as to why it is necessary to understand the dispute (and especially if it won't take too long). For example, one excellent judge I know was disturbed one morning when two eyewitnesses gave seriously contradictory testimony about a traffic accident. He questioned both in detail and then took the case under submission. That evening, he drove over to the relevant corner. Once there, it was clear that one of the witnesses couldn't possibly have seen the accident from the spot on which she claimed to be standing (in front of a particular restaurant). The judge decided the case in favor of the other party.

Don't waste a judge's time. Never ask a judge to take time to leave her court to view evidence if you can establish or prove the same point by other means, such as by presenting the testimony (or letter) of a witness or by showing the judge a photograph.

G. Testimony by Telephone

A surprising number of Small Claims Court judges will take testimony over the phone if a witness cannot be present because she is ill, disabled, out-of-state or can't take time off from work. While procedures vary, some courts will do this by setting up a conference call so that the opposing party has the opportunity to hear what is being said and to respond.

But don't assume that a particular judge will allow telephone testimony. If you think you'll need to have a witness who can't appear in court testify by phone, explain your problem to the court clerk well in advance. If you get a negative response, don't give up—ask the judge when you get into the courtroom. Be sure you also present a letter from the witness stating what he would testify to if he was present in court (for example, your opponent's car ran a red light and broadsided you) and explaining why it is impossible for him to be there. This type letter should look like the one in Section E, above, except the witness should add:

"Mr. Swift has asked me to testify on his behalf, and normally I would be happy to do so. However, I will be in New York City on business during the months of October, November and December 19__ and cannot be present.

"I have asked Mr. Swift to let me know the day and approximate time of the court hearing and have told him that I will give him a phone number where I can be reached. If you think it desirable, I will be pleased to give my testimony by phone."

■

Presenting Your Case to the Judge

A. Uncontested Cases—Getting a Judgment by Default

Presenting your case in court is normally easy if your opponent does not show up on the date of your hearing. After the judge checks to see that the defendant was properly served with court papers, you will normally be asked to briefly state the basic facts of your case, and possibly to show the judge some documentary evidence, such as a copy of the written contract you claim the defendant broke. (CCP Sec. 116.370.) Since the defendant is not present to contradict anything you say, you win as long as you have stated the bare bones of a valid legal claim.

Example: "Your Honor, I own the Racafrax Auto Repair Shop. On January 11, 199x, I repaired defendant's 1994 Eagle Talon. He paid me $500 and agreed to pay another $500 on March 1. He has not made the second payment. I have copies of the contract defendant signed and of several unpaid bills I sent him. I am asking for a judgment of $500 plus $55 for my court filing fee and the cost of having the papers served."

No need for a long-winded presentation: If the defendant isn't present, a judge only wants to hear the minimum number of facts necessary to support a judgment on your behalf. There is no need to make an extended argument, since in the absence of your opponent the judge will assume your version of what happened is true.

Assuming the judge is satisfied that there is no obvious defect in your case, she will enter a default judgment for the amount of your request. The defendant has no right to appeal this judgment to the Superior Court (see Chapter 23) unless he first gets the Small Claims Court judge to reopen the case by vacating the default judgment. If the defaulting party makes a motion to vacate the default within 30 days, the judge may—but does not have to—set it aside. The party who missed the first hearing always has the job of convincing the judge that the reason she didn't show up or phone earlier is good enough to justify vacating the default judgment. (See Chapter 10 for more on this procedure.) If the Small Claims judge decides not to set aside the default, the defendant can appeal the judge's refusal (but not the case itself) to Superior Court. If the Superior Court judge looks at the situation differently and does decide to vacate the default judgment and both parties are present and agree, the case can be heard immediately.

B. Contested Cases

Assuming now that both sides show up and step forward when the case is called by the clerk, what happens next? First, the judge will establish everyone's identity. Next, she will ask the plaintiff to briefly state his case. But before we focus on the plaintiff's and defendant's presentations, here are a few tips both parties should find helpful. These are not rules written on golden tablets, only suggestions. You may want to follow some and ignore others.

- Stand when you make your initial presentation to the judge. Standing gives most people a sense of presence and confidence at a time when they may be a little nervous. It's fine to sit while your opponent is talking. If the judge interrupts your opponent's presentation to ask you a quick question that requires a short answer, there is no need to leap to your feet to answer it.

- Be as brief as you can and still explain and document your case thoroughly.

- Start with the end of the story, not the beginning. That is, describe your loss and how much you are asking for. Then go back and tell your story chronologically.

- Don't read your statement. Reading in court is almost always a bore. But you may find it helpful to make a few notes on a card to serve as a reminder in case you get nervous or forget something. If you decide to do this, list the headings of the various points you want to make in an outline form. Be sure your list is easy to read at a glance and that the topics are in the correct order. (See Chapter 13, Section K, for a sample list.)

- Never interrupt your opponent or any of her witnesses, no matter how outrageous their "lies." You will get your chance to respond.

- Try to present any portion of your case that is difficult to explain verbally in another way. This often means bringing your used car parts, damaged clothing or other exhibits, such as photographs or canceled checks, and presenting them to the judge in an organized way.

- There will be a blackboard in court. If drawings will be helpful, as is almost always true in cases involving car accidents, be sure to ask the judge for permission to use it. You will want to draw clearly and legibly the first time, so it's wise to practice in advance.

- If you are the defendant, don't repeat uncontested facts already presented by the plaintiff (for example, that the two of you had a fender bender at a certain corner in a certain city at a certain time during certain weather conditions). Instead, focus on the facts of your principal disagreement (whether the light facing you was green or red, for example) and introduce evidence to prove that point.

- Recognize that a judge who is convinced that one side is morally in the right will bend over backwards to find a legal reason to rule in that person's favor. For example, if you lent a friend money in an emergency and he is now trying to wriggle out of his obligation based on a legal technicality (claims the loan was really a gift), make sure the judge understands the trouble your opponent's bad act has caused you (you can't afford to pay college tuition).

Practice your presentation early and often. As emphasized throughout this book, it pays to practice making your oral presentation ahead of time. Have a tough-minded friend or family member play the part of judge and be ready to ask questions and try to poke holes in your best points. Run through your presentation several times until you get it right.

1. From the Plaintiff's Side

The plaintiff should clearly tell the judge what the dispute is about before she starts describing the details of what happened. I call this starting with the end, not the beginning, of your story.

> If your case involves a car accident, you might start by saying,
>> "This case involves a car accident at Cedar and Rose Streets in which my car suffered $872 worth of damage when the defendant ran a red light and hit my front fender,"

not
>> "It all started when I was driving down Rose Street after having two eggs and a danish for breakfast."

Only occasionally have I seen a case where the plaintiff's initial presentation should take longer than five minutes. As part of his statement, the plaintiff should present and explain the relevance of any papers, photos or other documentary evidence. These should be handed to the clerk, who will pass them on to the judge. The plaintiff should also be sure to tell the judge if he has any witnesses to present. If either the plaintiff or defendant has done legal research and believes that a statute or court decision supports his position, he should call it to the attention of the judge as part of his oral presentation. If possible, it's also a good idea to back this up with a brief written memo. Begin with the name and number of your case. Then list the official citation of the statute, ordinance or court case you think helps your case and briefly explain why. (See Chapter 1, Section D, for an explanation of how to cite statutes and cases.) In court, give one copy of the memo to the clerk to hand to the judge and another to your opponent.

MEMO

Lee vs. Yew Small Claims #127654

To: Small Claims Judge

From: Robert Yew, Defendant

Re: California law on boundary trees

This case involves Mr. Lee, my next door neighbor, suing me because he claims my Monterey Pine tree drops debris on his roof and yard. Although he is asking for a judgment of $500 for clean-up costs, what he really wants is for me to pay several thousand dollars to remove the 80-foot tree.

There is only one problem with Mr. Lee's argument—because the tree touches our boundary line, the tree is half his. That's because California law, as set forth in Civil Code Section 834, clearly states that "Trees whose trunks stand partly on the land of two or more coterminous owners, belong to them in common."

Mr. Lee will argue that the tree was planted 100% on my property by the person who owned my house before I bought it and that the tree is still 90 percent on my side of the property line. Both contentions are true, but as you can see under Civil Code Section 834, it makes no difference. As long as the tree touches the boundary line—which the photographs I have presented the court clearly prove—the tree belongs to both of us as co-owners (tenants in common), (*Anderson v. Weiland* (1936) 12 CA 2d 730.)

I have offered to try and mediate the dispute, but so far Mr. Lee says "no." I hope he will change his mind.

Respectfully submitted,

August 10, 19__ Robert Yew

Your witness will normally be given a chance to speak after you complete your presentation. The witness should be well prepared to state her key information in an organized way (for example, that she inspected an apartment immediately after you did your final clean-up and found it to be clean). Too often, when a witness is asked to testify, she either leaves out important points or is so disorganized that the force of her testimony is lost.

Just as is true with your presentation, the best way to be sure your witness really will be able to succinctly and concisely explain to the judge the key facts that support your case is to have her practice her testimony in advance. As long as she sticks to the truth, rehearsing the exact words she will say in court is completely legal. Again, the best way to rehearse is to meet with your witness and a friend you have asked to act as a mock judge. Start by presenting your case to the pretend judge exactly as you plan to do it in court. Then ask your witness to stand and explain her version of what happened. If at first your witness is a little disorganized or unsure, work with her to develop a cogent presentation that covers all key points. When she says something that sounds good, help her to write it down and ask her to practice several times before your court date.

When the plaintiff and any witnesses are finished—or sometimes even before the plaintiff has made a decent start—the judge is likely to interrupt to ask questions. Never put the judge off by saying you'll get to the point she is interested in later in your presentation. Far better to go with the judge's energy, and directly answer her questions. Just be sure that you and your witnesses eventually get a chance to make all of your key points. If you feel rushed, say so. The judge will normally slow things down a little.

2. From the Defendant's Side

Sooner or later it will finally be your turn. Defendants often get so angry at something the plaintiff has said that when they get to speak, they attack angrily. This is usually counterproductive. Far better to calmly and clearly present your side of the dispute to the judge. Start with the key point of contention and then fill in the details of what happened from your point of view. If the plaintiff has made significant false or misleading statements, these should definitely be pointed out, but normally it is best to do this towards the end of your presentation.

Example: "Your Honor, it's true that the bumper of my truck hit defendant's fender and pushed it in slightly. But the key thing I want you to understand is that this happened because defendant's pickup entered the intersection before it was clear and therefore the accident was his fault. Here is what happened. I was driving south on Cedar and entered the intersection just as the light first turned yellow. I slowed briefly near the center line behind a car that was turning left and then continued across, at which point defendant's car darted in front of me...."

Like the plaintiff, the defendant should be prepared to present documentary evidence and, if possible, witnesses that will back up her story. And if any statutes or court decisions are relevant, she should call them to the judge's attention by preparing a brief memo, as described in Section B1, just above.

C. A Sample Contested Case

Now let's look at how a contested case might be presented from both the plaintiff's and defendant's perspectives.

Clerk: "The next case is *John Andrews v. Robertson Realty*. Will everyone please come forward?" (Four people come forward and sit at the table facing the judge.)

Judge: "Good morning. Which one of you is Mr. Andrews? Okay, will you begin, Mr. Andrews?"

John Andrews: (stands) "This is a case about my failure to get a $700 cleaning deposit returned, your Honor. I rented a house from Robertson Realty at 1611 Spruce St. in Fresno in March of 199x on a month-to-month tenancy. On January 10, 199x, I sent Mr. Robertson a written notice that I was planning to move on March 10. In fact, I moved out on March 8 and left the place extremely clean. I know it was clean because I spent eight hours, a lot of them on my hands and knees, cleaning it. In addition, all of my rent was properly paid. A few days after I moved out, I asked Mr. Robertson to return my $700 deposit. He wrote me a letter stating that the place was dirty and he was keeping my deposit.

"I have with me a copy of a letter I wrote to Mr. Robertson on March 15 setting out my position in more detail. I also have some photographs that my friend, Carol Spann, who is here as a witness, took on the day I moved out. I believe the pictures show pretty clearly that I did a thorough cleanup." (John Andrews hands the letter and pictures to the clerk, who hands them to the judge.)

"Your Honor, I am asking not only for the $700 deposit, but also for $600 in punitive damages, which the law allows a tenant when a landlord improperly refuses to return a deposit." (See Chapter 20 for a thorough explanation of California's law covering the return of security deposits.)

Judge: "Mr. Andrews, will you introduce your witness?"

Andrews: "Yes, this is Carol Spann. She helped me clean up and move on March 7 and 8."

Judge: (looking at the pictures) "Ms. Spann, were you in the house the day John Andrews moved out?"

Carol Spann: (standing) "Yes, your Honor, I was—and the day before, too. I helped clean up and I can say that we did a good job. Not only did we do the normal washing and scrubbing, but we waxed the kitchen floor, cleaned the bathroom tile and shampooed the rugs."

Judge: (turning to Mr. Robertson) "Okay, now it's your turn to tell me why the deposit wasn't returned."

Harry Robertson: (standing) "I don't know how they could have cleaned the place up, your Honor, because it was filthy when I inspected it on March 9. Let me give you a few specifics. There was mildew and mold around the bathtub, the windows were filthy, the refrigerator hadn't been defrosted and there was dog—how shall I say it—dog manure in the basement. Your Honor, I have brought along Clem Houndstooth as a witness. Mr. Houndstooth is the tenant who moved in three days after Mr. Andrews moved out. Incidentally, your Honor, the place was so dirty that I only charged Mr. Houndstooth a $200 cleaning deposit, because he agreed to clean it up himself."

Judge: (looking at Clem Houndstooth) "Do you wish to say something?"

Clem Houndstooth: (standing) "Yes, I do. Mr. Robertson asked me to come down and back him up and I am glad to do it because I put in two full days cleaning that place up. I like a clean house, your Honor, not a halfway clean, halfway dirty house. I just don't think that a house is clean if the oven is full of gunk, there is mold in the bathroom and the insides of the cupboards are grimy. All these conditions existed at 1611 Spruce St. when I moved in. I just don't believe that anyone could think that that place was clean."

Judge: "Mr. Andrews, do you have anything to add?"

John Andrews: (standing up) "Yes, I sure do. First, as to the mildew problem. The house is forty years old and there is some dampness in the wall of the bathroom. Maybe there is a leaky pipe someplace behind the tile. I cleaned it a number of times, but it always came back. I talked to Mr. Fisk in Mr. Robertson's office about the problem about a month after I moved in and he told me that I would have to do the best I could because they couldn't afford to tear the wall apart. As to the cupboards and stove, they are both old. The cabinets haven't been painted in ten years, so, of course, they aren't perfect, and that old stove was a lot dirtier when I moved in than it is now, since I can tell you I personally worked on it with oven cleaner for over an hour."

Judge: "What about the refrigerator, Mr. Andrews? Was that defrosted?"

John Andrews: "No, your Honor, it wasn't, but it had been defrosted about three weeks before I moved out and I thought that it was good enough the way it was."

Judge: "O.K., if no one else has anything to add, I want to return your pictures and letters. You will receive my decision by mail in a few days."

Now, I have a little surprise for you. The case I just presented is based closely on a real Small Claims case. As they used to say on *Dragnet*, "Only the names have been changed to protect the innocent." And I have another surprise for you. I spoke to the judge after the court session. Here is how he decided the case.

> "This is a typical case in which both sides have some right on their side. What is clean to one person may be dirty to another. Based on what I heard, I would have to guess that the old tenant made a fairly conscientious effort to clean up and probably left the place about as clean as it was when he moved in, but that the new tenant, Houndstooth, had much higher standards and convinced the landlord that it was filthy. The landlord may not have needed too much convincing since he probably would just as well keep the deposit. But I did hear enough to convince me that Andrews, the old tenant, didn't do a perfect job cleaning up. My decision will be that Andrews gets a judgment for the return of $450 of the $700 deposit, with no punitive damages. I believe that $250 is more than enough to compensate the landlord for any damages he suffered as a result of the house 'being a little dirty.'"

I then asked the judge if he felt that the case was well presented. He replied substantially as follows:

> "Better than average. I think I got a pretty good idea of what the problems were. The witnesses were helpful and the pictures gave me a pretty good idea that the place wasn't a total mess. Both sides could have done better, however. Andrews could have presented a witness to testify to the condition of the house when he moved in if, in fact, it was truly a lot dirtier than when he left. Another witness to testify to the fact that the house was clean when he moved out would have been good, too. His friend, Carol Spann, seemed to be a very close friend and I wasn't sure that she was objective when it came to judging whether or not the place was clean. The landlord, Robertson, could also have done better. He could have presented a more disinterested witness, although I must say that Houndstooth's testimony was pretty convincing. Also he could have had pictures documenting the dirty conditions and an estimate from a cleaning company for how much they would have charged to clean the place up. Without going to too

much trouble, I think both sides could have probably done somewhat better with more thorough preparation."

D. Don't Forget to Ask for Your Costs

Both plaintiff and defendant are entitled to ask that a judgment in their favor include any recoverable costs, such as for filing and serving court papers or subpoenaing essential witnesses. Sometimes defendants have no costs, unless a necessary witness is subpoenaed. Costs that are recoverable by the winner include:

- The plaintiff's court filing fee (defendants pay no fee to appear unless they file a Claim of Defendant).

- Service of process costs. A plaintiff must always pay this fee, which can vary from a few dollars where certified mail is used, to considerably more if a professional process service is required. A defendant will normally only have to pay to serve papers if she files a Claim of Defendant (counterclaim).

- Subpoenaed witness fees must be approved by the judge. Both the plaintiff and defendant can incur this cost if a witness must be subpoenaed and claims a fee. Fees for subpoenaing witnesses and documents are only likely to be approved if the judge believes the presence of the witness in court was necessary to prove the case.

- The cost of obtaining necessary documents, such as verification of car ownership by the DMV. (Both plaintiffs and defendants can have these costs.)

If you forget to get your costs added to the judgment in court and want to go to the trouble, you can file a "Memorandum of Costs" with the Small Claims clerk within five days after judgment. Forms are available at the clerk's office. For information on recovering costs incurred after judgment when your opponent won't voluntarily pay the judgment, see Chapter 24, Section G.

Some costs are not recoverable. You can't recover for such personal expenses as taking time off from work to prepare for or attend court, or paying a babysitter, parking your car or making photocopies of evidence.

■

16

Motor Vehicle Repair Cases

Most Small Claims Court cases fall into a dozen or so broad categories, with perhaps another dozen subcategories. In the next six chapters, we look at the most common types of cases and discuss strategies to handle each. Even if your fact situation doesn't fit neatly in one of these categories, I recommend that you read this material. By picking up a few hints here and a little information there, you should be able to piece together a good plan of action. For example, many of the suggestions I make to handle motor vehicle repair disputes can also be applied to cases involving problems with fixing major appliances such as televisions, washers and expensive stereos.

Let's start by imagining that you go to the auto repair shop to pick up your trusty, but slightly graying, steed after a complete engine overhaul. The bill, as agreed to by you in advance, is $1,225. This always seemed a little steep, but the mechanic talked you into it based on his claim that he would do a great job and that, when the work was done, the engine should last another 50,000 miles. At any rate, you write a check and drive out of the garage in something approaching a cheerful mood. One of life's more disagreeable hassles has been taken care of, at least temporarily. Unfortunately, as most of us have learned through hard experience, "temporarily" can sometimes be a very short time. In this case, it lasts only until you head up the first hill. What's that funny noise, you think? Why don't I have more power? "Oh shit," you say (you rarely swear, but this is one of those rare times when nothing else will do). You turn around and drive back to the garage in a sour mood. Not only are you out $1,225, but your car runs worse than it did when you brought it in.

Funny, no one seems as pleasant as they did before. Odd, how hard it is to get anyone to even pay attention to your problem. Finally, after a bit of foot stomping, you get someone to say that they will look the car over. You take a bus home, trying not to be paranoid. The next day you call the garage. Nothing has been done. You yell at the garage owner and then call your bank to stop payment on the check. You are told that it has already been cashed. The next day the garage owner tells you that the problem is in a part of the engine they didn't work on. You only paid for a "short block job," they tell you. "Give us another $500 and we can surely solve this new problem," they add.

You go down and pick up your mechanical friend and drive it home—very slowly. You are furious and decide to pursue every legal remedy, no matter what the trouble. How do you start?

First, park your car, take a shower and have a glass of wine, milk or whatever seems calming. Nothing gets decided well when you're mad. Now, following the approach I have presented throughout this book, ask yourself these two key questions.

A. Have I Suffered a Loss?

That's easy. Your car works worse than it did before you paid a lot of money to have it fixed. Unless some divine power has suddenly intervened to create a new mechanical problem, you have suffered a loss.

B. Can I Prove the Defendant's Negligence Caused My Loss?

Ah ha, now we get to the nitty-gritty. Since the car now works less well than before you had it fixed, you are doubtless convinced that a lousy repair job caused your problem. But in this type of case, you can almost always expect the garage owner to claim they did their work properly and that the car simply needs more work. For all the judge knows, this may even be true. In short, to win this type of case it's your job to prove that the repair work was not up to a reasonable standard of competence (plain English for negligence done). Doing so will make your case; failing to do so will break it. You'd better get to work.

Step 1. Collect Available Evidence

First, gather all evidence where time is of the essence. In this situation, this means getting your used parts (it's a good idea to do this any time you have major work done). If the garage will not give them to you, make your request by letter, keeping a copy for your file. If you get the parts, fine—if you don't, you have evidence that the garage is badly run or has something to hide, since California law requires that your used parts be returned to you upon request.

Step 2. Have Your Car Checked by an Expert

Before you drive many miles, have your car checked by an experienced mechanic. Sometimes it is possible to get a free estimate from a repair shop if the owner thinks it will get the job of fixing your car. In this situation, however, you are probably better off paying for someone to look at the engine thoroughly, with the understanding that if the need arises, he will testify on your behalf in Small Claims Court, or at the very least, write a letter stating what's wrong with the engine. One way to try and accomplish this is to take your car to a garage that a friend patronizes and recommends.

Step 3. Try to Settle Your Case

By now you should have a pretty good idea what the first garage did wrong. Call them and ask that either the job be redone, or that they give you a refund of part or all of your money. Often the repair shop will agree to do additional work to avoid a hassle. If they agree to take the car back, insist on a written agreement detailing what they will do and how long it will take. Also, talk to the mechanic who will actually work on the car to be sure he understands what needs to be done. Understandably, you may be a little paranoid about taking your car back to the organization that just screwed it up. Nevertheless, unless they have been outrageously incompetent, this is probably your best approach since it's usually easier to get work redone than it is to get a big refund. Also, if you sue and the garage owner shows up in court and says he offered to work on the car again but you refused, it may weaken your case.

Step 4. Write a Demand Letter

If the garage isn't cooperative, it's time to write them a formal demand letter. Remember our discussion in Chapter 6. Your letter should be short, polite and written with an eye to a judge reading it. In this situation, you could write something like the one below.

Be sure to emphasize any promise (warranty) made by the garage. Most small independent garages don't make a written warranty or guaranty on their work. However, if you were given any promises in writing, mention them in your letter. Also, if you were promised things orally about the quality of the work the garage planned to do and you relied on these statements as part of your decision to authorize the repairs, make sure the judge knows about this express warranty. (See Chapter 2, Section G.)

Haig Mackey
15 Orange St.
Laguna Beach, CA

Happy Days Motors
100 Speedway
Corona Del Mar, CA

Dear People:

On August 13, 19_, I brought my 1993 Dodge to your garage. You agreed to do a complete engine rebuild job for $1,225. You told me, "Your car will be running like a watch when we're through with it." The car worked well when I brought it in, but was a little short on power. Two days later, when I picked up my car, it barely moved at all. The engine made such a clanging noise that I've been afraid to drive it.

I have repeatedly asked you to fix the car or to refund my money. You have refused. Shortly after the work was done, I asked for my used parts to be returned. You refused to give them to me, even though this is a violation of state law.

I've had two mechanics check out my car since you worked on it. Both agree you did your work improperly and even installed some used parts instead of new ones. The work you did on the engine rings was particularly badly done.

After receiving no response from you, I had the work redone at a cost of $900. My car now works well. Please refund my $1,225. Should you fail to do so within ten days, I will promptly file complaints with interested state and local agencies and take this dispute to Small Claims Court. I hope to hear from you promptly.

Haig Mackey

CC: California Dept. of Consumer Affairs
    Bureau of Automotive Repair
    10240 System Parkway
    Sacramento, CA 95827

Step 5. File Your Court Papers

If you still get no satisfactory response from the garage, file your papers at the Small Claims Court's clerk's office in the judicial district where the defendant does business.

Step 6. Prepare for Court

If you want the judge to understand your case, you must understand it yourself. Sounds simple, doesn't it? It did to me too until I got involved with a case involving a botched car repair. All I really knew was that after I had paid to have the engine fixed, the darn thing was not supposed to belch black smoke and make a disgusting noise. I really wasn't interested in the details.

Fortunately, I realized that for me to argue a case in Small Claims with this level of ignorance would likely end in a bad loss. To be able to convince a judge that the mechanic had ripped me off, I needed to do some homework. After all, I could expect the people from the garage to show up in court with a terrific-sounding story about the wonderful job they did with pistons, bearings and cam shaft. An additional reason why I knew I needed to prepare was that I had seen many people argue car repair cases knowing no more than "the car was supposed to be fixed, your Honor, and it's worse than ever." On some mornings when the roses are in bloom, the peaches are sweet and the angels are in heaven, this was enough to win—usually it wasn't.

It turned out that fifteen minutes' conversation with a knowledgeable expert was all I really needed to understand what the mechanic did wrong. (Also, my local library had several car manuals, complete with diagrams of my problem, which were a big help.) In court, armed with my new knowledge, I had no trouble explaining to the judge that the mechanic had done a substandard job and getting a judgment for the full amount I had paid.

Remember, the judge is probably not a mechanic. In Chapter 13, I mentioned that it's important to pay attention to the human being to whom you are presenting your case. It's no secret that many, if not most, Small Claims judges don't understand the insides of cars any better than you do. After all, lots of people become lawyers because they don't like to get their hands dirty. So be prepared to make a convincing presentation to a person who nods his head but doesn't really understand the difference between the drive shaft and the axle.

Step 7. Appearing in Court

When you show up in court, be sure that you are well organized. Bring all the letters you have written, or received, about your car problem, any written warranty, photographs if they are helpful and your used parts if they aid in making your case. If you have a witness to any oral statements (warranties) made by the garage, be sure to bring that person with you to court. Or if that's impossible, ask her to write a letter explaining what she heard. Also, be sure to present any letter(s) written by an independent expert(s) who has arranged to examine your car. Even one cogent letter from an experienced mechanic, explaining how the repair job was botched, when combined with your own informed presentation, can make you a winner.

If you are well prepared you should win the sort of case outlined here without difficulty. Judges drive cars and have to get them fixed; they tend to be sympathetic with this type of consumer complaint. Simply present your story (see Chapter 15), your documentation and your witnesses. If you feel that your opponent is snowing the judge with a lot of technical lingo, get His Honor back on the track by asking that all jargon be explained in ordinary English. This will be a relief to everyone in the courtroom except your opponent. You will likely find that, once his case is shorn of all the magic words, it will shrink from tiger to pussycat.

A good drawing can help. Several times in cases involving machinery, I have seen people give effective testimony by presenting a large drawing illustrating the screw-up. This approach is most effective when your expert appears in court and authoritatively points to the drawing to detail the problem.

Step 8: Ask for a Continuance in the Middle of Your Presentation If It Is Essential

The best-laid plans can occasionally go haywire. Perhaps a key witness doesn't show up, or maybe, despite careful preparation, you overlook some aspect of the case that the judge feels is crucial. If this occurs, you may want to ask the judge to reschedule the case on another day so that you can prepare better. It is perfectly proper to make this sort of request. Whether or not it will be granted is up to the judge. If she feels that more evidence isn't likely to change the result, or that you are making the request to stall, it will not be granted. If, despite the fact that you prepared conscientiously, there is a good reason for a delay, however, it will usually be allowed. But if you want a delay, you have to ask for it—the judge isn't going to be able to read your mind. ■

Motor Vehicle Purchase Cases

Occasionally someone buys a vehicle and drives it a short way, only to have it fall apart. And too frequently the seller of the defective vehicle won't stand behind the product and work out some sort of fair adjustment. What can you do if you are the victim of this kind of rip-off? Since there are major differences in how you should approach your problem depending on whether you purchased a new or used vehicle, let's look at each situation separately.

A. New Vehicles

A common problem with new vehicles occurs when you end up with a lemon—a car or truck with major manufacturing defects. Before considering Small Claims Court, you should fully understand your rights under the terms of California's lemon law (CC Sec. 1793.2).

The lemon law applies during the first 12 months or first 12,000 miles of the car's warranty period, whichever ends sooner. It applies to defects covered by the warranty that substantially reduce the use, value or safety of the car. The law entitles you to a new car or refund if you get stuck with a lemon—a car that cannot be repaired after at least three tries by the dealer and one by the manufacturer, or is out of service for any combination of defects for more than 30 days during the 12 year/12,000 mile period, not counting delays beyond the control of the dealer and manufacturer.

To get a new vehicle or a refund, you must give the dealer or manufacturer the opportunity to fix the vehicle.

Example: You trade in your rusty '88 bomb that served you well for longer than you want to remember and fork over a ridiculously large pile of money on a shiny new car. Your new horseless carriage runs fine for a few months, but then begins to vibrate uncontrollably whenever you drive over 50 mph. You take it back to the dealer, who tries to fix it, but it still shakes. You take it back again—and then again—and then again, but it's still not right. By now you're fed up. You paid for a new car that's supposed to work and you feel you should either get a full refund or a replacement. How can you do this?

If, as part of the repair process, a dispute arises, it must first be submitted to a "qualified third party dispute resolution process if one exists." (See CC Sec. 1793.2(e)(3) for details.) This is normally either an independent arbitration program run by the Better Business Bureau or a supposedly independent one established by the car company directly. If you are not satisfied with this decision, you may then take the case to court. The decision of the third party arbitrator shall be admissible in court, however.

Unfortunately, many disputes involving new vehicles don't fall under the lemon law. This would be the situation if the same defect didn't recur four times or if problems develop just after lemon law coverage period expires. Often, too, a problem starts to surface while the car is still under the manufacturer's warranty (this is almost always longer than the lemon law period) but the dealer makes inadequate repairs that last scarcely longer than the remainder of the warranty term. When the same problem develops again after the warranty has run out, the dealer refuses to fix it.

Even if your car is no longer covered by the lemon law or the auto manufacturer's warranty when trouble develops, you may have a winnable case. That's because when a relatively new car falls apart for no good reason, a good many Small Claims Court judges bend over backwards to look for a legal way to give you protection over and above the actual written warranty that comes with the vehicle. For example, even if your properly maintained car fails shortly after the warranty ends, you still may be able to recover some money under one of the following approaches:

- *Prove that mechanical problems began while your car was still under warranty.* Often a newish car that suffers serious mechanical problems soon after the warranty period runs out suffered similar problems earlier. If so, you will want to argue that the dealer made inadequate repairs in the first instance and should still be responsible for the subsequent problems.

> **Document your attempts to have your car repaired.** Make sure the judge knows about all the trips you have made to the dealer's repair shop. One way to establish this is by presenting copies of work orders you signed. If you don't have these or other records, sit down with a calendar and do your best to make an accurate reconstruction of the dates you brought your car in for repair. In court, give your list to the judge, explaining that it's your best estimate. He should accept it as being true unless the car dealer disputes it.

- *Investigate the possibility of a secret warranty.* After a model has been in production for awhile, a pattern of problems or failures always develops. Manufacturers are extremely sensitive to complaints in "high problem" areas—if for no other reason than to head off a possible federal safety recall. As a result, the company may have even issued an internal memo telling dealers to fix certain types of problems upon request. How can knowing this benefit you? By giving you the opportunity to pressure the company where it is most vulnerable. If your car develops a serious problem after the warranty period ends but before it reasonably should, start by talking to people at independent garages that specialize in repairing your model. Especially if they tell you the problem is widespread and that the company has fixed it without charge for some persistent customers, your next step is to write a demand letter to the car dealer and manufacturer.

(See Chapter 6.) Mention that if your problem is not taken care of, you will sue in Small Claims Court and you will subpoena all records having to do with this defect. (See Chapter 14.) This may well cause the company to settle with you. If not, follow through on both threats.

Not long ago I saw a Small Claims case involving a typical newish car problem. A man—let's call him Bruno—who owned an expensive European car was suing the local dealer and the parent car company's West Coast representative. Bruno claimed that he had repeatedly brought the car into the dealer's repair shop with engine problems while it was still under the manufacturer's written warranty. Each time adjustments were made that seemed to eliminate the problem. But each time, after a month or so, the same problem reappeared. A few months after the written warranty ran out, the engine died. Even though the car was only a little over a year old, and had gone less than 50,000 miles, both the dealer and the parent car company refused to repair or replace it. Their refusals continued even though the owner repeatedly wrote to them, demanding action.

How did Bruno go about dealing with his problem? First, because he needed his car, he went ahead and had the repairs made. Then, although the repairs cost slightly in excess of $5,000—the Small Claims limit—he decided that because it was too expensive to hire a lawyer and sue in Municipal Court, he would scale down his claim and sue for the Small Claims maximum. Because the dealer was located in the same city as he was, Bruno sued locally. In this situation it would have been adequate to sue only the local dealer and not the car company, but it didn't hurt to sue both following the general rule, "when in doubt, sue all possible defendants."

In court, because Bruno was well prepared he had a reasonably easy time. Both he and his wife testified as to their trials and tribulations with the car. They gave the judge copies of the several letters they had written the dealer, one of which was a list of the dates they had taken the car to the dealer's shop while it was still under warranty. They also produced a letter from the owner of the independent garage that finally fixed the engine, stating that when he took the engine apart, he discovered a defect in its original assembly. The new car dealer simply testified that his mechanics had done their best to fix the car under the written warranty. He then contended that, once the written warranty had run out, he was no longer responsible. The dealer made no effort to challenge the car owner's story, nor did he bring his own mechanics to court to testify as to how they had repaired the car while it was still under warranty. Bruno won. Not only had he presented a convincing case that the defect had never been fixed when it should have been under the written warranty, but the dealer produced no evidence to rebut it.

As the judge noted to me after the hearing, a $65,000 car should come with an engine that lasts a lot longer than this one did. Bruno would have had made an even stronger case if he had had the independent garage mechanic who discovered the engine defect testify in court. But the mechanic's letter, along with Bruno's testimony and that of his wife, were adequate in a situation where the dealer didn't put up much of a defense.

B. Used Vehicle Dealers

Recovering from used vehicle dealers can be tricky for several reasons. Unlike new vehicle dealers, who are usually somewhat dependent upon their reputation in the community for honesty, a fair percentage of used vehicle dealers don't have a good reputation to start with and survive by becoming experts at self-protection. Also (and don't underestimate this one), judges almost never buy used vehicles and therefore aren't normally as sympathetic to the problems used vehicle owners encounter. Chances are a judge has had a problem getting her new car fixed under a warranty, but has never bought a ten-year-old Plymouth in "tip-top shape," only to have it die two blocks after leaving Honest Al's.

The principal self-protection device employed by used vehicle dealers is the "as is" designation in the written sales contract. The salesperson may praise a car to the sky, but when you read the fine print of the contract, you will see it clearly stated that the seller takes absolutely no responsibility for the condition of the vehicle and that it is sold "as is."

Time and again I have sat in court and heard hard luck stories like this one:

"I bought the car for $3,200 two months ago. The dealer at Lucky Larry's told me that the engine and transmission seemed solid. I drove the car less than 400 miles and it died. I mean really died—it didn't roll over and dig itself a hole, but it may as well have. I had it towed to an independent garage and they told me that, as far as they could see, no engine or transmission work had ever been done. They estimated that to put the car right would cost $800. I got one more estimate which was even higher, so I borrowed the $800 and had the work done. I feel I really got taken by Lucky Larry's. I have with me the canceled check for the $800 in repairs, plus a letter from the mechanic who did the work, stating that the engine was in horrible shape when he saw it."

Unfortunately, this plaintiff will probably lose. Why? Because going way back to the issues I discuss in Chapter 2, Section B, he has proven only half of a case. He has shown his loss (he bought a $3,200 car that wasn't worth $3,200), but he has not dealt with the issue of the defendant's responsibility to make the loss good ("liability"). Almost surely, the used car dealer will testify that she "had no way of knowing how long a ten-year-old Plymouth would last and that, for this very reason, she sold the car 'as is.'" She will then show the judge the written contract that not only contains the "as is" designation, but "this written contract is the entire agreement between the parties and that no oral statements or representations made by the dealer or any salesperson are part of the contract."

How can you fight this sort of cynical semi-fraud? It's difficult to do after the fact. The time for self-protection is before you buy a vehicle, when you have the opportunity to have it checked by an expert. In addition, you have the opportunity to refuse to close the deal unless the salesperson's claims about the great condition of the car are put in writing. Of course, after the damage has been done, good advice such as this isn't worth much. If you have just been cheated on a used car deal, you want to know what, if anything, you can do now. Here are some suggestions.

- If the car broke almost immediately after you took it out of the used car lot, you can file in Small Claims and argue that you were defrauded. Your theory is that, no matter what the written contract said, there was a clear implication that you purchased a car, not a junk heap. When the dealer produces the "as is" contract you signed, argue that it is no defense to fraud. I discuss fraud in more detail in Chapter 2, Section H.

- If the dealer made any promises, either in writing or orally, about the good condition of the vehicle, he may be required to live up to them. Why? Because, as noted in Chapter 2, Section G, statements about a product that you rely on as part of deciding whether to purchase constitute an express warranty. This is true even if the seller had you sign an "as is" statement that disclaims all warranties. The key to winning this sort of case is to produce a witness to the dealer's laudatory statements about the vehicle, copies of ads that state the car is in good shape plus anything else that will back up your story.

- If the seller of a used car provides any written warranty at all (for example, a 30-day warranty on parts only), the buyer is automatically entitled to the implied warranty of fitness. (Civil Code Sec. 1793, 1795.5.) (See Chapter 2, Section G, for an explanation.) This implied warranty cannot be disclaimed, and lasts for the same period as the written warranty, but not less than 30 days or more than 90 days. The point of knowing all of this is, of course, that if a used car breaks soon after purchase and you have received even a minimal warranty, you should tell the judge this and argue that the defects in the car constitute a breach of the implied warranty of general fitness and merchantability. In other words, the car you bought was so defective that it didn't meet the reasonable standards expected of even a used car.

- You may also want to consider having the car towed back to the lot and then refusing to make future payments. This is a radical remedy and should only be considered in an extreme situation. But it does have the beauty of shifting the burden of taking legal action to the other side, at which point you can defend on the basis of fraud. If you take this approach, be sure you have excellent documentation that the car was truly wretched. And be sure to set forth in writing the circumstances surrounding your extreme difficulties with the dealer, along with a convincing statement that, taken as a whole, the dealer's conduct amounts to consumer fraud. Send copies to the dealer and the bank or finance company to whom you pay your loan. Of course, you will probably have already made a down payment, so even in this situation you may wish to initiate action in Small Claims Court to try to recover it.

Look for signs of fraud. If you really suspect you have been defrauded, have your car   checked by an experienced mechanic who will be willing to write a letter explaining what she finds. If this person can find affirmative evidence that you were cheated, you will greatly improve your Small Claims case. The mechanic might, for example, find that the speedometer had been tampered with in violation of state law, or that a heavy grade of truck oil had been put in the crankcase so that the car wouldn't belch smoke. Also, this is the sort of case where a Subpoena Duces Tecum (subpoena for documents) might be of help. (See Chapter 14.) Specifically, you might wish to subpoena the car dealer's records, including any that indicate his purchase price and the condition of the car when he purchased it. It might also be helpful to learn the name of the car's former owner, with the idea of contacting him. With a little digging you may be able to uncover helpful information (for example, that the odometer was turned back) that will enable you to convince a judge that you have been defrauded.

• Consider other remedies besides Small Claims Court. In California, the Department of Motor Vehicles licenses used car dealers and can often be very helpful in getting disputes resolved, particularly where your complaint is one of many against the same dealer for similar doubtful practices. Also, contact your local district attorney's office. Most now have a consumer fraud division that can be of great help. If you can convince them that what happened to you smells rotten, or your complaint happens to be against someone they have already identified as a borderline criminal, they will likely call the used car dealer in for a chat. In theory, the D.A.'s only job is to bring a criminal action, which will be of no direct aid in getting your money back, but in practice, negotiations often go on which can result in restitution. In plain words, this means that the car dealer may be told, "Look buddy, you're right on the edge of the law here (or maybe over the edge). If you clean up your act, which means taking care of all complaints against you and seeing that there are no more, we will close your file. If you don't, I suggest you hire a good lawyer, because you are going to need one."

C. Used Vehicles From Private Parties

Normally it is easier to win a case against a private party than against a used vehicle dealer. This often runs counter to both common sense and fairness, as a private party may be more honest than a dealer. But fair or not, the fact is that a nondealer is usually less sophisticated in legal self-protection than is a pro. Indeed, in most private party sales the seller does no more than sign over the title slip in exchange for the agreed-upon price. No formal contract is signed that says the buyer takes the car "as is."

If trouble develops soon after you purchase the vehicle and you are out money for unexpected repairs, the fact that you have not signed an "as is" statement should be a big help in your efforts to recover. As is true with a used vehicle purchased from a dealer, your problem is usually not with proving that the vehicle you purchased is in poor shape and needs expensive repairs (in short, that you suffered a loss). No, the key to winning is usually to show the judge that the seller of the vehicle is responsible ("liable") to make your loss good. To do this, you normally must prove that the seller claimed that the vehicle was in better shape than, in fact, it was, and that you relied on these promises when you purchased it.

Recently, I watched Barbara, a 20-year-old college student, succeed in proving just such a case. She sued John for $3,500, claiming that the BMW motorcycle she purchased from him was in far worse shape than he had advertised. In court, she ably and convincingly outlined her conversations with John about the purchase of the motorcycle, testifying that he repeatedly told her that the cycle was "hardly used." She hadn't gotten any of John's promises in writing, but she did a creative job of developing and presenting what evidence she had. This included:

- A copy of her letter to John that clearly outlined her position, such as the following letter.

14 Stockton St.
Corte Madera, Calif.
January 27, 19__

John Malinosky
321 South Zaporah
Albany, Calif.

Dear Mr. Malinosky:

This letter is a follow-up to our recent phone conversation in which you refused to discuss the fact that the 19__ BMW motorcycle I purchased from you on January 15 is not in the "excellent condition" that you claimed.

To review: on January 12, I saw your ad for a motorcycle that was "almost new— hardly used—excellent condition" in the local flea market newspaper. I called you and you told me that the cycle was a terrific bargain and that you would never sell it except that you needed money for school. I told you that I didn't know much about machinery.

The next day, you took me for a ride on the cycle. You told me specifically that:

1. The cycle had just been tuned up.

2. The cycle had been driven less than 30,000 miles.

3. The cycle had never been raced or used roughly.

4. If anything went wrong with the cycle in the next month or two, you would see that it was fixed.

I didn't have the cycle more than a week when the brakes went out. When I had them checked, the mechanic told me that the carburetor also needed work (I confirmed this with another mechanic—see attached estimate). The mechanic also told me that the cycle had been driven at least 75,000 miles (perhaps a lot more) and that it needed a tune up. In addition, he showed me caked mud and scratches under the cycle frame that indicated to him that it had been driven extensively off the road in rough terrain and had probably been raced on dirt tracks.

The low mechanic's estimate to do the repairs was $1,150. Before having the work done, I called you to explain the situation and to give you a chance to arrange for the repairs to be made, or to make them yourself. You laughed at me and said, "Sister, do what you need to do—you're not getting dime one from me."

Again I respectfully request that you make good on the promises (express warranty) you made to me on January 15. I relied on the truth of your statements (express warranty) when I decided to buy the bike. I enclose a copy of the mechanic's bill for $1,150, along with several higher estimates that I received from other repair shops.

Sincerely,

Barbara Parker

- Copies of repair bills (and estimates) dated within two weeks of her purchase of the cycle, the lowest of which came to $1,150.
- A copy of John's newspaper ad that she answered. It read: "BMW 500 c.c., almost new—hardly used—excellent condition—$3,500."
- Finally, Barbara presented the judge with this note from the mechanic who fixed the cycle:

To Whom It May Concern:

It's hard for me to get off work, but if you need me, please ask the judge to delay the case a few days. I have been in the motorcycle-repair business for 20 years, and have repaired hundreds of BMWs. All I have to say is this: the BMW that Barbara Parker brought to me was in fair shape. It's impossible to be exact, but I guess that it had been driven at least 75,000 miles and I can say for sure that it was driven a lot of miles on dirt.

> Respectfully submitted,
>
>
> Al "Honker" Green
>
> February 3, 19__

Barbara quickly outlined what happened for the judge and emphasized that she had saved for six months to get the money to make the purchase. True, testimony about financial hardship isn't relevant, but a quick tug on the judge's heartstrings never hurts. As an old appeals court judge who had seen at least 75 summers told me when I graduated from law school and was proud of my technical mastery of the law, "Son, don't worry about the law—just convince the judge that truth and virtue are on your side and he will find some legal technicality to support you." No one ever gave me better advice.

Next, John had his turn. He helped Barbara make her case by acting like a weasel. His testimony consisted mostly of a lot of vague philosophy about machinery. He kept asking "How could I know just when it would break?" When the judge asked him specific questions about the age, condition and previous history of the cycle, he clammed up as if he was a mafioso called to testify by a Senate anti-racketeering committee. When the judge asked him if he had, in fact, made specific guarantees about the condition of the bike, John began a long explanation about how when you sell things, you "puff them up a little" and that "women shouldn't be allowed to drive motorcycles anyway." Finally, the judge asked him to please sit down.

Even a little tangible evidence is better than none. In this type of case, absent a written warranty such as an ad that states the vehicle is in great shape, it's often one person's word against another's. Any shred of tangible evidence that the seller really did make an express verbal warranty as to the condition of the goods which the seller relied on to make the purchase can be enough to shift the balance to that side. Of course, if you have a friend who witnessed or heard any part of the transaction, her testimony will be extremely valuable. Getting a mechanic to check over a vehicle and then testify for you is also a good strategy. Sometimes you can get some help from publications that list wholesale and retail prices for used cars. Several times I have seen people bring these publications into court to back up their assertion that they paid above the "Blue Book" price for a used car "because the car was represented to be in extra good shape." This type of evidence doesn't constitute much in the way of real proof that you were ripped off, but it is helpful to at least show the judge that you paid a premium price for unsound goods. ∎

Bad Debts: Initiating and Defending Cases in Which Money Is Owed

A. Small Claims Court Is a Good Place to Sue on Bad Debts

A large percentage of Small Claims cases involve a claim that the defendant has improperly failed to pay the plaintiff a sum of money. Usually this means a bill for goods or services hasn't been paid, but it also can involve failure to pay a promissory note (for example, a loan from a friend or relative), or even a civil fine for something as simple as the failure to return a library book. In over 90% of these cases the plaintiff wins (often because the defendant defaults), illustrating how effective Small Claims Court can be as part of any business's collection strategy. But paradoxically, Small Claims Court can also work well for a defendant who believes that no money is owed or that the plaintiff is asking for too much and, as a result, puts up a spirited defense. In large part this is because, unlike formal court, in Small Claims, a defendant needn't file complicated paperwork or jump through other legal hoops to present her side of the story. Indeed, all a defendant need do is show up on the appointed day and make a convincing, well-documented presentation.

Some business people and professionals don't often use Small Claims Court to collect unpaid bills because they think it takes too much time or is "undignified." You will have to worry about your "dignity" yourself, but realize that Small Claims Court actions can be handled with very little time and expense once you get the hang of them. And the job of actually appearing in court can often be delegated. By contrast, business people who don't use Small Claims Court as part of a self-help debt collection strategy must normally either write off the loss or turn the bill over to a collection agency.

Unincorporated businesses can often send a representative to Small Claims Court. As discussed in Chapter 7, a bookkeeper, financial manager or other employee of a sole proprietorship or partnership can appear and present a case in Small Claims Court if the case can be proved by virtue of presenting a business record (showing that a bill hasn't been paid, for example), and if there is no other issue of fact involved in the case. (CCP Sec. 116.540(d).) And, of course, a corporation or limited liability company has the right to send any authorized representative to court.

B. Bad Debt Cases From the Plaintiff's Point of View

The job of the plaintiff in a case where he is suing for nonpayment of a debt is often easy. That's because in the majority of cases, the debtor doesn't show up (defaults, in legalese). In the absence of a defendant, the plaintiff need only introduce evidence that a valid debt exists and it has not been paid. To accomplish this, simply present written proof of the debt in the form of a contract, work order, promissory note or purchase order signed by the defendant. Even if a debt is based on an oral contract, it's usually easy to get a judgment since the defendant isn't present to contradict the plaintiff's version of events.

Here are a few suggestions plaintiffs who plan to sue to collect a debt will want to think about:

1.   Don't Bother Suing on Some Types of Debts

Although using Small Claims Court as part of your debt collection process often makes sense, there are exceptions. Here are the principal ones:

- **When there isn't enough money at stake.** For disputes involving a few hundred dollars or less, your costs of filing, preparing and presenting a Small Claims case are likely to be unacceptably high relative to what you are likely to recover. Of course, this is doubly true if you doubt whether a court judgment will be collectible.

- **When the defendant is a deadbeat.** As discussed in more detail in Chapter 3, most court judgments are fairly easy to collect, because the defendant has a job, bank account, investments or real property. However, it's also true that some people are judgment-proof and are likely to stay that way. Although probably making up only between 10%–20% of the U.S. population, people who have so little money or property that they can effectively thumb their noses at creditors undoubtedly run up a disproportionate share of bad debts. One thing is sure— you don't want to spend your time and energy taking people to court who are never likely to have enough money to pay the resulting judgment. Better to write off the debt and tighten up your credit-granting procedures. (See Chapter 3.)

- **When you want or need to get along with the person in the future.** Any court action, even a Small Claims lawsuit, tends to polarize a dispute, with the result that the parties become angrier at one another. This isn't a big problem when dealing with people or businesses you don't plan to have future contact with. But in other circumstances, such as a situation where a relative or local business owes you money, it's possible that your ongoing relationship with a debtor may be more important than collecting all that you are owed. In these situations, it makes sense to try to minimize conflict by trying to work out your dispute through mediation. (See Chapter 6, Section B.)

A rubber check may be worth three times its face value. Every merchant is stuck with a bad check now and then. Until recently, it usually didn't pay to take a bad check writer to court, especially for smaller checks. Today, however, California law allows a person receiving a bad check to obtain a judgment for a significant amount of money in damages in addition to the amount of the check. I discuss how to take advantage of this law in Chapter 4, Section C1b.

2.   Ask for Your Money Before You Sue

In Chapter 6 I discuss techniques to settle your case without going to court. Because writing an effective letter demanding payment frequently produces a check by return mail, you should always do this before filing in Small Claims Court. Unfortunately, instead of doing this many businesses rely on fill-in-the-blanks past due notices and dun letters purchased from commercial sources. While sending one of these is better than doing nothing, it's far more effective to write your own, more personal, letter (see the sample in Chapter 6), or at least to customize a form letter enough so the debtor can see it's really aimed at him. But realize that whenever you demand payment of a debt, a number of laws protect the debtor from overzealous collection techniques. For the legal do's and don'ts of collecting bills, see *The Legal Guide for Starting and Running a Small Business*, by Fred Steingold (Nolo).

Plan in advance to counter any claim that your bill wasn't paid for a good reason. If you provide goods or services, it's wise to include a statement on all your bills and collection letters requesting that the debtor notify you if goods are defective or services substandard. Bring copies of these notices to court. Then, if the debtor shows up and, for the first time, claims he didn't pay because the goods or services he purchased were somehow defective, you will be prepared to counter his claim. Do this by first showing the judge your many notices asking that any quality problem be brought to your attention and then testifying that the defendant never made a complaint. This should go far towards convincing the judge that the defendant is fabricating, or at least exaggerating, his current complaint in an effort to avoid paying you.

3.   It Pays to Bring Debt Collection Cases Promptly

For maximum success in collecting on bad debts, file suit as soon as you conclude that informal collection methods are unlikely to work. For starters, you'll be pleasantly surprised that a small but significant number of debtors will quickly pay up—or call you to work out a payment plan—to avoid having a court judgment appear in their credit records. But fast action is also advisable for other reasons, the most important being that people who owe you money are likely to have other debts as well, and may be considering bankruptcy. The quicker you act, the faster you'll get a judgment and be eligible to start collection activities, such as a wage garnishment or property attachment. In addition, if you file promptly, you will avoid having to worry about whether you are within the legal filing deadline, called the "statute of limitations." Depending on the type of debt, this can be anywhere from one to four years. (You will find a discussion of the statutes of limitations applicable to different sorts of debts in Chapter 5.)

4.   Special Rules Apply to Installment Debts

If you lend money or sell an item with payments to be made in installments, and a payment is missed, you normally are only entitled to sue for the amount of the missed payment, not the whole debt. Before you can sue for the entire amount, you must wait until all payments are missed. But there is a major exception to this rule: You can immediately sue for 100% of the debt—plus any interest—if your contract contains an "acceleration clause" stating that if one payment is missed, the whole debt is due. To see if this type of provision is present, carefully read your installment contract.

5.   Written Contracts—Bring Documentation to Court

Most debts are based on a written contract. This may be a purchase order, credit agreement, lease or formal contract. It normally makes no difference what your document is called, as long as you have something in writing with the defendant's signature.

Always bring your written documentation to court on the day your case is heard and be ready to show it to the judge. Also, bring any ledger sheets, computer printouts or other business records documenting the payments that have been made or missed.

Take your responsibility to be organized seriously. Sometimes I have seen otherwise sensible-looking business people show up with botched records and become flustered when closely questioned by the judge. The courtroom is not the place to straighten out a poor accounting system.

6. How to Prove Debts Covered by Oral Contracts

Generally, a debt based on an oral contract is legal as long as the contract was (or could have been) carried out in one year and is not for the sale of real estate or of goods (personal property) worth more than $500. (See Chapter 22 for more on written documentation requirements for the sale of goods.) Of course, you may face a problem proving that the debt exists if the defendant denies that he borrowed the money or bought the goods or services. Your best bet is to attempt to come up with some written documentation that your version of what occurred is true. For example, even if there is no written agreement, the defendant may have written you a down payment check or a letter asking for more time to pay. Either would be a huge help in convincing the judge that a debt exists. If you can't come up with anything in writing, try to think of a person who has firsthand knowledge of the debt and who is willing to testify. For example, if you asked the defendant to pay you and he said in the presence of a friend, "I know I owe you $1,000. I'll pay you next month," or even "Too bad you will never get your money back," or anything similar that indicates that the loan existed, bring your witness to court or have him write a letter explaining what he heard and show it to the judge.

Unfortunately, in many oral contract situations you'll have no witness to help prove its existence. If so, you'll want to consider whether you can establish the debt's existence by looking at the conduct of the parties. (In law school, this is referred to as establishing the existence of an "implied contract.") It is often particularly easy to do this when you haven't been paid for services you provided in a commercial context. After all, if the other party accepted your labor, there is almost always an implication that payment is expected.

Example: Jane, a commercial illustrator, works as a freelancer for a number of ad agencies, publishers and other clients. One day she got a call from Harold, a dress designer, asking her to do a series of drawings of his new line of evening wear. Jane does the drawings and submits her bill for $2,000. Harold refuses to pay, claiming both that payment was conditional on the drawings being published in a fashion magazine (they weren't) and that even if a contract did exist, Jane is charging too much. Jane files in Small Claims Court. The judge has no trouble finding the existence of an oral contract based on Harold's admission that he asked Jane to do the work. However, the judge only awards Jane $1,400, because she can't document her claim that she was to be paid $100 an hour, and Harold made a convincing presentation that illustrators with similar qualifications customarily charge no more than $70 per hour. (See Chapter 2, Section C, for more on oral and implied contracts.)

C. Debt Cases From the Debtor's Point of View

Over 20 years ago, when I first observed debt collection cases, I did so with scant attention. Especially where individuals were being sued by businesses, I assumed they mostly did owe the money. I even wondered why most defendants bothered to show up—knowing in advance that they had no realistic defense.

But over the years a curious thing happened. As I sat in on more Small Claims Court sessions, I realized that many debtors simply did not fit the stereotyped deadbeat role I initially assigned them. Instead of shuffling in with heads down, saying something like "I didn't pay that bill because I'm short of money right now," they often presented well-thought-out, convincing defenses, with the result that the judge reduced the amount the plaintiff asked for, or occasionally even ruled that no debt existed.

My observations have been corroborated by a prominent study of Small Claims Court cases, which finds that when a defendant shows up to contest a case, the plaintiff's chance of winning 100% of the amount asked for declines substantially ("Small Claims and Traffic Courts," by John Goerdt (National Center for State Courts)). In fact, defendants win outright in 26% of debt cases and pay half or less of what the plaintiff asked for in an additional 20%.

Here are some examples of cases in which I have observed a defendant succeed in whole or part:

- A local hospital sued an unemployed man for failure to pay an emergency room bill for $678. It seemed an open and shut case—the person from the hospital had all the proper records, and the defendant hadn't paid. Then the defendant told his side of it. He was taken to the emergency room suffering from a superficial but painful gunshot wound. Because it was a busy night and he was not about to die, he was kept waiting four hours for treatment. When treatment was given, it was minimal and he suffered later complications that might have been avoided if he had been treated more promptly and thoroughly. He said he didn't mind paying a fair amount, but that he didn't feel he got $678 worth of care in the 20 minutes the doctor spent with him. The judge agreed and gave judgment to the hospital for $250, plus court and service of process costs. After the defendant explained that he had only his unemployment check, the judge ordered that he be allowed to pay the judgment at the rate of $25 per month.

- A large local tire retailer sued a woman for not paying the balance on a tire bill. She had purchased eight light truck tires manufactured by a major tire company and still owed $612.50. The tire company properly presented the judge with the original copy of a written contract along with the woman's payment record, and then waited for judgment. It is still waiting. The woman, who ran a small neighborhood gardening and landscaping business, produced several advertising flyers from the tire company which strongly implied that the tires would last at least 40,000 miles. She then testified and presented a witness to the fact that the tires had gone less than 25,000 miles before wearing out. The defendant also had copies of four letters she had written over the past year to the headquarters of the tire company in the Midwest complaining about the tires. Both in the letters, and in court, she repeatedly stated that the salesperson at the tire company told her several times that the tires were guaranteed for 40,000 miles. Putting this all together, the judge declared the total price of the tires should be prorated on the basis of 25,000 miles and, after figuring what the defendant had already paid, gave the tire company a judgment for only $350, instead of the $612.50 requested. The woman wrote out a check on the spot and departed feeling vindicated.

• A rug company sued a customer for $1,486 and produced all the necessary documentation showing that the carpet had been installed and that no payment had been received. The defendant testified that the rug had been poorly installed, with a seam running down the center of the room. He brought pictures that left little doubt that the rug installer was either drunk, blind or both. The defendant also presented drawings that illustrated that there were obviously several better ways to cut the carpet to fit the room. The rug company received nothing.

Of course, the real point of these examples is not to be found in their individual facts situations—yours will surely differ. Rather, they illustrate the fact that if you can convince the judge that goods or services were substandard, chances are good that you'll win at least a partial victory.

1. Kinds of Defenses Common to Debt Cases

As discussed in more detail in Chapter 2, defenses in cases where a bill was not paid include:

• *Breach of contract:* The other party failed to live up to (perform) the terms of the contract within the correct period of time, with the result that you are no longer obligated to keep your payment obligation. For example, you contracted to have your kitchen counter remodeled using white ceramic title, and ended up with beige plastic tile. Or, you hired a florist to provide fresh flower arrangements for a party and the flowers arrived half dead, and six hours late.

> ⚠️ **Trivial defects won't void a contract.** To succeed with a breach of contract defense, you must show that the other party's breach was significant (lawyers say "material")—enough that it prevented you from receiving all or at least a substantial amount of the benefits you entered into the contract to obtain. For example, if you order light yellow flowers for a wedding, and refuse to pay the bill because cream-colored flowers are delivered, you can be pretty sure the judge will decide in favor of the plaintiff, especially if you used the flowers. By contrast, if you had ordered yellow flowers and received dark red ones, which obviously clashed with your color scheme, your chances of winning would be much better.

- *Fraud:* The other party intentionally lied to you about a key fact in a transaction. For example, you purchased a used car with 75,000 miles on the odometer. Later, you meet the vehicle's first owner who says it really had gone 125,000 miles and that the odometer said so when he sold it to the used car dealer who sold it to you.

- *Breach of warranty:* An express written or implied warranty (assurance) made by the seller of goods is breached. For example, a roofer claims in writing that your new roof will last 20 years. In fact, it leaks in the first big storm.

- *Violation of statute:* Many federal and state laws require the seller of a particular type of goods or service to comply with specific rules. For example, the Federal Trade Commission provides that a seller of door-to-door goods and services for more than $25 must give you notice of your right to cancel within three days, along with a cancellation form. If he fails to do so, your right to cancel continues indefinitely. For example, if you buy an expensive vacuum cleaner from a door-to-door salesperson and ask to cancel the deal the next day, you have a good defense if the vacuum cleaner company sues you.

2. Evidence to Defend Your Case

To successfully defend a suit claiming you owe money, you'll normally need to document a very good reason why the goods or services you received were inadequate or for some other reason you are not legally required to pay for them. Sorry, but this means you'll normally need to do more than tell the judge a sad story. If shoddy goods are involved, show them to the judge, or bring a picture or written report from an expert. (See Chapter 14, Section E.) If you received truly bad service, bring a witness (see Chapter 14) or other supporting evidence to court. For example, suppose the new paint on your recently refinished boat immediately began to chip and peel and, as a result, you notified the boat yard that you would not pay for the job. In case you are later sued, you will want to take pictures clearly showing the problem, and get a written opinion from another boat refinisher stating the work was substandard, as well as an estimate to fix or redo the job.

3. Appearing in Court

There is often a tactical advantage for the debtor in the fact that the person who appears in court on behalf of the creditor is not the same person with whom he had dealings. If, for example, you state that a salesperson told you X, Y and Z, the salesperson probably won't be present to state otherwise. This may tilt a closely balanced case to you. It is perfectly appropriate for you to point out to the judge that your opponent has only books and ledgers, not firsthand knowledge of the situation. The judge may sometimes continue (delay) the case until another day to allow the creditor to present the testimony of the employee(s) you dealt with, but often this is impossible because the person in question has moved on.

You can always ask for a little more time to pay. In California, the judge has considerable discretion to order that a judgment be paid in installments. (CCP Sec. 116.610.) Specifically, if you lose your case in whole or part, the judge can allow you to pay off the judgment in small monthly payments, instead of all at once. If you are financially pressed, installment payments can obviously be extremely helpful, since as long as you meet the payment schedule the creditor can't initiate a wage levy (garnishment) or other collection activity. So don't be shy about asking the judge to establish time payments— she won't know that you want them if you don't ask. Fortunately, even if you don't make your request in court, it's not too late. Even after a judgment is entered, you can file a form entitled "Request to Pay Judgment in Installments" along with a completed Financial Declaration with the court clerk. Your proposal may be approved promptly, or a court hearing may be scheduled to consider it.   ■

Vehicle Accident Cases

It is a rare Small Claims session that does not include at least one fender bender. Unfortunately, these cases are often badly prepared and presented, with the result that the judge commonly makes a decision at least partially by guess. I know from personal experience when I sat as a "pro tem" judge that it sometimes wouldn't have taken much additional evidence for me to completely reverse a decision.

Personal injury cases rarely belong in Small Claims Court. Cases involving all but the most minor personal injuries should be filed in Municipal Court (up to $25,000) or Superior Court (over $25,000). But before you hire a lawyer to represent you in a formal court, take a few hours to read *How to Win Your Personal Injury Claim*, by Joseph Matthews (Nolo). You may be able to settle your case on your own for a larger net amount than you would end up with after subtracting a lawyer's fee from your court judgment.

The average vehicle accident case that ends up in Small Claims Court doesn't involve personal injury, but is concerned with damage to one, or both, parties' vehicles. Many are extremely hard fought. Because of some quirk deeply embedded in our overgrown monkey brains, it is apparently almost impossible for most humans to admit that they are even occasionally bad drivers or could possibly be at fault in a car accident. Out of fantasies such as these are lawsuits made.

In Chapter 2, Section D, I discuss the legal concept of negligence. Please reread this material. To recover in a vehicle accident case, you have to prove either that the other person was negligent and you were driving safely or, if both of you were negligent, that you were less so. Normally, dealing with concepts of negligence in a vehicle accident is a matter of common sense; you probably have a fairly good idea of the rules of the road and whether you or the other driver screwed up. One key is often whether you or the other party was cited for breaking a law having to do with highway safety (see Section D, below). When a safety-related law is broken, negligence is usually presumed.

Don't assume you will lose if you were partially at fault. You can still win, or at least partially win, a case involving negligence even if you were not completely in the right. Under the doctrine known as "comparative negligence," if the other person was significantly more at fault than you were, you still have a good case. (See Chapter 2, Section D, for more on comparative negligence.)

A. Who Can Sue Whom?

The owner of a vehicle is the person who should file a claim for damage done to the vehicle, even if he wasn't driving when the accident occurred. The lawsuit should be brought against the negligent driver and—if the driver is not also the vehicle's owner—the registered owner. To find out who owns a car, contact the Department of Motor Vehicles. As long as you can tell them the license number, they can tell you the registered owner. (See the discussion in Chapter 8, Section F.)

B. Was There a Witness to the Accident?

Because the judge has no way of knowing what happened unless one or more people tell her, a good witness can make or break your case. It is better to have a disinterested witness than a close friend or family member, but any witness is far better than none. If the other guy is likely to have a witness who supports his point of view (even though it's wrong) and you have none, you will have to work extra hard to develop other evidence to overcome this disadvantage. Reread Chapter 14 for more information on witnesses. If you do have an eyewitness but can't get that person to show up in court voluntarily, present as evidence his written statement explaining what happened.

C. Police Accident Reports

When you have an accident and believe the other person was more at fault than you were, it is almost always wise to immediately call the police so that a police report can be prepared (in some areas, accident reports are only prepared if someone claims to be injured). A police report is admissible as evidence in Small Claims Court. The theory is that an officer investigating the circumstances of the accident at the scene is in a better position to establish the truth of what happened than is any other third party. So, if an accident report was made, buy a copy for a few dollars from the police station. If it supports you, bring it to court. If it doesn't, be prepared to refute what it says. This can best be done with the testimony of an eyewitness. If both an eyewitness and a police report are against you, try prayer.

D. Determining Fault

In Chapter 2, Section D, I discuss the general concept of negligence. While that discussion is fully applicable to motor vehicle cases (go back and read it if you haven't already), negligence can also be determined in these types of cases by showing that the other driver caused the accident (in whole or in part) as a result of a safety-related Vehicle Code violation. For instance, if Tommy runs a red light (prohibited by the Vehicle Code) and hits a car crossing the intersection, Tommy is presumed to be negligent (unless he can offer a sufficient excuse for his action). On the other hand, if

Tommy is driving without wearing his seatbelt (also prohibited by the Vehicle Code) and has an accident, the violation cannot be said to have caused the accident and therefore can't be used to presume negligence.

If there is a police report, the reporting officer will have noted any Vehicle Code violations that occurred relative to the accident. The report may even conclude that a Vehicle Code violation caused the accident. Obviously, if the other driver was cited, this is terrific evidence and you'll want to show it to the Small Claims judge. If there is no police report, you may wish to do a little research on your own. The Vehicle Code is available in most large public libraries, all law libraries and sometimes at the Department of Motor Vehicles. You can use its index to very quickly review dozens of driving rules that may have been violated by the other driver. If you discover any violations that can fairly be said to have contributed to the accident, call them to the attention of the judge.

BEWARE! Professional drivers have an incentive to bend the truth. Be particularly wary when you are opposing a bus or truck driver. Many of these people will suffer job problems if they are found to be at fault in too many accidents. As a result, they often deny fault almost automatically. Judges usually know this and are often unsympathetic when a bus driver says that there has never been a time when he "didn't look both ways twice, count to ten and say the Lord's Prayer" before pulling out from a bus stop. Still, it never hurts to ask the driver in court as to whether his employer has any demerit system or other penalty for being at fault in an accident.

E. Diagrams

With the exception of witnesses and police accident reports, the most effective tool in presenting an accident case is a good diagram. I have seen a meritorious case lost because the judge never properly visualized what happened, and several iffy cases won because plaintiffs made very persuasive drawings. All courtrooms have blackboards, and it is an excellent idea to draw a diagram of what happened as part of your presentation. If you are nervous about your ability to do this, prepare your diagram in advance and bring it to court. Use crayons or magic markers and draw on a large piece of paper about three feet square. Do a good job, with attention to detail. When it's your turn to speak, ask the judge if you can display your drawing (this will be easy if you have attached it to a piece of corkboard or similar stiff surface).

Here is a sample drawing such as you might prepare to aid your testimony if you were going eastbound on Rose St. and making a right-hand turn on Sacramento St. when you were hit by a car that ran a stop sign on Sacramento. Of course, the diagram doesn't tell the whole story—you have to do that.

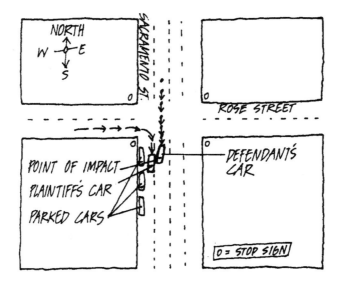

F. Photos

Photographs can sometimes be of aid in fender bender cases. This is especially true if they back up your story about how an accident occurred. For example, if you claim that you were sideswiped while you were parked, a photo showing a long series of scratches down the side of your car is likely to be convincing. Assuming they help you tell a convincing story, it can also be effective to show the judge pictures of the defendant's car (if you can manage to get them).

G. Estimates

Whenever you attempt to recover for damage done to your vehicle, it is important to show the judge several estimates for the cost of repairing it. Although not required by law, three is usually a good number. If you have already gotten the work done, bring your canceled check or receipt from the repair shop, along with the estimates you didn't accept. Be sure to get your estimates from reputable shops. If, for some reason, you get an estimate from someone you later think isn't competent, simply ignore it and get another. You have no legal responsibility to get your car fixed by anyone suggested to you by the person who caused the damage. Indeed, common sense often dictates that you don't. Unfortunately, you can't recover money from the other party to cover the time you put in to get estimates, to take your car to the repair shop or to appear in court.

In addition to damage to your car, you can also recover for the fair market value of anything in your car that was destroyed. You must be prepared not only to establish the fact of the damage, but the dollar amount of the loss. (See Chapter 4 for a discussion of what is involved in doing this.) You can also recover for the cost of alternate transportation while your car is disabled. However, a judge will usually only allow car rental fees for the minimum period of time it reasonably should have taken to get your car fixed. Thus, if you could reasonably have arranged to get a fender fixed in two days, you are only entitled to be reimbursed for renting a car for that time, not the days it took for an overworked body shop to get around to it.

Defendants should be on their guard against plaintiffs who try to pad their repair bill. Although it's a nasty practice, sometimes plaintiffs dishonestly try to fix existing damage to their car as part of getting legitimate accident work done. If you think the plaintiff is asking for too much money, try to develop evidence that this is so. For example, if you can present evidence that the plaintiff's car was already damaged at the time of your accident, but that she is suing you for 100% of her repair costs, the judge should award her less—maybe a lot less—than the amount she is demanding. Also, remember that the plaintiff is only entitled to get repairs made up to the total value of the car before the accident. If the car was worth only $1,500 and the repairs would cost $2,500, the plaintiff is only entitled to $1,500. (See Chapter 4.)

H. Your Demand Letter

Here again, as in almost every other type of Small Claims Court case, you should write a letter to your opponent with an eye to the judge reading it. See the sample letters in Chapter 6. Here is another:

18 Channing Way
Fullerton, California
August 27, 19__

R. Rigsby Rugg
27 Miramar Crescent
Anaheim, California

Dear Mr. Rugg:

On August 15, 19__, I was eastbound on Rose Street in Fullerton, California, at about 3:30 on a sunny afternoon. I stopped at the stop sign at the corner of Rose and Sacramento and then proceeded to turn right (south) on Sacramento. As I was making my turn, I saw your car going southbound on Sacramento. You were about 20 feet north of the corner of Rose. Instead of stopping at the stop sign, you proceeded across the intersection and struck my car on the front left fender. By the time I realized that you were coming through the stop sign, there was nothing I could do to get out of your way.

As you remember, after the accident the Fullerton police were called and cited you for failure to stop at a stop sign. I have gotten a copy of the police report from the police and it confirms the facts as I have stated them here.

I have obtained three estimates for the work needed on my car. The lowest is $612. I am proceeding to get this work done as I need my car fixed as soon as possible.

I will appreciate receiving a check from you as soon as possible. If you wish to talk about any aspect of this situation, please don't hesitate to call me, evenings at 486-1482.

Sincerely,

Sandy McClatchy

I. Appearing in Court

Here's how a motor vehicle accident case may be presented in court:

Clerk: "Next case, *McClatchy v. Rugg.* Please come forward."

Judge: "Please tell me what happened, Ms. McClatchy."

Sandy McClatchy: "Good morning. This dispute involves an auto accident that occurred at Rose and Sacramento Streets on the afternoon of August 15, 19_. I was coming uphill on Rose (that's east) and stopped at the corner. There is a four-way stop sign at the corner. I turned right, or south, on Sacramento Street, and as I was doing so, Mr. Rugg ran the stop sign on Sacramento and crashed into my front fender. Your Honor, may I use the blackboard to make a quick diagram?"

Judge: "Please do, I was about to ask you if you would."

Sandy McClatchy: (makes drawing like the one in Section E above, points out the movement of the cars in detail and answers several questions from the judge) "Your Honor, before I sit down, I would like to give you several items of evidence. First, I have a copy of the police accident report from the Fullerton police which states that Mr. Rugg got a citation for failing to stop at the stop sign in question. Second, I have some photos that show the damage to the front fender of my car. Third, I have my letter to Mr. Rugg trying to settle this case, and finally I have several estimates as to the cost of repairing the damage to my car. As you can see from my canceled check, I took the lowest one."

Judge: "Thank you, Ms. McClatchy. Now, Mr. Rugg, it's your turn."

R. Rigsby Rugg: "Your Honor, my case rests on one basic fact. Ms. McClatchy was negligent because she made a wide turn into Sacramento Street. Instead of going from the right-hand lane of Rose to the right-hand or inside lane on Sacramento Street, she turned into the center lane on Sacramento Street. (Mr. Rugg moves to the blackboard and points out what he says happened.) Now it might be true that I made a rolling stop at the corner. You know, I really stopped, but maybe not quite all the way—but I never would have hit anybody if she had kept to her own side of the road. Also, your Honor, I would like to say this—she darted out; she has one of those little foreign cars and instead of easing out slow like I do with my Lincoln, she jumped out like a rabbit being chased by a red fox."

Judge: "Do you have anything else to say, Ms. McClatchy?"

Sandy McClatchy: "I am not going to even try to argue about whether Mr. Rugg can be rolling and stopped at the same time. I think the policeman who cited him answered that question. I want to answer his point about my turning into the center lane on Sacramento Street, instead of the inside lane. It is true that, after stopping, I had to make a slightly wider turn than usual. If you will look again at the diagram I drew, you will see that a car was parked almost to the corner of Sacramento and Rose on Sacramento. To get around this car, I had to drive a little farther into Sacramento before starting my turn than would have been necessary otherwise. I didn't turn into the center lane, but as I made the turn, my outside fender crossed into the center lane slightly. This is when Mr. Rugg hit me. I feel that since I had the right of way and I had to do what I did to make the turn, I wasn't negligent."

Judge: "Thank you both—you will get my decision in the mail."

(The judge decided in favor of Sandy McClatchy and awarded her $612 plus service of process and filing costs.) ■

20

Landlord–Tenant Cases

Small Claims Court can be used by a tenant to sue for money damages for such things as the failure of a landlord to return a cleaning or damage deposit, invasion of the tenant's privacy by the landlord, the landlord's violation of his duty to provide safe and habitable premises and rent control violations, to name but a few. In addition, a group of tenants or neighbors can individually (but simultaneously) sue a landlord who allows drug dealing on the rental property. For example, if ten tenants sued a landlord who tolerated drug dealing for $5,000 each, the landlord would face a $50,000 suit.

While the majority of cases are initiated by tenants, landlords can and do also use Small Claims Court—for example, to sue a current or former tenant for unpaid rent or for damages done to the rental property. However, as we discuss in Section G, it is no longer possible to do evictions in Small Claims Court. Landlords who sue or defend small claims cases do not need to show up in court. Instead, they can send their man-

ager as long as that person really manages the property involved in the lawsuit and has
not been hired just to represent the owner in Small Claims Court (CCP 116.540). In
addition, the manager must file a declaration with the court stating that this is true.

FURTHER READING ON LANDLORD–TENANT LAW

To minimize your chances of ending up in Small Claims Court, and to more effectively fight your case if a dispute ends up in court, we highly recommend the
following Nolo books, which provide detailed California-specific information on
landlord–tenant law and specific advice, checklists and forms to avoid disputes
involving security deposits, housing code violations, late rent and rent withholding,
inspections (tenants' privacy rights), discrimination, illicit tenant activity and more.

- For tenants: *Tenants' Rights,* by Myron Moscovitz and Ralph Warner.

- For property owners and managers: *The Landlord's Law Book, Vol. 1:
  Rights and Responsibilities,* by David Brown and Ralph Warner.

- We also recommend LeaseWriter (Nolo), software designed to help
  small landlords easily and quickly create legally binding leases.

A. Security Deposit Cases

Disagreements about whether or not a landlord properly withheld all or part of a
tenant's security deposit account for a large percentage of the landlord–tenant disputes
that end up in Small Claims Court.

Problems involving security deposits often arise like this:

- The tenant moves out, making what she considers to be a reasonable effort to
  clean the place.

- The landlord keeps all or part of the deposit, stating that the place was left
  damaged or dirty.

- The tenant is furious, claiming the landlord is illegally withholding the deposit.

If the tenant and landlord can't reach a compromise, the tenant's best remedy is to
sue the landlord for the money withheld, leaving it up to the Small Claims Court judge
to decide who is telling the truth.

Whether you're a tenant filing a case or a landlord defending one, it's important to understand state law on security deposits.

1. State Deposit Law

California law dictates how large a deposit a landlord can require, how it must be used, when the deposit must be returned and more.

a. Legal definition of security deposits

Start by understanding that any "payment, fee, deposit, or charge," including last month's rent (but not first month's rent), paid by a tenant at the time she moves in is, legally, a security deposit (CC Sec. 1950.5), subject to being refunded if the tenant moves out and leaves the rental unit clean and undamaged. Or put another way, in California there is no such thing as a nonrefundable security or cleaning fee.

b. Dollar limits on deposits

For unfurnished property, the deposit (including last month's rent) can't exceed two months' rent; for furnished property, the deposit can't exceed three months' rent. (CC Sec. 1950.5(c).) If the tenant has a waterbed, the maximum allowed deposit increases by half a month's rent—to 2.5 times the monthly rent for unfurnished property and 3.5 times the monthly rent for furnished property. (CC Sec. 1940.5(h).)

c. Refundability of deposits

All security deposits are potentially refundable. Again, it's illegal to collect non-refundable fees or deposits, or to charge a "hidden" non-refundable deposit by charging considerably more rent for the first month than for later months. For example, a landlord can't require tenants to pay a nonrefundable cleaning fee, a fee for cleaning drapes or carpets or a fee to cover possible damage caused by a pet. All such fees are legally considered security deposits, and must be refundable in full—including interest on the deposit if required by the city—if when the tenant moves out the rental unit is left clean and undamaged and the tenant is paid up in rent. (CC Sec. 1950.5.)

Exceptions to Rules on Refundability of Security Deposits: There are two exceptions to the law that all deposits and fees must be refundable. Landlords don't need to refund:

- Credit check fees they charge prospective tenants for getting a report of their credit history (but the fee must be reasonable).

- Holding deposits that tenants pay to hold or bind a deal before a lease or rental agreement is signed. The law is very unclear as to what portion of a holding deposit a landlord can keep if a would-be tenant changes his mind about renting the property or doesn't come up with the remaining rent and deposit money. The basic rule is that a landlord can keep an amount that bears a "reasonable" relation to the landlord's costs, for example, for more advertising and for pro-rated rent during the time the property was held vacant. A landlord who keeps a larger amount is said to be imposing an unlawful "penalty" and may be sued by the prospective tenant in Small Claims Court. In general, holding deposits do landlords little or no good from a business point of view, and all too often result in misunderstandings or even legal fights.

d. Basic rules for returning deposits

Within three weeks after a tenant who has paid a deposit leaves—whether voluntarily or by eviction—the landlord must mail the following to the tenant's last known address:

1. The tenant's entire deposit, or

2. A written, itemized accounting of deductions for back rent and costs for necessary cleaning and damage repair, together with payment for any deposit balance.

When two or more co-tenants rent under the same rental agreement or lease, the landlord does not have to return or account for any of the deposit until all of the tenants leave.

If a deposit is not returned within three weeks from the time the tenant moves out, and if the landlord acted in bad faith in retaining the deposits, the tenant may be entitled to $600 in statutory damages over and above the actual amount of the withheld deposit. (CC Sec. 1950.5.) Whether or not the tenant is actually awarded punitive damages is left up to the judge, but it normally makes sense for tenants to bring a suit for an amount that includes punitive damages—especially if the tenant has proof that the landlord commonly withholds deposits or makes improper deductions from them.

Judges are more likely to grant punitive damages when the landlord is a bad actor. If a landlord had a pretty good reason for not returning a tenant's deposit, the tenant is unlikely to get punitive damages even if the judge rules that the deposit should have been returned. On the other hand, if the judge concludes that the landlord had no good reason to withhold the deposit, there is an excellent chance that up to $600 in punitive damages will be awarded.

2. Deposit Cases From the Tenant's Point of View

How should a tenant prepare a case involving a landlord's failure to return deposits? Ideally, preparation should start when the tenant moves in. Any damaged or dirty conditions should be noted as part of the lease or rental agreement, signed by both landlord and tenant. The tenant should also take photographs of substandard conditions and have neighbors or friends look the place over. When the tenant moves out and cleans up, she should do much the same thing—take photos, have friends (or even better, a disinterested person, such as another tenant in the building) check the place over, keep receipts for cleaning materials and, once the place is cleaned up, try and get the landlord to agree in writing that it is in satisfactory condition. Often the best way to do this is to have the tenant and landlord (or manager) tour the apartment together and check for any damage or dirty conditions (checking it against the inventory sheet at move-in, if one was made). Landlord and tenant should try to work out any disputes on the spot. If they can't and the dispute later ends up in Small Claims Court, the tenant should be prepared to bring at least one witness (such as a person who helped clean) to court who will support her position. In addition, it's wise to take some photos and keep all receipts for cleaning and repair materials.

Now let's assume that you are a tenant and have not gotten a $900 security deposit returned even though you moved out of an apartment more than three weeks ago, having paid all your rent and having given proper notice. Start by writing the landlord a letter like this:

October 25, 19__

Adam Anderson
Anderson Realty Co.
10 Rose St.
Costa Mesa, CA

Dear Mr. Anderson:

As you know, until September 30, 19__, I resided in apartment #4 at 1700 Walnut Street and regularly paid my rent to your office. When I moved out, I left the unit cleaner than it was when I moved in.

As of today, I have received neither my $900 security deposit nor any accounting from you for that money. Please be aware that I know my rights under California Civil Code 1950.5 and that, if I do not receive my money within the next week, I will regard the retention of this deposit as showing "bad faith" on your part and shall sue you, not only for the $900 deposit plus interest, but also for the $600 punitive damages allowed by Section 1950.5 of the California Civil Code. May I hear from you soon?

Sincerely,

Farah Shields
456 Main St.
Costa Mesa, CA

Be specific when requesting the return of a deposit. If your landlord has returned only part of your security deposit, deducting more for cleaning or damages than you thought was reasonable, your demand letter should detail exactly why you believe the deductions were improper. For example, if the landlord says a door was damaged and cost $200 to fix, you might claim that the work could have been done competently for $75. If you get no satisfactory response from your landlord, file your case.

WHOM SHOULD TENANTS SUE
IN SMALL CLAIMS DEPOSIT CASES?

A tenant who knows who owns the building should sue this person or business. However, sometimes it is hard to know who to sue, since rent is often paid to a manager or other agent instead of the owner. A tenant who doesn't know who owns his building is safe if he sues both the person to whom he pays his rent and the person who signed the rental agreement. Landlords must provide tenants with this information under state law (CC Sec. 1962):

1. The rental agreement must state the name and address of both the manager and the owner (or person authorized by him to receive notices, demands and lawsuits against the owner). The property owner must keep this information current and inform the tenant of all changes. If a tenant receives notice that the building has been transferred to a new owner, he should sue the new owner.

2. Instead of putting this information in each rental agreement, the owner may choose to post notices containing the same information in the building.

If the owner fails to follow this law, then the person who rented the dwelling for the owner—for example, the resident manager or property management firm—automatically becomes the owner's agent for receiving lawsuits, notices and demands. If no one has been designated as described in Section 1, above, and there is no manager, the tenant may serve legal papers on the landlord by sending them by certified or registered mail to the address where the tenant sends the rent (CC 19627).

On court day, a well-prepared tenant would show up in court with as many of the following pieces of evidence as possible:

- Photos or a video of the apartment on moving in that show any dirt or damage that already existed. (If you don't have these, it's not fatal; if you do, it helps.)

- Photos or a video of the apartment on moving out showing clean conditions.

- A copy of an inventory of conditions when moving in and moving out, signed by the landlord and tenant, if one or both was prepared.

- Receipts or canceled checks for any cleaning supplies used in the final cleanup.

- A copy of your written lease or rental agreement.

- A copy of a demand letter to the landlord, such as the one set out above, showing that you made the required demand before suing. Although the judge will normally pay far more attention to what you say in court than what you said in the demand letter, presenting the court with a well-organized written statement of the facts usually helps.

- One or, preferably, two witnesses who were familiar with the property, saw it after you cleaned up and will testify that it was in good shape. Incidentally, the testimony or written statements of people who actually scrubbed an oven or toilet are particularly effective. If you also have a witness who saw the place when you moved in and who will say that it wasn't perfectly buffed (or that damage already existed), so much the better.

Proceedings in court should go something like this:

Clerk: "*Shields v. Anderson Realty.* Please step forward."

Judge: "Good morning. Please tell me your version of the facts, Ms. Shields."

Farah Shields: "I moved into the apartment at 1700 Walnut St. in Costa Mesa in the spring of 19__. I paid Mr. Anderson, here, my first and last months' rent, which totaled $800. I also paid him a $450 damage 'security deposit' and a $450 'cleaning deposit.' I moved out on September 30 of this year. Three weeks after I moved out, Mr. Anderson had not yet returned my $900 deposit, so I wrote him a letter asking for my money back. I have yet to hear from him. As I believe this constitutes a willful denial of my rights under Civil Code Section 1950.5, I am asking for the $900 Mr. Anderson owes me, but also $600 in punitive damages, for a total of $1,500 plus my court costs. Here is a copy of the rental agreement (hands it to the clerk), which specifically states my deposit is to be returned to me if the apartment is left clean and undamaged.

"When I moved into #4 at 1700 Walnut, it was a mess. It's a nice little apartment, but the people who lived there before me were sloppy. The stove was filthy, as was the bathroom, the refrigerator, the floors and just about everything else. In addition, the walls hadn't been painted in years. But I needed a place to live and this was the best available, so I moved in despite the mess. I painted the whole place—everything. Mr. Anderson's office gave me the paint, but I did all of the work. And I cleaned the place thoroughly, too. It took me three days. I like to live in a clean home.

"Here are some pictures of what the place looked like when I moved in (hands photos to clerk, who gives them to the judge). Here is a second set of photos that were taken after I moved out and cleaned up (again hands pictures to clerk). Your Honor, I think these pictures tell the story—the place was clean when I moved out. I also have receipts (hands to clerk) for cleaning supplies and a rug shampooer that I used during the cleanup. They total $45.25. I have also brought two people who saw the place the day I left and can tell you what it looked like when I moved out."

Judge: (looking at one of the witnesses) "Do you have some personal knowledge of what this apartment looked like?"

John DeBono: "Actually, I helped Farah move in and move out. I simply don't understand what the landlord is fussing about. The place was a smelly mess when she moved in, and it was spotless when Farah moved out."

Judge: (addressing the second witness) "Do you have something to add?"

Puna Polaski: "I never saw 1700 Walnut when Farah moved in because I didn't know her then. But I did help her pack and clean up when she moved out. I can tell you that the windows were washed, the floor waxed and the oven cleaned, because I did it. And I can tell you that the rest of the apartment was clean, too, because I saw it."

Judge: "Mr. Anderson, you may now tell your side of the story. I should remind you that you have the burden of proving that the amounts you withheld were reasonable."

Adam Anderson: "Your Honor, I am not here to argue about whether or not the place was clean. Maybe it was cleaner when Miss Shields moved out than when she moved in. The reason I withheld the deposit is that the walls were all painted odd, bright colors and I have had to paint them all over. Here are some color pictures of the walls taken just after Miss Shields moved out. They show pink and purple walls, two of which are adorned with rainbows. And in one of the bedrooms, there were even animals painted on the walls. I ask you, your Honor, how was I going to rent that place with a purple bulldog painted on the wall? It cost me more than $300 to have the place painted over white."

Judge: (looks at the pictures and gives up trying to keep a straight face, which is okay, as everyone in the courtroom is laughing except Mr. Anderson) "Let me ask a few questions. Was it true that the place needed a new coat of paint when you moved in, Ms. Shields?"

Farah Shields: "Yes."

Judge: "Do you agree, Mr. Anderson?"

Adam Anderson: "Yes, that's why my office paid her paint bills, although we never would have if we had known about that bulldog, not to mention the rainbows."

Judge: "How much did the paint cost?"

Adam Anderson: "$125."

Judge: "I normally send decisions by mail, but today I am going to explain what I have decided. First, the apartment needed repainting anyway, Mr. Anderson, so I am not going to give you any credit for paying to have the work done. However, Ms. Shields, even though the place looked quite—shall I say, cheerful—when you moved out, Mr. Anderson does have a point in that you went beyond what is reasonable. Therefore, I feel that it's unfair to make Anderson Realty pay for paint twice. My judgment is this: The $125 for the paint that was given to Ms. Shields is subtracted from the $900 deposit. This means that Anderson Realty owes Farah Shields $775 plus $11 for costs (the filing fee plus service by certified mail). I am not awarding any punitive damages because I do not believe that Anderson Realty acted in bad faith in retaining the deposit."

3. The Landlord's Perspective: Defending Deposit Cases

Your best protection against spending hours haggling over security deposits is to follow the law scrupulously when a tenant moves out and it is your responsibility to return his deposit or explain why you are withholding some or all of it. But no matter how meticulous you are about properly accounting to your tenants for their deposits, sooner or later you may be sued by a tenant who disagrees with your assessment of the cost of cleaning or repairs.

This section shows landlords how to defend themselves in tenant-initiated Small Claims Court cases. The following section covers the occasional necessity of taking a tenant to Small Claims Court for unpaid rent, damage or cleaning bills not covered by the deposit. See *The Landlord's Law Book, Vol.1: Rights and Responsibilities*, by David Brown & Ralph Warner (Nolo), for advice on protecting yourself from security deposit disputes through inspection of the rental unit when the tenant moves in and moves out, an inventory of conditions, regular maintenance and safety updates, a clear lease or rental agreement clause regarding the use and return of security deposits and prompt return of security deposits with a detailed itemization of deductions. Regular maintenance and safety updates will also be useful if tenants withhold rent, claiming the unit needs substantial repairs. (See Section B3, below.)

After inspecting the premises and documenting the dirty or damaged conditions, send the tenant a written itemization of deductions for repairs, cleaning and unpaid rent within three weeks. Include details on the costs of any cleaning or damage repair, including a reasonable hourly charge if you or your employees do any necessary cleaning or repainting and an itemization if work is done by an outside firm. Be sure to keep receipts for costs of damage repair such as new carpets or repainting. If you use an outside cleaning service, ask the service if they will testify in Small Claims Court, if necessary, or at least write a letter describing what they did in detail if the tenant contests your deposit deductions.

Before your court hearing, you, or your properly authorized property manger if you won't be appearing in person, should gather all evidence that the premises needed cleaning or were damaged. It's important to understand that the landlord has the legal burden of proving one or both of these facts. If he fails to do that, the tenant will win. In other words, all a former tenant needs to prove to win is that a residential tenancy existed, that she paid you a deposit and that you didn't return all of it.

To make a winning case, a landlord or authorized manager should show up in court with as many of the following items of evidence as you can:

- Photos or a video of the premises before the tenant moved in which shows how clean and undamaged the place was.

- Photos or a video taken after the tenant left that shows a mess or damage.

- If they were prepared, copies of inventory sheets detailing the condition of the rental unit when the tenant moved in and out, signed by the landlord and tenant. (These are particularly valuable if they show that an item that is now broken was in good shape when the tenant moved in.)

- An itemization of hours spent by you or your repair or cleaning people working on the unit, complete with the hourly costs for the work.

- A copy of the written security deposit itemization you sent the tenant detailing deductions.

- Any damaged items appropriate to be brought into the courtroom (for example, a curtain with a cigarette hole would be effective evidence).

- Receipts for professional cleaning or repair services.

- One or, preferably, two witnesses who were familiar with the property, saw it just after the tenant left and who will testify that the place was dirty or that certain items were damaged. People who helped in the subsequent cleaning or repair or the new tenant who saw the place before you cleaned it are likely to be particularly effective witnesses. Written statements or declarations under penalty of perjury can be used, but they aren't as effective as live testimony. A sample written statement is shown below.

SAMPLE DECLARATION

DECLARATION OF PAUL STALLONE, CLEANER

I, Paul Stallone, declare:

1. I am employed at A & B Maintenance Company, a contract cleaning and maintenance service located at 123 Abrego Street, Monterey, California. Gina Cabarga, the owner of an apartment complex at 456 Seventh Street, Monterey, California, is one of our accounts.

2. On May 1, 199_, I was requested to go to the premises at 456 Seventh Street, Apartment 8, Monterey, California, to shampoo the carpets. When I entered the premises, I noticed a strong odor, part of what seemed like stale cigarette smoke. An odor also seemed to come from the carpet.

3. When I began using a steam carpet cleaner on the living room carpet, I noticed a strong smell of urine. I stopped the steam cleaner, moved to a dry corner of the carpet, and pulled it from the floor. I then saw a yellow color on the normally white foam-rubber pad beneath the carpet, as well as smelled a strong urine odor, apparently caused by a pet (probably a cat) having urinated on the carpet. On further examination of the parts of the carpet, I noticed similar stains and odors throughout the carpet and pad.

4. In my opinion, the living room carpet and foam-rubber pad underneath need to be removed and replaced and the floor should be sanded and sealed. I declare under penalty of perjury under the laws of the State of California that the foregoing is true and correct.

DATED: June 15, 199_

SIGNATURE: _____

Paul Stallone

If the tenant is suing you but has not demanded payment of the security deposit, as legally required, point this out to the judge, who may dismiss the suit on that basis.

B. Unpaid Rent, Rent Withholding and Other Money Damage Cases

Landlords most commonly initiate Small Claims actions to sue for unpaid rent—for example, if the tenant has already moved out and the security deposit (if any) doesn't cover the unpaid rent. Typically, the tenant will have broken the lease early or skipped out on a month-to-month tenancy without providing adequate notice. In theory, the tenant may still be residing on the premises, but in this case it's usually better to request damages as part of an unlawful detainer (eviction) action in Municipal Court.

If you are a landlord who decides that it is worthwhile to go after your tenant for money owed, your first step is to write a letter asking her to pay the amount of your claim. If the tenant has already moved out, a written statement itemizing how you applied the tenant's security deposit to the charges for cleaning and damage repair and requesting payment of the balance, is legally considered to be such a demand.

1. No Defense by Tenant

Often the tenant has already moved out and doesn't bother to show up in court. If this happens, the landlord briefly states her case and, assuming it's credible, will win by default. Sometimes the tenant does show up, but presents no real defense (often he is there only to request the judge to allow him to pay the judgment in installments. (See Chapter 24.) Again, the landlord should easily prevail.

The landlord (or manager who complies with rules set out in Chapter 7, Section F) should bring the lease or rental agreement to court and simply state the time periods for which rent is due, but unpaid. Nothing else is required unless the tenant presents a defense as discussed below. Sometimes a landlord will sue for three times the amount of rent owed (triple damages) under a lease or rental agreement that states that he is entitled to them if the tenant fails to pay rent, but stays in the rental unit. Doing this will almost guarantee that the tenant will put up a fight. In my experience landlords are rarely awarded more than their actual out-of-pocket loss, and it makes little sense to request more.

2. When a Tenant Breaks a Lease

A tenant who leaves before the expiration of a fixed-term lease (whether or not she notified the landlord that she's leaving) and refuses to pay the remainder of the rent due under the lease is said to have "broken the lease." This means the tenant is liable for the entire rent for the entire lease term (except where the landlord breaches an important lease provision first). However, the tenant's liability to pay all rent still due under the lease when she leaves too soon is limited by the landlord's duty to "mitigate damages." Stated in plain English, the landlord has a legal duty to try to find a new tenant as soon as reasonably possible. (CC Sec. 1951.2.)

What all this adds up to is that a landlord whose tenant breaks a lease with no good reason is entitled to:

1. The remaining rent due under the lease,

minus

2. Any portion of this amount that can have been reasonably recovered by obtaining a new tenant,

plus

3. Any reasonable advertising expenses incurred in finding a new tenant.

A landlord can deduct the total of these items, plus necessary repair and cleaning charges from the tenant's security deposit (see Section A, above) and sue for the remainder in Small Claims Court. See Chapter 4, Section C1, for a discussion of the "mitigation of damages" concept.

3. Lawsuits Regarding Defective Conditions or Damage to the Premises

Now let's look at Small Claims suits where a tenant stops paying rent based on a claim that the rental unit is seriously defective (uninhabitable). Although this issue most often comes up in the context of an eviction (unlawful detainer) lawsuit which can't be filed in Small Claims Court (see Section G, below), occasionally a landlord brings a separate Small Claims suit for unpaid rent.

a. From the tenant's point of view

There are several valid defenses to a landlord's suit based on a tenant's failure to pay rent. The principal one is where the tenant claims that rent was withheld because the condition of the premises was "uninhabitable." This amounts to the tenant saying to the landlord: "I won't pay my rent until you make essential repairs." This defense is based on the fact that under California law, every landlord makes an implied promise that a dwelling will be fit for human habitation—whether or not the promise is written down in a lease or rental agreement. If the landlord does not keep the place in a habitable condition at all times, he is said, in legalese, to have "breached the implied warranty of habitability." That breach justifies the tenant's withholding of rent. For a tenant to legally withhold rent, the problems must not have been caused by the tenant, the defects must be serious ones that threaten the tenant's health or safety and the tenant must have given the landlord reasonable notice of the problem.

Under California law it is also legal for a tenant to have repairs done himself under some circumstances and deduct the cost from one month's rent. (CC Secs. 1941-42.) The details of how this remedy can be used up to twice a year are discussed in detail in Nolo's *Tenants' Rights* and *The Landlord's Law Book, Vol 1: Rights and Responsibilities*.

Several state and local laws set housing standards for residential rental property. These laws require landlords to put their rental apartments and houses in good condition before renting them and keep them that way while people live there. If a landlord doesn't meet these requirements—for example, if the property has a leaky roof—a tenant may well be excused from paying all or part of the rent.

The important thing for a tenant to understand is that rent withholding is not legal where the landlord is slow to fix some minor defect. For rent to be legally withheld (whether or not the tenant actually hires someone to make the repairs), the condition needing repair must be sufficiently serious as to make the home "uninhabitable," unhealthy or unsafe. Thus, a broken furnace that a landlord refuses to fix in February would qualify as a condition making a home uninhabitable, but lack of heat in the summer for a few days probably would not.

A tenant normally has the responsibility of convincing a judge that the rent withholding was reasonable under the circumstances (lawyers call this the "burden of proof"), unless the landlord took more than 60 days to fix a very serious defect and a local health or building inspection department official insisted it be repaired following an inspection. (CC Secs. 1942.3 and 1942.4.) In this case, the burden falls on the landlord to prove the tenant was wrong to withhold rent.

If you are involved in a rent withholding case as a tenant, your job is to prove—with pictures, witnesses and other evidence—that the condition that caused you to withhold rent is indeed serious. Thus, you might call the building inspector or an electrician to testify that the wiring was in a dangerous state of decay. The landlord, of course, will probably testify that the rental unit is in fundamentally sound shape, even though there may be some minor problems. A landlord has the right to inspect the property as long as she gives the tenant reasonable notice. (See Section E, below, for the legal rules in this area.)

State law also requires tenants to use rented premises properly, refrain from damaging or defacing the premises and keep them clean. (CC Sec. 1941.2.) To protect a landlord against a tenant's careless damage to the property, lease and rental agreements commonly make the tenant financially responsible for repair of damage caused by the tenant's negligence or misuse. For example, if a refrigerator no longer works because the tenant defrosted it with a carving knife, it's the tenant's responsibility to make the repairs or to reimburse the landlord for doing so. If a tenant refuses to repair or pay for the damage he caused, the landlord can sue the tenant in Small Claims Court for the cost of the repairs.

Theoretically, a tenant can withhold an amount of rent equal to the dollar amount the unfixed defect lowers the value of the property. As a practical matter, however, the tenant can withhold as much rent as the landlord—or a judge, if the matter gets to court—will allow under the circumstances. A judge will make a decision based on what she thinks is the rental value of the premises, in light of the seriousness of the defect.

A landlord who fails to maintain property can be sued by a tenant for failing to provide a habitable dwelling. The tenant, whether or not he remains in the property, can sue the landlord for the following:

- Partial or total refund of rent paid while conditions were substandard;

- The value, or repair costs, of property lost or damaged as a result of the defect—for example, furniture ruined by water leaking through the roof;

- Compensation for personal injuries—including pain and suffering—caused by the defect. Landlords may be liable for physical injuries caused by faulty premises, such as a broken step, inadequate lighting or substandard wiring. Tenants can sue for medical bills, lost earnings and pain and suffering in Small Claims Court. (See Chapter 2, Section E, and Chapter 4, Section C4, for more on this.) A landlord is not protected from liability by a provision in a lease or rental agreement in which the tenant purports to give up the right to sue the landlord. These clauses are illegal and will not be enforced by courts.

A landlord may not retaliate against a tenant—for example, with a rent increase or termination notice—who complains to authorities about conditions in the property or who files a lawsuit and stays in the property.

b. From the landlord's point of view

If you are a landlord involved in a rent withholding case, you're probably either responding to a tenant's suit based on claimed substandard conditions or, more likely, are suing the tenant for the portion of the rent he withheld based on his claim that the rental unit was uninhabitable. Either way, be prepared to prove the following:

- The claimed defect was not so serious or substantial as to render the property legally uninhabitable and, therefore, to justify the tenant's decision to withhold rent under the reasoning of *Green v. Superior Court,* 10 Cal.3d 616 (1974). One good way to establish that the problem was not serious (for example, a hot water heater was noisy, but still functioning), is to have the repairperson who eventually corrected the problem write a letter or testify in person.

or

- Even if the defect was substantial, that the tenant didn't give you adequate notice and a chance to fix it. Especially if you regularly solicit and respond quickly to tenant complaints about potential safety problems, install and maintain basic security features and have a detailed complaint procedure for tenants to report potential safety hazards or maintenance problems, you'll want to explain your system to the judge to convince him that if the tenant had made a timely complaint, the problem surely would have been taken care of.

or

- Assuming there was a substantial defect that you didn't fix within a reasonable time, this defect justifies only the withholding of a small amount of rent (not the amount the tenant withheld) because it didn't inconvenience the tenant much.

4. Tenants Suing Co-Tenants for Unpaid Rent

When two or more people rent property together, and all sign the same rental agreement or lease, they are co-tenants. Each co-tenant shares the same rights and responsibilities under the lease or rental agreement. For example, all co-tenants, regardless of agreements they make among themselves, are liable for the entire amount of the rent, and a co-tenant who fails to meet this responsibility may be sued by the other co-tenant in Small Claims Court.

Example: James and Helen sign a month-to-month rental agreement for an $800 apartment. They agree between themselves to each pay half of the rent. After three months, James moves out without notifying Helen or the owner, Laura. As one of the two co-tenants, Helen is still legally obligated to pay all the rent and may be able to recover James's share by suing him in Small Claims Court. In the same way, Laura, the owner, may sue Helen, the tenant, for the full amount of the rent in Small Claims Court.

5. Rent Control Cases

State law provides that in rent-controlled cities that require landlords to register their rental property, a landlord who charges illegally high rent can be sued by the tenant for up to three times the rent collected in excess of the level certified by the local rent control board, plus attorney fees and costs. (CC Sec. 1947.11.)

C. Drug Dealing and Neighborhood Nuisances

A tenant or neighbor may sue the landlord for damages for maintaining a legal nuisance—a serious and persistent condition that adversely affects the tenant's (or neighbor's) enjoyment of the property—even if no physical injury occurs. For example, a tenant, plagued by the stench of garbage scattered about because the landlord hasn't provided enough garbage cans for the apartment building, can sue the landlord for the annoyance and inconvenience of putting up with the smell. A tenant or neighbor—or a group of them—may sue a landlord who does nothing to evict a drug-dealing tenant.

Increasingly, tenants have gotten together to hold landlords accountable for negligence in failing to fulfill their legal responsibility to maintain rental property in a habitable condition. Recently, tenants and homeowners have extended this group action approach to sue landlords for failing to protect tenants and neighbors from drug dealers, neighborhood gangs or other tenants who are creating excessive noise, running an illegal business or throwing trash in common areas. Similarly, homeowners have filed multiple suits to collect damages from neighbors who allow their teenage children to create disturbances that keep the neighborhood awake all night.

As noted in Chapter 7, Section E, this technique of using Small Claims Court for groups of individual actions was instigated when a neighborhood group banded together to bring hundreds of Small Claims suits against the City of San Francisco to recover damages for the nuisance created in their neighborhood from the noise from the city airport. (*City & Co. of S.F. v. Small Claims Division, San Mateo Co.,* 190 Cal.Rptr. 340 (1983).)

Despite the fact that this approach is legal and effective, some judges have viewed the filing of many simultaneous lawsuits with verbal disapproval. Nonetheless, a number of claimants in such cases have been successful in obtaining a quick and inexpensive resolution of their neighborhood disputes when other channels for solving their problems had failed. It appears that unless society or the legal system creates another efficient, economic alternative to the Small Claims Court system for dealing with neighborhood problems such as these, judges will be facing a growing number of this type of claim, whether they like it or not.

One problem that often arises in this type of case is how much to sue for. Assuming the annoyance is serious and persistent and the landlord or other source of the problem does not take reasonable steps to reduce or eliminate it after receiving a written demand to do so, it often makes sense for each claimant to sue for the Small Claims maximum and let the judge scale this back if she feels that less damages are appropriate.

1. Drug-Dealing Tenants

Trafficking in illegal drugs, most notably cocaine, has turned some formerly placid neighborhoods into battle zones. Drug dealing has hurt law-abiding landlords and tenants alike. It causes lower rents and property values for landlords and reduces safety and security for tenants and neighbors. To combat this seemingly intractable problem, the law is making landlords who rent to dealers liable for the interference with neighbors' enjoyment of their property.

The legal theory boils down to this: Landlords have a responsibility to keep their properties safe. That means it's up to the landlord to keep dealers out or, failing that, to kick them out pronto when they are discovered. When landlords allow drug-dealing tenants to annoy, frighten or even prey upon other tenants and neighbors, law-abiding tenants may start withholding rent, and neighbors or the government may bring costly lawsuits against the landlord.

a. Rent withholding

Although no statute specifically allows it, some courts have said that tenants may withhold rent if the landlord fails to protect their security. A landlord who does nothing about a tenant's drug dealing is certainly open to this accusation.

Even if the landlord tried to evict the complaining tenants for nonpayment of rent, a court could well rule that the tenants were within their rights to withhold rent until the property again became reasonably safe and peaceful.

b. Lawsuits against landlords

Tenants and others who become victims of the crime that surrounds a drug dealer's home may also sue a landlord who does nothing to stop drug dealing on his property. In recent years, exasperated neighbors have brought individual lawsuits against such landlords in Small Claims Court—and won. Clusters of such claims can quickly add up to tens of thousands of dollars.

In 1989, 19 neighbors plagued by the crime, noise and fear generated by a "crack house" in Berkeley won Small Claims Court judgments of $2,000 each (the California Small Claims maximum has since risen to $5,000) against an absentee owner who had ignored their complaints for years. In San Francisco, a similar rash of Small Claims suits cost one landlord $35,000. Soon after the verdicts, both landlords evicted the drug-dealing tenants. In the years since, dozens of other neighborhood groups have filed similar Small Claims suits, many of which have succeeded.

For more information on how to organize and file these types of Small Claims Court lawsuits, contact Safe Streets Now!, 408 - 13th Street, Oakland, CA 94612, telephone 510-836-4622, fax 510-836-8959.

D. Obnoxious Behavior

Occasionally a particular landlord or tenant can get pretty obnoxious. This is also true of plumbers, physics teachers and hair stylists, but since this chapter is about landlord–tenant disputes, we will concentrate on these folks.

From the start, there is a major difference between how landlords and tenants handle problems. This is because landlords have two advantages tenants don't have. First, they can charge deposits, and if a tenant fails to pay rent or damages the place, a landlord can often recover her loss by subtracting the amount in question from the deposit. In addition, the landlord usually has the right to ask a tenant to move out. (If the tenant has a lease or the unit is located in a city requiring just cause for eviction, this right is restricted.) Tenants, on the other hand, have neither of these rights and, as a result, are much more likely to sue for money damages in Small Claims Court when they are seriously aggrieved.

Typically, tenants have problems with landlords who cannot stop fidgeting and fussing over their property. Smaller landlords tend to develop this problem to a greater extent than do the larger, more commercial, ones. Nosy landlords are always hanging around or coming by, trying to invite themselves in to look around and generally being pests. In addition, a tenant may also run into a manager or owner who sexually harasses tenants or is on a power trip.

If a landlord or manager is difficult or unpleasant to deal with, she can make a tenant's life miserable. There is no law that protects a tenant from a landlord's disagreeable personality, and, if the tenant has no leases, he is especially unprotected from all but the most outrageous invasions of privacy, sexual harassment or trespass (discussed in Section E, below). However, if the landlord's or manager's conduct is truly obnoxious, courts recognize that tenants have a right to sue for the intentional infliction of emotional distress. In the case of *Newby v. Alto Riviera Apts.*, 60 Cal.App.3d 288 (1976), the court found that it was necessary to prove four things in this sort of lawsuit:

1. Outrageous conduct on the part of the landlord;

2. Intention to cause, or reckless disregard of the probability of causing, emotional distress;

3. Severe emotional suffering; and

4. Actual suffering or emotional distress.

See Chapter 4, Section C5, for advice on determining the dollar amount of a suit for emotional or mental distress.

E. The Landlord's Right of Entry and the Tenant's Right of Privacy

One area where tenants are easily and understandably upset is when they feel their privacy is invaded. Landlords, on the other hand, have a legal right to enter their rental units in certain situations. Sometimes a tenant's need to be left alone and a landlord's need to enter conflict. If they do, it is extremely important that both parties understand their rights.

CC Sec. 1954 establishes the circumstances under which a landlord can enter his tenant's home, and CC Sec. 1953(a)(1) provides that these circumstances cannot be expanded, or the tenant's privacy rights waived or modified, by any lease or rental agreement provision. The first thing to realize is that there are only four broad situations in which a landlord may legally enter while a tenant is still in residence. They are:

1. To deal with an emergency;
2. To make needed repairs (or assess the need for them);
3. To show the property to prospective new tenants or purchasers; or
4. The tenant gives permission (for example, invites the landlord to enter).

In most instances (emergencies and invitations by tenant excepted), a landlord can enter only during "normal business hours" (usually thought to be 9:00 a.m. to 5:00 p.m. Monday through Friday, though the statute doesn't say specifically and some people claim that Saturday should be a business day) and then only after "reasonable notice," presumed to be 24 hours. If a landlord does not follow these rules, a tenant's first step is to politely ask him to do so. If violations persist, a follow-up letter is in order. If this doesn't help, it is possible to sue in Small Claims Court for invasion of privacy if the landlord's conduct is persistently outrageous.

One difficulty faced by a tenant who sues his landlord for entering the tenant's unit without permission (lawyers call this "trespass") is that it is hard to prove much in the way of money damages. (A judge will want to know why the landlord's improper entry justifies a good-sized monetary award.) However, if a tenant can show a repeated pattern of trespass (and the fact that he asked the landlord to stop it) or even one clear example of outrageous conduct, he may be able to get a substantial monetary recovery. In this situation, the landlord may be guilty of a number of "torts" (legal wrongdoings) including trespass, invasion of privacy, harassment (CCP Sec. 527.6), breach of the tenant's implied covenant of quiet enjoyment (the tenant's right to enjoy his home free from interference from his landlord), intentional infliction of emotional distress and negligent infliction of emotional distress (discussed in Section D, above).

Assuming you are a tenant who faces this situation, how much do you sue for? There is no easy answer, but one approach is to keep or reconstruct a list (or diary) of each incident, complete with a fair amount of detail about the distress it caused you. Then read it over and assign a reasonable dollar value to each hour of distress. For example, if a landlord's repeated illegal entries into your house caused you 75 hours of serious upset, and you value your time at $25 per hour, you would sue for $1,875.

If a landlord is sued, but believes that his entry or conduct was legal, he should be able to document this. For example, if a tenant claims that the landlord entered his apartment without 24-hour notice, to prove his case, a landlord should be able to show a copy of a formal 24-hour notice to enter to make needed repairs (any notes of related phone conversations would also be useful) and testimony by a repairperson or other witness that entry was made 24 hours later. Also, the landlord may be able to explain that the urgent nature of the repair required less than 24 hours' notice. If there is a good reason—for example, a repairperson is available to make urgently needed repairs on a few hours' notice—a landlord can legally give a reasonable but shorter notice. Under state law, a 24-hour notice is presumed to be reasonable, but it is not absolutely required.

If a landlord repeatedly encounters unreasonable refusals to let the landlord or his employees enter during normal business hours for one of the legitimate reasons cited above, the landlord can legally enter anyway, provided he do so in a peaceful manner. In this case, a wise landlord should bring someone along who can later act as a witness in case the tenant claims some of her property is missing.

F. Discrimination

It is illegal for a landlord to refuse to rent to a tenant, or to engage in any other kind of discrimination (such as requiring higher rent or larger deposits), on the basis of any group characteristic such as nationality, race, religion, sex, physical disability, sexual orientation, being on public assistance or being a family with children. A landlord's attempted or actual termination of a tenancy for a discriminatory reason, or discrimination in providing services such as the use of a pool or other common area, is also illegal and can provide the discriminated-against tenant with a defense to an eviction lawsuit as well as a basis for suing the landlord for damages. Essentially, any discrimination that is not rationally related to a legitimate business reason is now against the law. Even an innocent owner whose agent or manager discriminates without the owner's knowledge can be sued and found liable. A landlord who unlawfully discriminates against a tenant or prospective tenant may end up in federal or state court, including Small Claims Court, or before a state or federal housing agency facing a tenant's allegations of discrimination. Because most of these cases involve amounts in excess of the Small Claims maximum, I do not discuss them in detail here. Your most effective remedy is to sue the offending landlord in formal court. For more information on how to spot and prove discrimination, see *Tenants' Rights*, Myron Moskovitz & Ralph Warner (Nolo). To find a lawyer who handles this type of lawsuit, contact an organization in your area dedicated to civil rights and fighting discrimination.

G. Evictions

It is illegal in California for a landlord to try to physically force or scare a tenant out of the property, no matter how obnoxious the tenant. Only the sheriff, marshal or constable is legally allowed to physically evict a tenant, and then only after the landlord has obtained a court order, known as an unlawful detainer judgment, allowing the eviction to take place.

Until February 1992, landlords could, in some circumstances, use Small Claims Court to evict a tenant. This is now illegal, and eviction lawsuits may only be brought in Municipal Court. (CCP Sec. 116.220.) See *The Landlord's Law Book, Vol. 2: Evictions*, by David Brown (Nolo), for clear step-by-step instructions on how to properly terminate a tenancy and prepare and file the necessary Municipal Court eviction papers. Tenants who want advice on going to court and defending themselves against an eviction lawsuit should see *Tenants' Rights*, by Myron Moskovitz & Ralph Warner (Nolo).   ■

Miscellaneous Cases

By now you should have a pretty clear idea of how a Small Claims case should be researched and presented. The facts of each situation will vary, but the general approach will not. Here I will very briefly discuss a few of the common types of cases not covered in the previous few chapters. Unfortunately, given the huge number of fact situations that commonly result in Small Claims disputes, I still may not cover your situation in detail. It will be up to you to adapt the approaches I have outlined in Chapters 13–20 to your situation.

A. Clothing (Alteration and Cleaning)

A number of years ago, before I started attending Small Claims Court regularly, I stopped by one morning when I had a few free moments to kill before a criminal hearing. The case being argued involved an elderly German-American gentleman with a strong accent suing an equally aged Armenian-born tailor, who was also seriously uncomfortable with the English language. The dispute centered around whether a suitcoat that the tailor had made for the plaintiff should have had two or three buttons.

After ten minutes of almost incomprehensible testimony, I understood little more than that the plaintiff had never owned a suit with two buttons and the tailor had never made one with three. The two men ended by standing and facing one another—each pulling a sleeve of the suitcoat and each yelling as loud as he could in his own language, apparently about how many buttons a suit ought to have. Much to her credit, the judge just sat and listened. What happened? I don't know. I was still actively practicing law then and had to bustle off to argue before another judge that my client thought the two pounds of marijuana he was selling in small plastic bags was really oregano. You can probably guess how that argument ended.

While I have never seen another clothing case quite as colorful as that of the two-button suit, I have been consistently surprised at how often I have encountered people in Small Claims Court clutching an injured garment. Given how often we humans seem to react with a level of indignation out of proportion to our monetary loss when a favorite item is damaged, we really must view our clothing to be an extension of ourselves. Unfortunately—no matter how much we love a favorite coat, dress or sweater—winning a significant monetary recovery in a case where clothing is damaged or destroyed is difficult. That's because—as also discussed in Chapter 4, Section C3—while it's often fairly easy to prove that the defendant mutilated your garment, most used clothing simply isn't worth much. Remember, in theory, at least, you are only legally entitled to the fair market value of the item of clothing just before it was damaged or destroyed, not its replacement value. To get more, you'll normally need to engage the sympathies of the judge. Here are some possible ways to do this:

- Bring the damaged clothing to court. It's hard for a tailor to say much in his own defense when confronted with a coat two sizes too big or featuring three sleeves.

- Be ready to prove the original purchase price with a canceled check, newspaper ad or credit card statement. If the item was purchased at a pricey store, let the judge know where. Most judges at least occasionally shop at stores like Nordstrom, Saks or Macy's, and may be sympathetic if an item you just paid top dollar for was destroyed.

- If you only wore the damaged or destroyed item a few times, make sure the judge knows it. For example, if you paid $500 for a good-quality suit you planned to wear to work 50–100 times over the next three years and a dry cleaner screwed it up after just five wearings, try to get the judge to value it at close to $500.

- Be sure that the person you are suing (tailor, cleaner, seamstress) really caused the problem. As noted in the example of the suede coat in Chapter 2, Section C, some problems that develop during cleaning or alterations may be the responsibility of the manufacturer.

Don't let the cleaners take you to the laundry! Cleaners are particularly apt to offer "proof" from "independent testing laboratories" to the point that the damage caused to your garment during cleaning was really the fault of its manufacturer. Start by understanding that since these labs work almost exclusively for the dry cleaning industry, the idea that they are independent is a joke. If you are faced with one of these reports, you will want to ask the defendant:

✔ "How much did you pay the testing lab for the report?"

✔ "How many times have you used the same testing lab before?"

✔ "How did you know about the testing lab (for example, does it place ads in dry cleaners' trade journals that say, 'Let us help you win in court')?)?"

B. Dog-Related Cases

No question. Dogs can be frustrating, especially to non-dog owners. As a result, lots of dog-related cases end up in Small Claims Court. Since many of these involve neighbors who will benefit by maintaining or establishing a pleasant relationship, trying to work out the dispute through mediation is often a good first step. (See Chapter 6.)

1. Dog Bites

California law makes dog owners liable for injuries their dogs cause—no ifs, ands or buts. (CC Sec. 3342.) The portion of this law that affects most people reads as follows:

> *The owner of any dog is liable for the damages suffered by any person who is bitten by the dog while in a public place or lawfully in a private place, including the property of the owner of the dog, regardless of the former viciousness of the dog or the owner's knowledge of such viciousness. A person is lawfully upon the private property of such owner within the meaning of this section when he is on such property in the performance of any duty imposed upon him by the laws of this state or by the laws or postal regulations of the United States, or when he is on such property upon the invitation, express or implied, of the owner.*

Of course, like any other laws, the language of this statute is open to interpretation. What does it mean to invite someone onto your property, for example? Fortunately, California courts have dealt with this legal issue in written opinions in previously decided dog bite cases. It can be extremely helpful to review the brief digests of the fact situations of these cases with an eye towards learning how appellate courts ruled in cases such as yours. To do this, locate a copy of either West's or Deering's Annotated California Codes. (See Chapter 1, Section D, for more on legal research.) You'll find the material you need following Civil Code Sec. 3342. If you find a ruling that seems to support your position, read the entire case and then write a memo telling the Small Claims Court judge about it. (See Chapter 15, Section B, for a sample memo.)

Once in court, be ready to prove the extent of your injury, the place where it occurred and the amount of your money damages. As discussed in Chapter 4, Section C4, this consists of the value of any uncompensated time you took off work, out-of-pocket medical expenses, and the value of your pain and suffering. Particularly if the dog is mean-looking, show its picture to the judge.

2. Barking Dogs

Noise produced by barking dogs is often regulated by local city or county ordinance. Sometimes there is a separate ordinance involving animals; other times dogs are covered by a more general noise ordinance. Start by understanding what the law requires and if your local governmental entity will help enforce it. In addition, the owner(s) of a barking dog that interferes with a homeowner's or renter's ability to enjoy her home have committed a civil wrong (tort) called a "nuisance." As with any other tort, the dog's owner(s) are liable for money damages for the harm caused.

Assuming negotiation and, possibly, mediation with the owner of a noisy beast fail and you file in Small Claims Court, you will face two main problems:

1. To establish that the barking dog really has damaged your ability to enjoy your property (life). One good way to do this is to get a number of neighbors to write letters or, better yet, testify in court to the point that the animal in question is truly a noisy menace. (Don't forget to bring a copy of the local dog-barking ordinance to establish that it is also a law breaker.) Also, if your municipality has cited the dog's owner for violating the noise ordinance, make sure the judge knows about it.

2. To prove money damages. Establishing money damages caused by a noisy dog is obviously a subjective task. One approach is to try to put a money value on each hour of your lost sleep. For example, if you can convince the judge that each hour you lay awake tossing is worth a certain amount (perhaps $10 or even $20), your damages will quickly add up. As a backup to your oral testimony about how miserable it is to be denied sleep by a howling canine, keep a log of the dates and times you are awakened and present it to the judge. I once observed a case where six neighbors kept a log for 30 days detailing how often a particular dog barked after 10 p.m. The number, which was over 300, was influential in convincing the judge to give the plaintiffs a good-sized judgment.

Dog Law, by Attorney Mary Randolph (Nolo), answers common legal questions about biting, barking, leash laws, problems with veterinarians and other common dog-related problems.

C. Damage to Real Property (Land, Buildings, Etc.)

There is no typical case involving damage to real property, since individual fact situations vary greatly. So instead of trying to set down general rules, I'll explain how one person (let's call her Babette) coped with a property damage problem. Hopefully some of the legal lessons Babette learned will apply to your fact situation.

Babette owns a cinder-block building that houses two stores. One morning, when she came to work, she noticed water pouring in through the back of her building. Because the building was set into a hill, it abutted about eight feet of her uphill neighbor's land (let's call her neighbor Boris). After three days of investigation involving the use of green dye in Boris's plumbing system, it was discovered that the water came from an underground leak in Boris's sewer pipe. At this point, Babette had spent considerable effort and some money to pay helpers to get the water mopped up before it damaged anything in the stores.

Instead of fixing the leak promptly, Boris delayed for four days. All of this time, Babette and her helpers were mopping frantically and complaining loudly to Boris. Finally, when Boris did get to work, he insisted on digging the pipe out himself, which took another four days. (A plumber with the right equipment could have done it in one.) In the middle of Boris's digging, when his yard looked as though it was being attacked by a herd of giant gophers, it rained. The water filled the holes and trenches instead of running off, as it normally would have. Much of it ran through the ground into Babette's building, bringing a pile of mud with it.

When the flood was finally over, Babette figured out her costs as follows:

First three days (before the source of the water was discovered)	$148 (for help with mopping and cleaning)
Next four days (while Boris refused to cooperate)	$188 (for help with mopping and cleaning)
Final four days (including the day it rained)	$262 (for help with mopping and cleaning)
One secondhand water vacuum purchased during rain storm	$200
Her own time, valued at $8.00 per hour.	$600

Assuming that Boris is unwilling to pay Babette's mopping and cleanup costs, how much should she sue for and how much is she likely to recover? Remembering the lessons taught in Chapter 2, before Babette can recover for her very real loss, she must show that Boris was negligent or caused her loss intentionally. Probably, she can't do this for the first three days when no one knew where the water was coming from, and it's also likely to be difficult to convince a judge that Boris was negligent for failing to replace a pipe that, up until then, had worked fine. (But Babette might try to show that the pipe was so old it was likely it would break and Boris should have anticipated this by replacing it.) However, once the problem was discovered and Boris didn't take steps to fix it as fast as possible, he was clearly negligent, and Babette can recover at least her out-of-pocket loss ($450 for her labor and $200 for the water vacuum). Can Babette also recover for the value of her own time? The answer to this question is "maybe." If Babette could show she had to close her store or take time off from a job to stem the flood and as a result she lost income, she probably could recover. But if she was retired and lost no pay as a result of her efforts to stem the flood, it would be more difficult. If I were Babette, I would sue for about $1,250 ($450 for labor she paid for, $200 for the vacuum and $600 for the value of her own labor) and count on getting most of it.

D. Police Brutality/False Arrest Cases

Now and then actions against the police end up in Small Claims Court. Usually, the plaintiff is an irate citizen who has tried and failed to get an attorney to represent him in a larger suit and, as a last resort, has filed for the maximum amount his Small Claims Court will allow. Put simply, most of the people I have seen bringing this sort of case ended up losers. Why? Because the police and jailers have excellent legal advice and usually aren't afraid to bend the truth to back each other up. It's no secret that the unwritten rule in any law enforcement agency is to protect your own behind first and to protect your buddies' derrieres right after that. Or put another way, few police officers are going to tell the whole truth if doing so means collecting a black mark on their (or a buddy's) service record. Add to this the fact that most law enforcement people have testified many times, and know how to handle themselves in court. If you still doubt how hard it is to win these cases, ask yourself what chance Rodney King would have had of prevailing if there had been no videotape of his beating.

The reason many plaintiffs must use Small Claims Court to sue law enforcement personnel pretty much tells the story. Lawyers normally won't invest their time and money in these sorts of cases because they find them almost impossible to win. Does this mean I believe that people bringing false arrest, police brutality and similar types of cases are wasting their time? Balancing the trouble involved against the unlikely chance of success, I would have to say that unless the facts of the particular case really are compelling, the answer is "often, yes." That said, let me add that I admire people who will fight for principle against arrogant public employees who illegally abuse their positions even though they have small chance of winning.

If you do sue a police officer, jailer or anyone else with a badge, be sure that you have several witnesses or other evidence to back you up. Again, never, never rely on one officer to testify against another; they will almost never do it. You would also be wise to spend a few dollars and talk to a lawyer who specializes in criminal cases. For a small fee, you can probably pick up some valuable pointers on how to convince the judge that you were treated in an illegal and unreasonable way.

Sue the city or county as well as the officer. In most cases where you claim police misconduct, you will want to sue the city, county or state government that employs the officer, as well as the individual involved. But remember, before you can sue a government entity, you must first promptly file an administrative claim. (See Chapter 8.)

E. Defamation (Including Libel and Slander)

In California, libel and slander cases may be brought in Small Claims Court. However, many judges don't take them seriously, since most untrue statements don't really result in serious damage. To prevail, you need to show that the statement was false, that others saw and heard it and, most important, that it really did harm your reputation in a significant way. In addition, if you are a public figure (politician, actor, media celebrity), the law requires that you not only need to show that the statement was false, but that the defendant either knew it was false or made it in reckless disregard of whether or not it was true. In short, the fact that the defendant's statement was just plain wrong isn't enough to make you a winner if you are a public figure.

Example: Your nutty neighbor tells everyone on the block you are an idiot. You wonder if you have grounds to sue. Probably not, since chances are you haven't been harmed—after all, since everyone in the neighborhood knows he is a kook, chances are no one has taken his comments seriously. However, if he writes and distributes a leaflet all over town which falsely accuses you of having sex with minors, your chances of winning are much better. One reason is that at least some people who receive the flyer won't know that the writer isn't very reliable and therefore may take it seriously.

To learn more about the many intricacies of defamation law, a good place to start is with a law student course outline on torts (a negligent or intentional "wrong" that results in damage). These are carried by all law bookstores (usually located near law schools) and are also available from Nolo's self-help law stores (510-704-2248). ∎

Disputes Between Small Businesses

Because they have learned that it is a relatively fast and cost-efficient way to resolve intractable-seeming problems, more and more small business owners are turning to Small Claims Court to settle business disputes that they have been unable to resolve through negotiation or mediation. Unfortunately, when the Legislature increased the Small Claims Court jurisdictional amount to $5,000, it also adopted a provision to prevent plaintiffs from bringing more than two claims for over $2,500 within a calendar year. This limit was largely the result of intensive lobbying activity on behalf of collection agencies, who proved far more influential with the California Legislature than small business groups. So while small businesses continue to be able to utilize Small Claims Court to provide speedy resolution to business disputes under $2,500 (and up to two disputes between $2,500 and $5,000 per calendar year), they are forced to resort to more expensive procedures—such as turning bad debts over to collection agencies—for most disputes over $2,500.

Unfortunately, limiting the number of larger lawsuits small businesses can file each year also ends up hurting defendants. That's because many businesses which are prevented from filing in Small Claims Court instead sue in Municipal Court (often through a collection agency). Unfortunately, this means that instead of just showing up and having her say in Small Claims Court, a defendant must cope with filing legal pleadings and then, once in court, cope with formal rules of evidence. Even worse for the defendant, if the plaintiff wins in formal court, they are often entitled to tack their attorney's fee onto the judgment.

This chapter didn't appear in the first few editions of this book because I naively assumed that Chapter 18—"Bad Debts: Initiating and Defending Cases in Which Money is Owed"—provided sufficient information to help business people cope with their Small Claims cases. It's here now because I have had so many requests from friends who own their own small businesses asking for additional information. It turned out, of course, that although many disputes between small business people involve a simple failure to pay money, a significant number are more complicated. Commonly these more complex disputes involve people who have had a continuing business relationship and find themselves in the midst of a major misunderstanding that goes beyond the refusal to pay a bill. Often both parties are in court because they feel badly used— perhaps even "ripped off" or "cheated"—by the other.

I have been asked for advice on preparing Small Claims Court cases by a surprising variety of business people. They include:

- A dentist who was furious at a dental equipment wholesaler who passed off slightly used equipment as new.

- An architect who wasn't paid for drawing preliminary plans for a small retail complex when the development failed to get financing.

- A phototypesetter who refused to pay her former accountant in a dispute involving the value of the latter's services.

- A landscape designer who tried to enforce a verbal agreement, which he claimed allowed him to increase his fee when he accommodated a client by making changes to final plans.

- An author who claimed that her publisher had taken too long to publish her book.

- A client who claimed that his lawyer's incompetence was a prime reason he had to pay too much to settle a case.

A. Remember: You Didn't Always Hate Your Opponent

Although the disputes listed above seem very different, they all have one thing in common—in each situation, the disputing parties had previously enjoyed a friendly business or personal relationship. And in each case, at least part of the reason the plaintiff brought the dispute to court was that he was just plain mad at the defendant.

In short, disappointment is a significant factor driving many small business disputes. Unfortunately, feeling let down by the other party doesn't help you evaluate whether you have a good case. Nor does it help you prepare for court or collect your money should you win. In fact, aside from its value as a goad to taking action, it often gets in the way of the clear thinking necessary to make good decisions. It follows that your first job is to try and cool your emotions. If you are having trouble doing this, enlist another small business person as your mentor. First carefully explain both sides of the dispute. Then ask your mentor for a frank evaluation both of the merits of the argument and whether there really is enough at stake to warrant taking the case to court.

Mediation may offer the best way to settle your dispute. Assuming you really do have a good case and the defendant is solvent, going to Small Claims Court is a quick and cost-efficient way to put dollars in your pocket. But like all courts, Small Claims Court tends to polarize disputes and deepen enmities. In some circumstances—especially where business people will benefit from working together, or at least being civil to each other, in the future—attempting to arrive at a compromise settlement through mediation is a better initial choice. (See Chapter 6, Section B, for more on mediation.)

B. Organizing Your Case

When it comes to preparing for court, small business people normally have two advantages over run-of-the-herd mortals. First, as a matter of course, they maintain a recordkeeping system. Depending on the type of business, this typically includes a good filing system to maintain bids, contracts and customer correspondence, as well as a bookkeeping system that tracks payables and receivables. Taken together, these resources normally contain considerable raw material helpful to successfully proving a Small Claims case. The second advantage is more subtle, but no less real. It involves the average small businessperson's organizational skill—that is, her ability to take a confused mess of facts and organize them into a coherent and convincing narrative. Of course, when one business person sues another, those advantages often cancel out, meaning that both sides are likely to be well-organized and prepared.

Throughout this book I talk about how to decide if you have a good case (Chapter 2) and, assuming you do, how to prepare and present it in court (Chapters 13–20).

Since there is no point in repeating this information, I'll instead use the rest of this chapter to supplement it with material of particular interest to small business people.

1. Most Business Disputes Involve Contracts

The majority of business cases involve one business claiming that the other has broken a contract. (See Chapter 2, Section C, for more on contract law.) Start by taking a close look at any contract involved in your case. Specifically, ask yourself, what were your obligations and expected benefits from the deal? Similarly, what was the other person supposed to do and how was he going to benefit?

Oral contracts are usually legal. Most oral contracts—except those that involve the sale of real estate or of goods (tangible property) worth $500 or more, or which can't be carried out in one year—are legal and enforceable if they can be proven. But when nothing has been written down, proving that a contract existed can sometimes be difficult. An exception to this rule applies when you did work for someone and weren't paid (you are a commercial photographer and spend a day taking pictures of a hat designer's new creations), since the judge is likely to agree with your contention that, by implication, you wouldn't have done the work unless the defendant had promised to pay you.

You should also understand that a written contract need not be a formal negotiated document with both parties' signatures at the end. Under the Uniform Commercial Code (UCC)—which has been adopted in all states and applies to the sale of goods, but not services—to be a contract, a letter or other written document doesn't even have to state the price or time of delivery, only that the parties agree on the sale of goods and the quantity of goods sold. If it meets this modest requirement, any letter, fax or other writing can constitute a contract. (See Sidebar, "The Sale of Goods.")

Example: *Hubert, a pest control operator, sends a fax to Josephine, the business manager of a company that manufactures rodent traps, saying, "I would like to order 1,000 gopher traps at $14 per trap." Josephine faxes back, "Thank you for your order. The traps will be sent next week." There is a contract. Indeed, even if Josephine didn't reply but instead promptly sent the traps, a contract would be formed based on the circumstances of the transaction.*

You should also be aware that the business usage and practices in a particular field are commonly viewed as being part of a contract and can be introduced as evidence in Small Claims Court to support or thwart your case. Thus, if Hubert ordered rodent traps in February and Josephine didn't send them until September, Hubert could present evidence to the judge that everyone in the rodent control business knows that traps are only saleable in the summer when rodents attack crops, and that Josephine's failure to deliver the traps in the correct season constituted a breach of contract.

Finally, keep in mind that contracts can be, and often are, changed many times as negotiations go back and forth and circumstances change. The important agreement is the last one.

THE SALE OF GOODS

The Uniform Commercial Code (UCC), adopted by all states, contains special rules affecting contracts for the sale of goods. While it requires that you produce something in writing if you want to enforce a contract for a sale of goods and the price is $500 or more, it provides that this writing can be very brief—briefer than a normal written contract. Under the UCC, the writing need only:

- indicate that the parties have agreed on the sale of the goods, and
- state the quantity of goods being sold.

If items such as price, time and place of delivery or quality of goods are missing, the UCC fills them in based on customs and practices in the particular industry. And where specially manufactured goods are ordered, the UCC doesn't require any writing at all once a party makes a significant effort towards carrying out the terms of the contract.

Example: A restaurant calls and orders 200 sets of dishes from a restaurant supply company. The dishes are to feature the restaurant's logo. If the supply company makes a substantial beginning on manufacturing the dishes and applying the logo, the restaurant can't avoid liability on the contract simply because it was oral.

2.   Presenting Your Evidence in Court

In addition to the normal techniques of efficiently presenting evidence in court (discussed in Chapters 14 and 15), this section reviews several additional approaches of special interest to small business people.

Start by understanding that in business disputes, the problem is often having *too much* evidence, rather than too little. If this is your situation, your job is to separate the material that is essential to proving your case from that which is less important. The best approach is to organize both your verbal presentation and the backup evidence around the heart of the dispute, rather than trying to first fill in all the background information.

Example: Ted, an interior decorator, is hired by Alice, the owner of Ames Country Inn, to freshen up the decor of her bed and breakfast. Ted submits an estimate, which Alice verbally accepts by telephone. Later, Alice stops by Ted's office to drop off a set of detailed architectural drawings. Ted works for three days on the new decor plan before Alice suddenly calls and cancels the deal because, "on second thought, I don't like the colors you are proposing." After Ted's bills are not paid and his demand letter is ignored, Ted files in Small Claims Court, asking for three days' pay plus the money he is out of pocket for supplies. In court, Ted very sensibly begins his presentation like this: "Your Honor, the defendant hired me to prepare a detailed plan to redecorate the Ames Country Inn. I worked on the job for three days and bought $200 worth of supplies before she canceled our contract. Today, I'm asking for a judgment for my normal rate of pay of $80 per hour for the 24 hours I worked, plus the $200 for supplies. The total is $2,120."

Of course, there is more to Ted's story, which means, after stating the crux of his claims, he will need to fill in the key points. Were I Ted, I would next make these points:

- He and Alice had worked together before and his work had always been acceptable and paid for.

- He really did the 24 hours of work he claimed, as documented by drawings and worksheets presented.

- He has canceled checks covering an itemized list of supplies he purchased for the job ready to show the judge .

This should be enough to make Ted a winner. But as is true of all Small Claims litigants, Ted should also try to anticipate and deflect what he anticipates will be the other side's key points. For example, in this instance, if Ted is pretty sure Alice is going to claim she canceled because Ted was using a design theme and colors she had specifically ruled out, he would be wise to make it clear that no such restrictions were contained in their contract.

Many business people have employees, partners or business associates who have intimate knowledge of the dispute. By all means, bring them to court as witnesses. A witness who is knowledgeable about the transaction is almost always worth more than a stack of documentary evidence.

Example: Assume Ted's assistant, Doris, attended a preliminary meeting with Alice at which Ted asked Alice for a list of her suggestions. Also assume Doris can truthfully testify that when the subject of color came up, Alice just waved her hand and said, "You know I don't like purple too much, but it's really up to you—you're the designer." Aided by Doris's testimony, Ted should be a winner, even if Alice claims he violated their agreement not to use purple.

In some situations, having a witness testify as to the normal business practices in a field can also be helpful. Thus, if in your field goods are normally shipped within five to 15 days after an order is received (unless written notice of a delay is sent), but the person you are having a dispute with is claiming you must pay for goods that were shipped 90 days after your order was received, it would be a good idea to present an "expert" witness—or a letter from someone knowledgeable about relevant business practices—who could testify that unfilled orders are never good for more than 30 days.

C. The Drama of the Distraught Designer

Now let's review a typical small business case, with an eye to identifying good strategies. Don Dimaggio is a successful architect and industrial designer who heads his own small company, which specializes in designing small manufacturing buildings. He has his offices in a converted factory building near the University of California and prides himself on doing highly innovative and creative work. Recently Don did some preliminary design work for an outfit that wanted to build a small candle factory. When they didn't pay, he was out $6,500. In Don's view, the dispute developed like this:

"Ben McDonald, who makes custom candles, had a good year and wanted to expand. He called me and asked me to rough out a preliminary design. McDonald claims now that we never had a contract, but that's simply not true. What really happened is that McDonald authorized me to do some preliminary work before his company got their financing locked down. When interest rates went through the roof, the whole deal collapsed. I had already completed my work, but they got uptight and refused to pay. My next step was to get Stephanie Carlin, a lawyer who

has done some work for me, to write McDonald a letter demanding payment. When that didn't do any good, I took Stephanie's advice and filed a Small Claims Court suit against McDonald. True, I had to scale my claim back to $5,000, the Small Claims maximum. But since I obviously couldn't afford to pay Stephanie $200 an hour to file in formal court, it seemed like the best approach."

Don's most immediate problem was that he had never used Small Claims Court before. He wasn't sure how he needed to prepare, but knew, at the very least, he had to develop a coherent plan—if for no other reason than to overcome his anxiety. Here is how I coached him to do this:

RW: "Your first job is to establish why McDonald owed you money. Presumably it's because you claim he broke a contract with you that called for him to pay you for your work."

DD: "True, but unfortunately, nothing was written down."

RW: "Oral contracts to provide services are perfectly legal if they can be proven, and judges typically bend over backwards to see that freelancers get paid. But don't be so sure you have nothing in writing. Tell me, how did McDonald contact you?"

DD: "Mutual friends recommended me to him. He phoned me and we talked a couple of times. There was some back and forth about how much I would charge for the whole job and how much for parts of it. After a little garden-variety confusion, we decided that I would start with the preliminary drawings and be paid $6,500. If the whole job came through, and we felt good about one another, I would do the entire thing. On big jobs, I always insist on a written contract, but this one was tiny and I couldn't see wasting the time. McDonald just stopped by with someone else from his business and we hashed out the whole thing in person."

RW: "Did you make notes?"

DD: "Sure. In fact, I made a few sketches, and they gave me specifications and sketches they had already made."

RW: "Do you still have those?"

DD: "Of course, in a file along with a couple of letters they sent later thanking me for my good ideas and making a few suggestions for changes. And of course, I have copies of the detailed drawings I made and sent them."

RW: "Well, that's it."

DD: "What do you mean, that's it?"

RW: "You've just told me that you can prove a contract exists. The combination of the sketches McDonald provided and the letters someone at his company wrote to you pretty convincingly prove they asked you to do the work. Of course, it helps your case that legally there is a strong presumption that when a person is asked to do work in a situation where compensation is normally expected, he must be paid when the work is completed." (In legalese, this presumption is called "quantum meruit." See Chapter 2.)

DD: "That's all there is to it? I just tell the judge what happened and I win?"

RW: "Not so fast. First, let me ask if you are sure you can present your case coherently? After you make your opening statement, you need to back it up with the key facts that show that McDonald hired you, that you did the work and that he broke the contract by failing to pay you. As discussed throughout this book, because so many people do a poor job making their oral presentation, I recommend that you practice ahead of time. Ask a savvy friend to serve as your pretend judge. Then present your case as if you were in court. Encourage your friend to interrupt and ask questions, since that's what a judge will likely do. Finally, be sure you have organized all your evidence, especially the plans and letters, so you are ready to present them to the judge at the appropriate time."

DD: "What about McDonald? Is he likely to show up?"

RW: "Many cases involving money being owed result in defaults, meaning the person being sued ignores the whole proceeding. (See Chapter 15.) But since you know that McDonald claims he doesn't owe you the money, it's my guess he will probably show up and claim no contract existed. Therefore, you should be prepared to counter the points he is likely to make."

DD: "You're right. Although it's a total crock, he will probably claim I agreed to do the work on speculation that he would get financing and that since the job fell through, he doesn't owe me anything."

RW: "And if your case is typical, McDonald will also probably try and claim your work was substandard. That way, even if you prove that a contract existed, the judge may award you less than you asked for."

DD: "But they wrote me that my design was of excellent quality."

RW: "Great, but don't wait until they raise the issue. Since you are pretty sure this point will come up, emphasize how pleased McDonald was with your work in your opening statement and present the letter to the judge. Now, what about McDonald's argument that there was no deal in the first place? Do you ever do preliminary work without expecting to be paid unless the deal goes through? And is that a common way to operate in your business?"

DD: "Me? Never! I don't have to. I suppose some designers do, or at least prepare fairly detailed bid proposals without pay, but I have so much work coming my way these days, I'm turning jobs down right and left, so when I do submit a bid, I make it clear to all potential clients that I charge for preliminary drawings. In this situation, as I said, we agreed on the price in advance."

RW: "What about witnesses to that conversation?"

DD: "Well, Jim, my partner, sat in on one of the early discussions. We hadn't agreed on the final price yet, but we weren't too far apart."

RW: "Was it clear to Jim that you intended to charge for your work and that McDonald knew you did?"

DD: "Yes, absolutely."

RW: "Great, bring Jim to court with you as a witness. Here is how I would proceed. Organize your statement as to what happened so it takes you no longer than five minutes to present it to the judge. Bring your sketches, and most important, the sketch that McDonald made, along with the letters they sent you, and show them to the judge. (See Chapter 15.) Then introduce your partner and have him state that he was present when money was discussed."

This little scenario is a simplified version of a real case. What happened? Don was given a judgment for the entire amount he requested and McDonald paid it

D. Old Friends Fall Out

Finally, let's review another typical Small Claims dispute. Toni, a true artist when it comes to graphics, is an ignoramus when it comes to dollars and cents. Recognizing this, she never prepares her own tax returns. For the past several years, she has turned all of her tax affairs over to Phillip, a local C.P.A. Price was discussed the first year, but after that Toni just paid Phillip's bill when the job was done.

One spring, things went wrong. As usual, Toni's records weren't in great shape, and she was late in getting them to Phillip. By this time Phillip, who was overly busy, put Toni's tax return together quickly, without discussing it with her in detail. When Toni saw the return, she was shocked by the bottom line. She felt that she was being asked to pay way too much to Uncle Sam.

She called Phillip and reminded him of a number of deductions that she felt had been overlooked. There was some discussion of whether Phillip should have known about these items or not. Things began to get a little edgy when Phillip complained about Toni's sloppy records and her delay in making them available, and Toni countered by accusing Phillip of doing a hurried and substandard job. But after some more grumpy talk back and forth, Phillip agreed to make the necessary corrections. In a week this was done and the return was again sent to Toni.

While her tax liability was now less, Toni was still annoyed, feeling that not all of the oversights had been corrected. Toni called Phillip again and this time they quickly got into a shouting match. When Phillip finally and reluctantly agreed to look at the return a third time, Toni replied, "Hell no, I'm taking my business to an accountant who can add."

True to her word, Toni did hire another accountant, who made several modifications to her return, resulting in a slightly lower tax liability. The second accountant claimed that because he needed to check all of Phillip's work to satisfy himself that it was correct, he ended up doing almost as much work as if he had started from scratch. As a result, he billed Toni for $2,300, saying that this was only $500 less than if he had not had the benefit of Phillip's work.

Phillip billed Toni $3,000. Toni, still furious, refused to pay. Phillip then sent Toni a demand letter asking to be paid and stating that most of the problems were created by Toni's bad records. He added that he had already made a number of requested changes and had offered to make relatively minor final changes at no additional charge. Phillip also suggested in his letter that he was willing to try and mediate the claim using a local community mediation center which charged very low fees.

When Toni didn't answer the letter, Phillip filed suit. Were I Phillip, here is how I would prepare my case:

Phillip's Case

Step 1. Phillip has already written a clear demand letter (see Chapter 6 for a discussion of how to do this) and suggested mediation—a good idea, since both he and Toni work in the same small city and Phillip has an obvious interest in not turning Toni into a vocal enemy. Unfortunately, Toni didn't bite on Phillip's suggestion of mediation.

Step 2. Phillip knows that Toni's business makes money, so he is pretty sure he can collect if he wins, which of course should be a big consideration in deciding whether to file any Small Claims case. (See Chapter 3.)

Step 3. In court, Phillip's main job will be to prove that he did a job that was worth $3,000 and to refute Toni's likely contention that his work was so bad it amounted to a breach of their contract. Bringing copies of the tax returns he prepared for Toni as well as his own worksheets is probably the simplest way for Phillip to accomplish this. The returns should not be presented to the judge page by page, but as a package. The purpose is to indicate that a lot of work has been done, not go into details.

Step 4. Phillip should then testify as to his hourly rate and how many hours he worked. He should emphasize that extra hours were required because Toni did not have her records well organized. To illustrate his point, Phillip should present to the judge any raw data Toni gave him that he still has (for example, a shoebox full of messy receipts). If he no longer has Toni's material, he might create something that looks like it, carefully pointing out to the judge that this is a reconstruction of Toni's data, not the real thing.

Step 5. So far, by testifying that he was hired to do a job, that he did it and that he wasn't paid, Phillip has presented facts necessary to establish a breach of contract case. However, he would be wise to go beyond this and anticipate at least some of Toni's defenses, which will almost surely involve the claim that Phillip broke the contract by doing poor quality work and doing it late. In addition, Phillip should anticipate Toni's backup claim that he charged too much and that the judge should award him less than $3,000. Were I Phillip, I would attempt to take the sting out of Toni's likely presentation by saying something along these lines:

"Your Honor, when I finished my work, my client pointed out that several deductions had been overlooked. I believed then and believe now that this was because the data she provided me with was disorganized and inadequate, but I did rework the return and correct several items that were left out. When my client told me that she felt the revised draft needed additional changes, I again told her that I would work with her to make any necessary modifications. It was at this point that she refused to let me see the returns and hired another accountant. In my professional opinion at this stage, very little work remained to be done—certainly nothing that couldn't be accomplished in an hour or two.

"Now, as to the amount charged—it took me ten hours to reconstruct what went on in the defendant's business from the mess of incomplete and incoherent records I was given. At $90 per hour, this means that $900 of my bill involved work that had to be done prior to actually preparing the return. Taking into consideration the difficult circumstances, I believe I charged fairly for the work I did, and that I did my work well."

Toni's Case

Okay, so much for looking at what happened from the point of view of the indignant accountant. Now let's see how Toni, the upset graphic artist, might deal with the situation.

Step 1. For starters, I think Toni made a mistake by refusing to negotiate or mediate with Phillip. Especially since this is the sort of dispute over the quality of work where a judge is likely to enter a compromise judgment, it would have saved time and anxiety for both her and Phillip to at least try to arrive at a compromise outside of court. (See Chapter 6.)

Step 2. Once Toni decided not to try and settle the case, she should write a letter of her own, rebutting Phillip's demand letter point by point. (See Chapter 6.) She should bring a copy of this letter to court and give it to the judge as part of her presentation. The judge doesn't have to accept Toni's letter (it's not really evidence of anything but the fact that Phillip's request for payment was rejected), but more often than not, the judge will probably look at both parties' letters.

Step 3. Next, Toni should testify that she refused to pay the bill because she felt that Phillip's work was so poorly done that she didn't trust Phillip to finish the job. To make this point effectively, Toni should testify as to the details of several of the tax issues Phillip overlooked. For example, if Toni provided Phillip with information concerning the purchase of several items of expensive equipment for which Phillip didn't claim depreciation, this would be important evidence of poor work. But Toni should be careful to make her points about tax law relatively brief and understandable. She won't gain by a long and boring rehash of her entire return. One good approach might be for Toni to submit pertinent sections of IRS publications or a privately published tax guide outlining the rules that require equipment to be depreciated.

Step 4. Toni should next present more detailed evidence that supports her claim that Phillip did poor work. The tax return as correctly prepared by the new accountant would be of some help, but it would be even better to have the second accountant come to court to testify about the details of Phillip's substandard work. Unfortunately for Toni, professionals are commonly reluctant to testify against one another, so this may be difficult to arrange. But Toni should at the very least be able to get a letter from the new accountant outlining the things that he found it necessary to do to change the return as prepared by Phillip.

Step 5. Toni should also present to the court her canceled checks, establishing the amounts paid Phillip for the last several years' returns, assuming, of course, that Phillip's previous bills were substantially less. For example, if Toni had been billed $1,700 and $1,900 in the two previous years, it would raise some questions as to whether Phillip's bill of $3,000 for the current year was reasonable.

Both Toni and Phillip should be prepared to answer the judge's questions. Especially in a case like this one involving a technical subject, the judge is almost sure to interrupt both Toni's and Phillip's presentations and ask for details. So in addition to preparing and practicing presenting their cases before a critical friend, both Phillip and Toni should be prepared to answer likely questions and then smoothly return to presenting their cases.

Since this little story is based on a real case, I can tell you what happened. Phillip was given a judgment for $1,800. The judge didn't explain his reasoning, but apparently felt that there was some right on each side and split the difference with a little edge to Phillip, probably because since Toni hired him in the first place and had worked with him for several years, she was on somewhat shaky ground claiming he was incompetent. This sort of compromise decision, where each side is given something, is common in Small Claims Court and again illustrates the wisdom of the parties' negotiating or mediating their own compromise. Even if Toni and Phillip had arrived at a solution where one or the other gave up a little more than the judge ordered, there would have been a savings in time and aggravation that probably would have more than made up the difference. ∎

Judgment and Appeal

A. The Judgment

The decision in your case will be mailed to the address on record with the clerk any time from a few days to a few weeks after your case is heard. The exception to this rule is when one side doesn't show up and the other wins by default. Default judgments are normally announced right in the courtroom. (See Chapter 10 for information on how to set aside a default.) The truth is that in the vast majority of contested cases, the judge has already made up his mind at the time the case is heard and jots down his decision before the parties leave the courtroom. Decisions are sent by mail because the court doesn't want to deal with angry, unhappy losers, especially those few who might get violent. However, despite the fact that an occasional person may be upset, some judges are willing to announce and explain their decisions in court, on the theory that both parties are entitled to know why a particular decision was reached. One progressive judge explained his policy in this regard as follows: "The only time I don't announce my decision in court is when I have phoning or research to do before finalizing it, or if I feel that the losing party will be unnecessarily embarrassed in front of the audience."

Legal Jargon Note: Now that a judgment has been entered, we need to expand our vocabulary slightly. The person who wins the case (gets the judgment) now becomes "the judgment creditor" and the loser is known as "the judgment debtor."

Often when a judgment is entered against a person, she feels that the judge would surely have made a different decision if he hadn't gotten mixed up, or overlooked a crucial fact, or had properly understood an argument. On the basis of my experience on the bench, I can tell you that in the vast majority of cases this is not true. Even if you had an opportunity to argue the whole case over, there is little likelihood that the judge would change his mind. Or put another way, chances are good the judge did understand your side of the case, but simply didn't agree that you were in the right. (See Section E, below, for appeal rights and Section F, below, for instructions on correcting and setting aside judgments based on error of fact.)

If you sued more than one person, the judgment should indicate who the judgment is against and for how much. Some defendants may not owe anything or their financial liability may be limited to a stated amount. If so, this is the maximum you can collect from them. However, in most instances where a judgment is against two or more defendants, they will be "jointly and severally liable." This means that each defendant is 100% liable to pay you the entire amount. For example, if you receive a $1,000 judgment against two defendants, you may collect it in any proportion from either defendant (for example, you could collect $800 from one defendant and $200 from another). If you collect a disproportionate amount from one defendant, she is left with the task of evening things out. (In this example, the defendant who paid the $800 could sue the other for $300.)

The words "joint and several liability" may not appear on the judgment. A judgment against two or more defendants will often simply list the names of the judgment debtors. This means they are jointly and severally liable for the entire amount. When one defendant's judgment debt liability is limited (say to $200), the judgment will make that clear.

The back of the Notice of Entry of Judgment form provides information for both the judgment creditor and the judgment debtor. It also contains an Acknowledgment of Satisfaction of Judgment, to be completed after the judgment is paid (discussed in Section D, below).

B. Time Payments

I have mentioned the fact that in California a judge may order that the loser—usually the defendant, but sometimes the plaintiff, if the defendant filed a Defendant's Claim—be allowed to pay the winner over a period of time, rather than all at once. But the judge normally won't make this sort of order unless you request it. So whether you have no real defense to the plaintiff's claim, or you do have a fairly good case but aren't sure which way the judge will rule, be sure the judge knows that if you lose, you wish to pay in installments. You might put your request this way:

- "In closing my presentation, I would like to say that I believe I have a convincing case and should be awarded the judgment, but in the event that you rule for my opponent, I would like you to allow me time payments of no more than [whatever amount is convenient] per month."

Or, if you have no real defense:

- "Your Honor, I request that you enter the judgment against me for no more than (an amount convenient to you) per month."

If you neglect to ask for time payments in court and wish to make this request after you receive the judgment, promptly obtain and file a Request to Pay Judgment in Installments form, along with a completed financial declaration form. The judgment creditor has ten days in which to accept your proposed payment schedule. If no agreement is possible, a court hearing will be held and the judge will decide.

REQUEST TO PAY JUDGMENT IN INSTALLMENTS

Name and Address of Court:

Ventura County Municipal Court
Small Claims Div.
800 So. Victoria Ave
Ventura, CA 93009

SMALL CLAIMS CASE NO.

PLAINTIFF/DEMANDANTE (Name, address, and telephone number of each):

Don Gonzalez
P.O. Box 6489
Ventura CA 93006
805-654-2610

Telephone No.:

Telephone No.:

DEFENDANT/DEMANDADO (Name, address, and telephone number of each):

Luke Smith
10 N. Main St.
Ventura, CA 93006
805-654-2609

Telephone No.:

Telephone No.:

[ ] See attached sheet for additional plaintiffs and defendants.

REQUEST TO PAY JUDGMENT IN INSTALLMENTS

1. I request the court to allow me to make installment payments on the judgment entered against me in this case in the amount and manner stated below.

2. My request is based on this declaration, the court records, my completed financial declaration (Form EJ-165—*obtain from court clerk*) attached to this declaration, and any other evidence that may be presented.

   NOTE: YOU MUST ATTACH A COMPLETED FINANCIAL DECLARATION WITH THIS REQUEST TO MAKE INSTALLMENT PAYMENTS.

3. Judgment was entered against me in this matter on (date): 8/31/__ in the amount of (specify): $1,004.91

4. Payment of the entire amount of the judgment at one time will be a hardship on me because (specify):

   I am currently unemployed.

5. I can and will make payments toward the judgment in the amount of (specify): $ 40.00 per [ ] week [X] month.

6. I request the court to order that I make payments as specified in item 5 and that execution on the judgment be stayed as long as I make payments according to this schedule.

I declare under penalty of perjury under the laws of the State of California that the foregoing is true and correct.

Date: 10/12/__

Luke Smith

.... (TYPE OR PRINT NAME)

▶ *Luke Smith*

(SIGNATURE OF JUDGMENT DEBTOR)

NOTICE TO JUDGMENT CREDITOR

The judgment debtor has requested the court to allow payment of the judgment in installments. Complete the following and return this form to the court within 10 days. You will be notified of the court's order, or, if a hearing is necessary, the date of the hearing.

1. I am the judgment creditor, and I have read and considered the judgment debtor's request to make installment payments on the judgment.

2. a. [ ] I am willing to accept the payment schedule the judgment debtor has requested.
   b. [ ] I am willing to accept payments in the amount of (specify): $ per [ ] week [ ] month.
   c. [ ] I am opposed to accepting installment payments because (specify):

I declare under penalty of perjury under the laws of the State of California that the foregoing is true and correct.

Date:

.... (TYPE OR PRINT NAME)

▶

(SIGNATURE OF JUDGMENT CREDITOR)

SEE REVERSE FOR HEARING DATE, IF ANY.

(Continued on reverse)

Form Approved by the
Judicial Council of California
SC-106 [New January 1, 1992]

REQUEST TO PAY JUDGMENT IN INSTALLMENTS
(Small Claims)

Code of Civil Procedure, § 116.620(b)

C. Paying the Judgment Directly to the Court

The judgment debtor may pay the money directly to the court, which will then notify the judgment creditor. This procedure is helpful for a judgment debtor who doesn't want to deal directly with the prevailing party. It's also an easy way for a judgment debtor who doesn't know the whereabouts of the judgment creditor to get the case resolved. Once the court receives payment, it—not the judgment creditor—is responsible for filing papers showing that the judgment was paid in full.

To pay money directly to the court, the judgment debtor must complete a Request to Pay Judgment to Court form, available from the Small Claims Court clerk. The judgment debtor must then pay the court the total amount due—including the amount of judgment, any interest due and the court fee for using this service (up to $25). The court will enter a "Satisfaction of Judgment." (See next section for more on this.)

Your Satisfaction of Judgment will be entered most quickly if you pay by money order, cash or certified or cashier's check. The payment should be made out to the court, not to the judgment creditor. Paying by a method other than these will result in a 30-day delay. Make sure you get a receipt, regardless of your payment method.

The court will notify the judgment creditor at her last known address that her money is available. Then it's up to her to claim it. If she fails to do so within three years, the money goes to the State of California. (CCP Sec. 116.860.)

Notify the court when you move. It's important to keep your current address on file if you've won a lawsuit but haven't yet been paid. That way, you won't miss out on your money in a situation where the losing party pays the court and the court can't find you.

D. The Satisfaction of Judgment

Once a judgment is paid, whether in installments or a lump sum, a judgment creditor (the person who won the case, remember) must acknowledge that the judgment has been paid by filing a Satisfaction of Judgment form with the court clerk. Doing this makes it clear to the world (and especially credit rating agencies) that the person who lost the case (the judgment debtor) has met her obligation.

If the judgment creditor has not recorded an Abstract of Judgment (see Chapter 24) to create a lien on real property, she can simply fill in and sign the Acknowledgment of Satisfaction of Judgment form printed on the back of the Notice of Entry of Judgment. This form must then be returned to the court.

If the judgment creditor has recorded an Abstract of Judgment with a county recorder, the procedure to file is a little complex. The judgment creditor must fill out a copy of a separate Satisfaction of Judgment form and sign it before a notary public. The judgment creditor must then record a certified copy with the county recorder's office in each county where the Abstract of Judgment was recorded. For more information on this, ask the Small Claims clerk.

If a judgment creditor who receives payment in full on a judgment fails to complete a Satisfaction of Judgment, the judgment debtor should send a written demand that this be done. A first class letter is adequate. It's important to make sure a Satisfaction of Judgment has been filed. Otherwise, the judgment will continue to appear on credit records and property records as unpaid. If, after written demand, the judgment creditor doesn't file his Satisfaction within 14 days and without just cause, the judgment debtor is entitled to file suit to recover all actual damages he or she may sustain by reason of such failure (for example, denial of a credit application) and, in addition, the sum of $50.

Here is a sample Satisfaction of Judgment form, which is available from the Small Claims Court clerk. Again, it should be signed by the judgment creditor when the judgment is paid and then filed with the court clerk. Don't forget to do this; otherwise, you may have to track down the other party later.

ACKNOWLEDGMENT OF SATISFACTION OF JUDGMENT

ATTORNEY OR PARTY WITHOUT ATTORNEY (Name and Address): TELEPHONE NO.: FOR RECORDER'S OR SECRETARY OF STATE'S USE ONLY

ATTORNEY FOR (Name):

NAME OF COURT: Mount Diablo Municipal Court
STREET ADDRESS: 1020 Ward Street
MAILING ADDRESS:
CITY AND ZIP CODE: Martinez, CA 94553
BRANCH NAME:

PLAINTIFF: Philip Yee

DEFENDANT: Eric Smith Motors Inc.

ACKNOWLEDGMENT OF SATISFACTION OF JUDGMENT
☐ FULL   ☐ PARTIAL   ☐ MATURED INSTALLMENT

CASE NUMBER
123456

FOR COURT USE ONLY

1. Satisfaction of the judgment is acknowledged as follows (see footnote* before completing):
   a. ☒ Full satisfaction
      (1) ☐ Judgment is satisfied in full.
      (2) ☐ The judgment creditor has accepted payment or performance other than that specified in the judgment in full satisfaction of the judgment.
   b. ☐ Partial satisfaction
      The amount received in partial satisfaction of the judgment is
      $
   c. ☐ Matured installment
      All matured installments under the installment judgment have been satisfied as of (date):

2. Full name and address of judgment creditor:
   Eric Smith Motors Inc.

3. Full name and address of assignee of record, if any:

4. Full name and address of judgment debtor being fully or partially released:
   Philip Yee

5. a. Judgment entered on (date): 7/21/2000
      ☐ (1) in judgment book volume no.: 127   (2) page no.: 6
   b. ☐ Renewal entered on (date):
      ☐ (1) in judgment book volume no.:   (2) page no.:

6. ☒ An ☒ abstract of judgment ☐ certified copy of the judgment has been recorded as follows (complete all information for each county where recorded):

COUNTY	DATE OF RECORDING	BOOK NUMBER	PAGE NUMBER
Contra Costa County	8/14/99	21	82

7. ☐ A notice of judgment lien has been filed in the office of the Secretary of State as file number (specify):

NOTICE TO JUDGMENT DEBTOR: If this is an acknowledgment of full satisfaction of judgment, it will have to be recorded in each county shown in item 6 above, if any, in order to release the judgment lien, and will have to be filed in the office of the Secretary of State to terminate any judgment lien on personal property. ▶

Date:

(SIGNATURE OF JUDGMENT CREDITOR OR ASSIGNEE OF CREDITOR OR ATTORNEY)

*The names of the judgment creditor and judgment debtor must be stated as shown in any Abstract of Judgment which was recorded and is being released by this satisfaction. A separate notary acknowledgment must be attached for each signature.

Form Approved by the
Judicial Council of California
EJ-100 [Rev. July 1, 1983] (Cor. 7/84)

ACKNOWLEDGMENT OF SATISFACTION OF JUDGMENT

CCP 724.060, 724.120, 724.250

It's easy to get a copy of a Satisfaction of Judgment. If either party ever needs it (for example, to correct an out-of-date credit report), the court clerk will provide a certified copy of a filed Satisfaction of Judgment. This form proves that the judgment was paid.

Sometimes people forget to get a Satisfaction of Judgment form signed when they pay a judgment, only to find that they can't locate the judgment creditor later. If this happens and you need a Satisfaction of Judgment to clean up your credit record or for some other reason, you can get it if you present the court clerk with the following documents:

1. A canceled check or money order written subsequent to the judgment by you the judgment debtor for the full amount of the judgment, or a cash receipt for the full amount of the judgment signed by the judgment creditor after the date the court awarded judgment; and

2. A statement signed by the judgment debtor under penalty of perjury stating all of the following:

- The judgment creditor has been paid the full amount of the judgment and costs;

- The judgment creditor has been requested to file a Satisfaction of Judgment and refuses to do so or can't be located;

- The document attached (for example, the check or money order) constitutes evidence of the judgment creditor's receipt of the payment.

SAMPLE STATEMENT

My name is John Elliot. On January 11, 19__ , a judgment was awarded against me in Small Claims Court in San Francisco, California (Case # 1234). On March 20, 19__, I paid Beatrice Small, the prevailing party, $1,200, the full amount of this judgment (or, if payments were made in installments—"I paid Beatrice Small, the prevailing party in this action, the final installment necessary to pay this judgment in full.")

I attach to this statement a canceled check (or other proof that the judgment was paid) for the full amount of the judgment endorsed by Beatrice Small. (If payment was made by money order or cash [with a receipt], modify this statement as needed.)

Beatrice Small did not voluntarily file a Satisfaction of Judgment. When I tried to contact her, I learned that she had moved and had left no forwarding address. (If the judgment creditor refuses to sign a Satisfaction of Judgment, or is otherwise not available to do so, modify this statement as necessary.)

I declare under penalty of perjury under the laws of the State of California that the foregoing is true and correct.

DATED: June 4, 19__.   _____

                                        John Elliot

E. Who Can Appeal

If, in the face of justice, common sense and all of your fine arguments, the judge turns out to be a big dummy and rules for your opponent, you can appeal, right? If you are the person or business that was sued (either the defendant, or the plaintiff on a claim of the defendant), the answer is "yes." Not only can you appeal, but if you do, you are entitled to a whole new trial (called a "trial de novo") in Superior Court.

What about the person filing suit? In theory, the plaintiff has no right to appeal (except from a judgment against her on a defendant's claim). Since the defendant can appeal, this, of course, raises a question of fairness. Isn't it unfair, maybe even unconstitutional, to allow appeal rights for defendants on the original claim and none for plaintiffs? I will leave it to you to decide the fairness issue, but it's not unconstitutional for the simple reason that a plaintiff knows before he files that he doesn't have a right to an appeal. He has a choice of bringing his suit in Small Claims Court, where there is no right for plaintiffs to appeal, or in Municipal Court, where both sides can appeal. The defendant doesn't have this opportunity to pick the court and, therefore, the legislature has decided that her appeal rights should be preserved. For the same reason, the defendant cannot appeal if she loses on a Claim of Defendant that she initiates.

That's the traditional theory, anyway. But since 1993, California law has been changed to allow courts to correct clerical errors in a judgment and to set aside or vacate a judgment on the ground of an incorrect or erroneous legal basis for the decision. (CCP Sec. 116.725.) Or put another way, plaintiffs now have at least a limited right of appeal if a decision was just plain legally wrong.

But doesn't this ability to petition a court also apply to the person who is sued (usually the defendant)? Yes, but remember that the defendant already has the right to appeal to Superior Court for a whole new trial. (See Section G, below.) So from a defendant's point of view, filing a motion to correct a clerical error or vacate a legally incorrect judgment is of limited value. After all, the motion might not even be considered before the defendant's 30 days to appeal are up.

F. Filing Your Request to Correct or Vacate Judgment

As noted above, while a losing plaintiff can't appeal, she can attempt to correct a clerical error or a legal mistake. Understanding what constitutes a clerical error is normally easy (the judge wrote $125 when he clearly meant $1,250). But what is a legal mistake? Normally it means a judge applied the wrong law or legal theory to your case, thereby arriving at an incorrect result. For example, if the judge didn't properly compute the statute of limitations and therefore wrongly dismissed your case, that's a legal mistake. Another example of a legal mistake involves California's bad check law. If after receiving a dud check, you follow the proper procedures and ask the writer to make it good and she fails to do so, it's a legal error if the judge fails to award you the extra damages called for by California's bad check law. (See Chapter 4, Section C1b.)

However, it's important to understand that this procedure to correct a legal mistake is not available in situations where you believe the judge made a wrong factual decision. For instance, if you and your witnesses claimed you left a rental unit clean, but the landlord claimed it was filthy and the judge sided with the landlord, you do not have the right to use this procedure to correct what you see as an obvious error. That's because the question of whether the apartment was clean or dirty is one of fact, not law. And as you should now understand, only the defendant has a right to appeal factual questions to Superior Court (see Section G, below), while plaintiffs don't.

Assuming now that you do wish to correct a clerical or legal error, how do you do it? First, contact the Small Claims clerk about its procedures. Some courts may let you correct a clerical error informally, such as by sending a letter or marked-up judgment showing the correction.

If the court requires a formal motion, or if you want to correct a legal error within ten days of the clerk's mailing the judgment, complete these steps:

Step 1:   Go to the court and get copies of the forms you need (see below).

Step 2:   On the form, check the box that indicates you are making a request or a motion to correct or to vacate a judgment. Include a brief description of the legal or clerical mistake in the space provided.

Step 3:   File your motion with the Small Claims Court clerk. You may need to appear at a court hearing.

Now let's look a each of these steps in more detail.

Step 1: Get Copies of the Form

If you want to correct a clerical error, get at least two blank copies of a Request to Correct or Vacate Judgment form from the Small Claims Court clerk. You can use this form to correct a legal error (and, in fact, it's intended to be used for that purpose), but you are probably better off using a Notice of Motion and Declaration. This is because the Request to Correct or Vacate gives the judge the opportunity to make a decision without having a hearing—that is, without you getting to explain to the judge in person what the mistake was. If you use the Notice of Motion and Declaration, the clerk will automatically schedule a hearing when you file the paper. If you want to vacate a judgment, you may use a Notice of Motion and Declaration, a Request to Correct or Vacate Judgment, or a Notice of Motion to Vacate Judgment and Declaration. (Chapter 10, Section E1, contains a sample of the latter form.)

Call or visit the Small Claims Court clerk and pick up copies of the form you plan on using. You may want to fill out and file your papers while you're at the court.

Step 2: Prepare Your Request Form

Fill out the top of the form the same way as other papers you filed in court. (See the sample that follows.)

On the form, you must convincingly explain what the error was. Be brief but, at the same time, thorough. Use an additional piece of paper if you need more room.

Here are two examples.

Example of Motion to Vacate Judgment Based on Legal Error: *Under CCP Sec. 116.725, a judgment may be set aside and vacated if it is based on a legal error or mistake. The court incorrectly applied the statute of limitations when it dismissed my case, because it did not take into consideration the fact that I was a minor when the accident occurred.*

My case is a personal injury case which, under the terms of Code of Civil Procedure Sec. 340, must normally be filed within one year of the date of my injury, which occurred on January 23, 1995. However, Sec. 352 of the Code of Civil Procedure states: "If a person entitled to bring an action, mentioned in Chapter 3 of this title, be, at the time the cause of action occurred, … under the age of majority … the time of such disability is not a part of the time limited for the commencement of the action."

At the time of my injury on January 23, 1995, I was 17 years and two months old. Therefore, I was still a minor until November 23, 1995, at which point I became 18. Therefore, under the terms of CCP Sec. 352, it was from this date (not from January 23, 1995) that the court should have begun counting the one-year statute of limitations that applies to personal injuries. Therefore, I was entitled to file my case until November 22, 1996. In fact, since I filed on June 27, 1996, I filed well within the allowed time.

In conclusion, I request that the judgment in this case be vacated and that I be granted a new Small Claims Court hearing.

Example of Request to Correct Clerical Error: *Under CCP Sec. 116.725, a clerical error may be corrected in a judgment. My request is based on the following clerical error. After entry of the judgment, I discovered that only defendant Janice James was named. The judgment was supposed to be against both Janice James and Brad James. I request that judgment be entered against both defendants Janice James and Brad James.*

REQUEST TO CORRECT OR VACATE JUDGMENT

Name and Address of Court: San Diego Municipal Court-Small Claims
Room 2005, County Courthouse
San Diego, CA 92101

SMALL CLAIMS CASE NO. 01234

PLAINTIFF/DEMANDANTE (Name, address, and telephone number of each):

John Michaelson
8950 Claremont Mesa Blvd.
San Diego, CA 92123

Telephone No.: (619) 694-2600

Telephone No :

DEFENDANT/DEMANDADO (Name, address, and telephone number of each):

Janice James
1501 Sixth Avenue
San Diego, CA 92101

Telephone No.: (619) 531-3151

Brad James
1501 Sixth Avenue
San Diego, CA 92101

Telephone No.: (619) 531-3151

☐ See attached sheet for additional plaintiffs and defendants.

REQUEST TO CORRECT OR VACATE JUDGMENT

FILING THIS REQUEST DOES NOT INCREASE THE TIME FOR FILING A NOTICE OF APPEAL

REQUEST TO [X] CORRECT ☐ VACATE JUDGMENT

1. I request the court to make an order to [X] correct ☐ vacate the judgment entered on (date):
2. My request is based on this declaration and the records on file with the court.
DECLARATION SUPPORTING MY REQUEST
3. I am the [X] plaintiff ☐ defendant in this action.
4. The facts supporting this request
    a. [X] to correct a clerical error in the judgment
    b. ☐ to set aside or vacate the judgment on the grounds of an incorrect or erroneous legal basis for the decision
    are as follows (specify facts, statute, rule of court case law, etc.):

On June 1, 19__, judgment was incorrectly entered against defendants Jan James and Jamie Brad. Defendants' correct names are Janice James and Brad James. Under Civil Code Sec. 116.725, a clerical error may be corrected in a judgment.

☐ Item 4 continued on attached page.
I declare under penalty of perjury under the laws of the State of California that the foregoing is true and correct.

Date: June 12, 19__

.........John Michaelson..................... ▶ *John Michaelson*
       (TYPE OR PRINT NAME)   (SIGNATURE)

5. If you wish to oppose this request, please file a response with the court within 15 days and serve a copy on the opposing side.

No hearing will be held unless ordered by the court.

CLERK'S CERTIFICATE OF MAILING

I certify that I am not a party to this action. A copy of this Request was mailed first class, postage prepaid, in a sealed envelope to the responding party at the address shown above. The mailing and this certification occurred
at (place):   , California,
on (date):

Clerk, by _____, Deputy

— The county provides small claims advisor services free of charge. —

Form Approved by the
Judicial Council of California
SC-108 [New January 1, 1994]

REQUEST TO CORRECT OR VACATE JUDGMENT
(Small Claims)

Code of Civil Procedure, § 116.725

Step 3: File Your Request or Motion With the Small Claims Court Clerk

Contact the Small Claims Court clerk and explain that you wish to file your request or motion to correct or vacate judgment. You may need to provide one or two extra copies. The clerk will mail copies to the other party. If you file a motion, the clerk will schedule a hearing. If you file a request, the judge may forego having a hearing if she agrees that your request has merit and that it can easily be corrected.

G. Filing and Presenting Your Appeal

Now let's look at the mechanics of the appeal. In California, the defendant must file a Notice of Appeal within 30 days of the day the court clerk mails the judgment to the parties (or hands it over, if a decision is made in the courtroom). This means if the decision was mailed, there will be less than 30 days to file an appeal from the day that the defendant receives the judgment. The date the judgment was mailed will appear on the judgment. If for some reason attributable to the magic of the U.S. Postal Service your judgment doesn't show up within 30 days after it was entered, and you are unhappy with the result and want to appeal, call the Small Claims clerk immediately and request help in getting an extension of time to file your appeal.

Just because you lost once, the deck is not stacked hopelessly against you. You may have heard scuttlebutt to the point that some Superior Court judges consider Small Claims Court appeals to be such a nuisance they try to discourage them by routinely upholding the original judgment. If there is any truth to this urban legend, it's very little. My experience is that most Superior Court judges will give you a fair hearing on appeal if you are well prepared and able to present a convincing case. So, if you believe you really were victimized by a bad decision in Small Claims Court and your case involves enough money to make a further investment of time and energy worthwhile, go ahead and appeal.

Both sides may be represented by a lawyer on a Small Claims appeal. However, this is not generally necessary, as appeals are conducted following informal procedures similar to Small Claims Court itself. And, of course, the amount of money involved does not really justify your hiring a lawyer. There is no right to a jury trial for Small Claims Court. (CCP Sec. 116.770(b).)

To file your Notice of Appeal, go to the Small Claims clerk's office and fill out a paper such as the one illustrated at the end of this chapter. Currently, the appeal fee is in the range of $30–$60 in most counties. There is no charge for the original plaintiff to appear in Superior Court on the defendant's appeal. When you file your appeal, the court will notify the other side that you have done so. You need not do this yourself. Typically, you will receive a court date within 60 days.

An appeal of a Small Claims judgment is not the sort of appeal that the U.S. Supreme Court hears. The Supreme Court, and the other formal appellate courts, are concerned with looking at the written record of what went on in a lower court with the idea of changing a decision when a judge has misinterpreted the law. Since no formal record has been made in Small Claims Court, the Superior Court has nothing to look over. Instead, they must start from scratch, just as if nothing had been said in Small Claims Court. You simply argue the case over from the start, presenting the same or different witnesses, documents and testimony, as you wish. Neither side may initiate formal discovery procedures such as depositions or interrogatories. (CCP Sec. 116.770(b).)

Even if a record is kept, you have the right to present your case again. In a few Small Claims Courts, videos are made of the original Small Claims proceeding and may be viewed by the Superior Court judge. But by law, the Superior Court judge must also permit both sides to present additional legal or factual points.

Of course, especially if you lost, you should give thought to how your presentation can be improved. Ask yourself: Did the judge decide against me because I presented my case poorly or because I didn't support my statements with evidence? Or did the judge simply misapply the law? To answer these questions, you may have to do some legal research. (See Chapter 1, Section D.) I suggest that you start preparing your appeal by making a list of ways to improve your case. Often you'll conclude that you need to make a better presentation (for example, explain a complicated series of events more clearly) and back it up with more convincing evidence (for example, show the judge a photo that backs up your central point). If you didn't take my often-repeated advice to practice presenting your case before going to court, do so now.

Be prepared for a somewhat more formal atmosphere in Superior Court. Depending on the judge, your testimony and that of any witnesses may be given from the witness box. In addition, in a few Superior Courts the judge may expect you to question your witnesses. But because rules are still informal, the Superior Court judge should not require you to follow lawyer-type rules of evidence (for example, prohibiting leading questions and banning hearsay testimony). In short, allowing for some differences in style, the judge should permit you to present oral and written testimony, witnesses and any other relevant evidence much as you did in Small Claims Court. (*Houghtaling v. Superior Ct.,* 17 Cal.App.4th 1128 (1993).)

Ask the judge to conduct your appeal as informally as possible. If you are worried about having to cope with the more formal atmosphere of Superior Court, on the day of your hearing ask the judge to conduct the proceeding as much like it was done in Small Claims Court as possible. Explain that, as a non-lawyer, you are thoroughly prepared to present the facts of your case, but that since you are unfamiliar with formal rules of evidence and procedure, you will appreciate it if your Small Claims appeal is conducted so that a citizen who has not spent three years at law school is given a fair opportunity to be heard. During your Small Claims appeal, if there is some terminology or procedure you don't understand, politely ask the judge for an explanation. If necessary, remind the judge that, under California law, you are entitled to understand the rules and procedures that control the presentation of your Small Claims appeal.

But what if your opponent takes advantage of her right to hire an attorney on appeal? Aren't you at a disadvantage in continuing to represent yourself? Not necessarily, because, as just mentioned, the appeal court must follow informal rules (Judicial Council Rule 155; *Houghtaling v. Superior Ct.,* 17 Cal.App.4th 1128 (1993)), similar to those used in Small Claims Court. This should put everyone on a fairly equal footing. If you have prepared carefully, you may even have an advantage; you carry with you the honest conviction that you are right, while a lawyer arguing a Small Claims appeal always seems a bit pathetic. If, despite this commonsense view of the situation, you still feel a little intimidated, the best cure is to go watch a few Small Claims appeals so you know what to expect and how to prepare for it. Ask the Superior Court clerk when they are scheduled.

After the appeal is concluded, the Superior Court may (but does not have to) award the winner up to $150 for attorney fees and up to an additional $150 for lost earnings, transportation and lodging costs. And if the judge decides that the appeal was meritless (intended only to harass or delay the plaintiff or encourage her to drop her claim) and made in bad faith, the judge may award up to $1,000 for attorney fees actually incurred in connection with the appeal, and up to $1,000 for any lodging and transportation costs, as well as any lost earnings. (CCP Sec. 116.790.)

Example: *Toshiro sues an electronics store for $2,000 when the big-screen TV he bought breaks and the store refuses to fix it under the warranty. He wins. The electronics store turns the case over to its lawyer, who appeals. In Superior Court, Toshiro convincingly presents his case again. After the electronics store comes up with a lame defense, Toshiro tells the judge that he believes that the defendant's appeal was filed to harass and intimidate him. He asks for and is awarded $250 damages based on his having to take off a day's work, drive 30 miles to and from the courthouse and pay for parking.*

WHAT CAN THE APPEALS COURT DECIDE IF THE DEFENDANT ALSO SUED?

Suppose A sues B for $1,000 and then B files a claim of defendant (counterclaim) for $2,000 against A? The Small Claims judge sides with A on both claims and awards her $1,000. As the losing defendant, B exercises her right to appeal. Clearly, if it believes the Small Claims judge was wrong, the appeals court has the power to reverse the $1,000 judgment against A. But can this court also award B the $2,000 he claims? At first you might say no, since B initiated the $2,000 claim and is therefore in the position of a plaintiff as far as it is concerned (and plaintiffs can't appeal, right?). You would probably be wrong. Although several California appellate courts have disagreed, the majority have concluded that once a Small Claims case is appealed, all claims of both the plaintiff and defendant which were considered by the Small Claims judge can be decided by the appellate court (*Universal City Nissan Inc. v. Superior Court*, 65 Cal. App. 4th 203, 75 Cal. Rptr. 2d 910 (1998), rev. denied, 1998 Cal. LEXIS 5493 (1998)). In short, if the court believes his case merits it, B gets his $2,000.

Appeal from the Appeal: If a defendant loses the appeal, there is no right to file a second appeal. However, in very rare instances (perhaps one case out of 100,000) the loser has good grounds to file what is called an "extraordinary writ" with the California Court of Appeal. You are eligible for the writ procedure if—and only if—both the Small Claims Court and Superior Court have made a fundamental legal mistake involving the power of the Small Claims Court (for example, rendered a judgment for more than the $5,000 limit or decided a case that shouldn't have been in Small Claims Court in the first place, such as an eviction or divorce). You are absolutely not eligible to file an extraordinary writ because you believe a judge decided your case incorrectly. Because Small Claims Courts rarely make fundamental mistakes, extraordinary writs based on Small Claims judgments are rarely filed. And even when they are, they are even more rarely granted. For these reasons, I do not cover this procedure here. For more information, see the case of *Houghtaling v. Superior Ct.,* 17 Cal.App.4th 1128 (1993), where this right is discussed in the context of Small Claims Court.

NOTICE OF APPEAL

Name and Address of Court:

SMALL CLAIMS CASE NO.

PLAINTIFF-DEMANDANTE (Name, address, and telephone number of each):

DEFENDANT/DEMANDADO (Name, address, and telephone number of each):

Telephone No.:

Telephone No.:

Telephone No.:

Telephone No.:

☐ See attached sheet for additional plaintiffs and defendants.

NOTICE OF FILING NOTICE OF APPEAL

TO: ☐ Plaintiff (name):
☐ Defendant (name):

Your small claims case has been APPEALED to the superior court. Do not contact the small claims court about this appeal. The superior court will notify you of the date you should appear in court. The notice of appeal is set forth below.	La decisión hecha por la corte para reclamos judiciales menores en su caso ha sido APELADA ante la corte superior. No se ponga en contacto con la corte para reclamos judiciales menores acerca de esta apelación. La corte superior le notificará la fecha en que usted debe presentarse ante ella. El aviso de la apelación aparece a continuación.

Date: Clerk, by _____ , Deputy

NOTICE OF APPEAL

I appeal to the superior court, as provided by law, from
☐ the small claims judgment **or** ☐ the denial of the motion to vacate the small claims judgment.

DATE APPEAL FILED (clerk to insert date):

▶

. . . .
(TYPE OR PRINT NAME)   (SIGNATURE OF APPELLANT OR APPELLANT'S ATTORNEY)

☐ I am an insurer of defendant (name) _____ in this case. The judgment against defendant exceeds $2,500, and the policy of insurance with the defendant covers the matter to which the judgment applies.

▶

. . . .
(NAME OF INSURER)   (SIGNATURE OF DECLARANT)

CLERK'S CERTIFICATE OF MAILING

I certify that
1. I am not a party to this action.
2. This Notice of Filing Notice of Appeal and Notice of Appeal were mailed first class, postage prepaid, in a sealed envelope to
   ☐ plaintiff
   ☐ defendant
   at the address shown above.
3. The mailing and this certification occurred
   at (place):   , California,
   on (date):

Clerk, by _____ , Deputy

Form Adopted by the
Judicial Council of California
SC-140 [Rev. January 1, 1992]

NOTICE OF APPEAL
(Small Claims)

Rule 982.7
Code of Civil Procedure, § 116.710

24

Collecting Your Money

You won. You undoubtedly want to collect every penny from the opposing party pronto. Not so fast. You need to be patient for a short while longer. Specifically, if the defendant showed up in court at the trial, you must legally wait 30 days after the day the Notice of Entry of Judgment form is mailed out (or handed to the defendant) to see if the defendant appeals. If you got your judgment on the basis of the defendant's failure to show up at the trial (it's a default judgment), you must also wait 30 days, this time to see if the defendant asks the court to set aside the default judgment. (See Chapter 10, Section E.) In either case, if 30 days passes with no action taken by the defendant, you can begin your collection efforts.

Let sleeping defendants lie. It is not illegal to ask for your money during the 30-day period after a judgment is entered, but it is unwise. Why? Because if you make your request for money, you may remind the defendant to take advantage of his right to appeal, or, in the case of a default judgment, to move to set it aside. (See Chapter

10, Section E.) If the defendant does appeal, you can no longer enforce the original Small Claims judgment until the appeal is decided or dismissed. Ten days after the appeal is decided by the Superior Court, this new judgment will be transferred back to Small Claims Court. If the appeal was decided in your favor, you can proceed to enforce the judgment immediately.

Once the 30-day waiting period is up, what should you do? Try asking politely for your money. This works in many cases, especially if you have sued a responsible person or business. If you don't have personal contact with the party who owes you money, try a note such as the sample below.

P.O. Box 66
Berkeley, California
February 15, 19___

Mildred Edwards
11 Milvia Street
Berkeley, California 94706

Dear Mrs. Edwards:

As you know, a judgment was entered against you in Small Claims Court on January 15 in the amount of $1,457.86. As the judgment creditor, I will appreciate your paying this amount within 10 days.

Thank you for your attention to this matter.

Very truly yours,

John Toller

As explained in Chapter 23, Section C, your judgment debtor may be willing to pay up—but may not want to deal directly with you. If so, a short note explaining that payment can be made directly to the court may make sense. (See sample, below.) A Small Claims Court judgment debtor always has the option of paying off a judgment directly to the court. The court can charge the debtor up to $25 for this service.

Once the court receives payment, it will notify you. The court is responsible for filing a Satisfaction of Judgment so that the Court's records indicate the judgment has been paid. If you fail to claim the payment within three years, the state gets to keep the money—which is an important reason to keep your current address on file.

P.O. Box 18-C
Byron, CA 94514
July 2, 19__

Donald Lee
Donald Lee Industries
14 Western Ave., S.W.
Byron, CA 94514

Dear Mr. Lee,

As you know, a judgment was entered against you in Small Claims Court on June 25 in the amount of $4,112.87. If you would prefer to pay the Small Claims Court rather than pay me directly, you can do so. However, please be aware that the court can charge up to $25 for processing your payment. As an alternative, you can send the payment directly to me. I would appreciate your handling this matter within ten days.

Thank you for your consideration.

Very truly yours,

Alice Andrews

If you receive no payment after sending a polite note, you will have to get serious about collecting your money or forget it. The emphasis in the previous sentence should be on the word "you." Much to many people's surprise, the court will not enforce your judgment for you—you have to do it yourself.

⚠ Don't harass the debtor. Now that you are a creditor, you are subject to the laws that protect debtors from abusive or unfair conduct. These rules are set out in detail in *Collect Your Court Judgment*, by Gini Graham Scott, Stephen Elias & Lisa Goldoftas (Nolo). Basically, they require that you don't call the debtor at odd hours or badmouth her in the community (of course, it's fine to talk about the judgment to officials who are helping with the collection process).

Fortunately, a few of the legal ways to collect money from a debtor are relatively easy to accomplish. Since I outlined these briefly in Chapter 3, hopefully, you gave some thought to collection before you brought your case. If you only now realize that your opponent really doesn't have the money to buy a toothbrush, you are better off not wasting more time and money trying to get her to pay up, at least for the present. In some situations, you may simply want to sit on your judgment, with the hope that your judgment debtor will show a few signs of economic life sometime in the future. But if the debtor owns real property, you'll want to establish your judgment as a property lien, even if her only property is a residence which is currently exempt from being sold under California's homestead law. (See Section F of this chapter.)

Your judgment is good for ten years from the date it was entered, and can be renewed for additional ten-year periods. To renew a judgment, just file an Application for a Renewal of Judgment form (available from the court clerk) at the court where your judgment was originally entered. You must also have the debtor served by mail or personally with a Notice of Renewal of Judgment form. But to renew your judgment, you must act while it's still good—that is, within ten years of the date it was entered. If more than ten years has lapsed, you cannot renew the judgment, and it becomes permanently unenforceable. The same applies to real estate liens, which are renewable upon the recording of an Application for a Renewal of Judgment form.

Nolo also publishes *Collect Your Court Judgment*, by Gini Graham Scott, Stephen Elias & Lisa Goldoftas, which is a far more thorough book on this subject. It outlines a number of collection strategies and deals with what to do if the debtor files a claim of exemption or threatens bankruptcy. There is also a pamphlet called

"Collecting Your Small Claims Judgment," which contains lots of practical information. It is available from the Department of General Services, Documents and Publications, P.O. Box 1015, North Highlands, CA 95660, for about $6.90. When ordering the pamphlet, refer to Item No. 445-1254-1301-0, as well as the title.

PLAN AHEAD IF THE DEBTOR MAKES PARTIAL PAYMENTS BY CHECK

Always make copies of any checks the debtor sends you as partial payment on your judgment. That's because, should the debtor fail to pay the entire judgment, you'll need to find a collection source for the unpaid portion. One good place is often the debtor's bank account. (See Section D3, below.)

If the debtor's check bounces, make a demand on the debtor by certified mail, requesting payment on the bounced check within 30 days. Keep photocopies of bounced checks, your demand letter to the debtor and the original signed, certified receipt. (See the instructions in Chapter 4, Section C1b.) If the debtor does not make the check good or pay the bad check charges, you can:

- Sue in Small Claims Court for the original amount of the bounced check plus three times that amount—with a minimum of $100 and a maximum of $1,500 (CC Sec. 1719); or

- See if your county's district attorney's office has a check diversion program. To avoid prosecution, the person who wrote a bad check must make the check good and comply with other rules. You cannot seek damages if you enlist the district attorney's help—but you'll be spared the hassle of another lawsuit.

A. If Installment Payments Aren't Made

When a court has ordered a judgment to be paid in installments and the judgment debtor misses one or more payments, the person holding the judgment (the judgment creditor) has the right to immediately collect the missed payments. But here is the problem: The judgment creditor can't collect the rest of the judgment (the part that hasn't come due yet) unless the court first sets aside the installment payment provisions and makes the entire judgment due and payable.

Example: *Phoebe gets a judgment against Ted for $3,000. The judge grants Ted's request for installment payments in the amount of $300 per month. Ted missed the first payment and Phoebe hears he soon plans to move out of state. She can immediately move to collect the $300. But to collect the rest, Phoebe must either wait until each subsequent payment is missed (and then try to collect each one) or go back to court and ask the judge to set aside the installment payments portion of the judgment, so that she can proceed to collect it all.*

To set aside an installment judgment, call the Small Claims clerk's office and ask if they have a form for this purpose. Since there is currently no statewide form in use, some local courts have developed their own. Below is a sample form you can copy if your court doesn't have its own form.

Make sure the form is served correctly and that the debtor receives copies of both the petition and the Proof of Service. (See Chapter 11.)

MUNICIPAL COURT, SMALL CLAIMS DIVISION, _____

___[PLAINTIFF'S NAME]___ , PLAINTIFF VS. ___[DEFENDANT'S NAME]___ , DEFENDANT

CASE NO. _____

PETITION OF JUDGMENT CREDITOR
TO SET ASIDE TERMS FOR PAYMENT OF JUDGMENT

The undersigned hereby declares the following:

1. The judgment was entered in the above-entitled action on ___[date]___ against the judgment debtor(s) _____[name(s)]_____ in the amount of: $_____ principal, $_____ interest and $_____ costs.

2. The judgment bore terms for payment of the above amount as follows: $_____ to be paid on ___[date]___ and $_____ to be paid on ___[specify]___ . (Complete the applicable item below.)

☐　No "grace period" for late payments was stated on the judgment.

☐　If payment is (specify): _____ days late, the entire balance is due and owing.

3. The judgment debtor(s) has defaulted in payment of the judgment and the balance owing is $_____, including interest and costs awarded at the time of judgment. The last payment by the judgment debtor(s) was made on ___[date]___ .

4. The judgment creditor therefore petitions the court for an order setting aside the terms for payment of the judgment so that execution on the entire balance of the judgment may issue forthwith.

5. I, the undersigned, am ___[specify: "the judgment creditor," or "the agent for the judgment creditor"]___ . I declare under penalty of perjury under the laws of the State of California that the foregoing is true and correct.

Date: _____

_____
Signature of Declarant

NOTICE TO THE JUDGMENT DEBTOR(S):

If you dispute any allegation made on this petition, you must file a declaration in opposition to the petition with the Small Claims office within 10 days of the mailing of the petition as stated on the Proof of Service by Mail.

B. Collecting a Judgment Against a Public Entity

If you have a Small Claims judgment against a public entity in California, you can't use any of the enforcement procedures outlined in the rest of this chapter. Instead, you'll need to follow special procedures to collect. Public entities include the State of California, counties, cities, districts, public authorities, public agencies and any other political subdivisions in the state. (CCP Sec. 708.710.)

As soon as you receive notice that the judgment has been entered, prepare the following:

1. A written declaration under penalty of perjury that specifies that you have a judgment, clearly identifies the public entity, states that you want to be paid as provided by law and indicates how much is owing. The sample declaration below contains all the required information.

2. A certified copy of the judgment or a form entitled Abstract of Judgment. You'll need to get this from the Small Claims Court clerk.

3. A small fee payable to the public entity (about $6). (CCP Sec. 708.785(a).)

Take or send the three items to the agency you have the judgment against. By law, you're then supposed to serve notice of the filing on the judgment debtor, even though doing so is redundant. To play it safe, have a friend mail photocopies of the declaration and judgment to the public entity and sign a Proof of Service. Keep the original documents in a safe place.

The public entity must notify its controller, who will deposit the money with the court. Make sure that you have your current address on file with the court—otherwise, you may never get paid. (See Chapter 23, Section C.)

> **SAMPLE DECLARATION**
>
> I, Steven Nakamura, declare as follows:
>
> 1. I have a judgment against the City of Los Angeles (Los Angeles Small Claims Court case #11212).
>
> 2. I desire the relief provided by CCP Secs. 708.710–708.795.
>
> 3. The exact amount required to satisfy the judgment is $2,312, plus interest at the rate allowable by law from February 16, 19__, until the judgment is paid in full.
>
>   I declare under penalty of perjury under the laws of the State of California that the foregoing is true and correct.
>
> Dated: February 16, 19__   _____
>
>   Steven Nakamura

C. Finding the Debtor's Assets

Collecting on your Small Claims judgment isn't normally difficult if the judgment debtor has some money or property and you know where it is. But what do you do if you suspect that money or other assets exist, but you have no idea how to find them? For example, you may know a person works, but not where, or that he has money in the bank, but not which one.

1. Judgment Debtor's Statement

Wouldn't it be nice to simply ask the judgment debtor a few questions about his assets that he must answer? Well, thanks to CCP Sec. 116.830, you can do just that. Here's how it works. When a Small Claims Court judgment is entered against a person or business, the loser (judgment debtor) must fill out a form entitled the Judgment Debtor's Statement of Assets. This form must be sent by the judgment debtor to the person who won the case (the judgment creditor) within 30 days after the Notice of Entry of Judgment is mailed out by the clerk unless the judgment debtor pays off the judgment, appeals or makes a motion to set aside or vacate the judgment. If a losing defendant appeals or files a motion to set aside a default judgment (or a losing plaintiff files a motion to vacate a default judgment against him) and subsequently loses, he has 30 days to pay or fill out the Judgment Debtor's Statement of Assets. If the judgment debtor fails to complete the statement, you may ask the court to issue a bench warrant for his arrest.

2.   Order of Examination

A judgment creditor can also ask the court clerk to issue a Declaration and Order of Examination. There is a small filing fee. This order, which must be personally served on the judgment debtor, requires the judgment debtor to show up in court and give information about his assets and financial situation. There are some limits to your use of this procedure. You can't require the judgment debtor to travel too far to participate, nor can you make him attend an examination if you've already examined him within the last 120 days. If the debtor fails to show up, the judge can issue a bench warrant for his arrest. Oh, and one hint.

You may want the judgment debtor to bring certain documents with her to the examination. For example, you may find bank statements, vehicle records and documents regarding property ownership helpful in trying to collect. To do this, you must ask the clerk to issue a Subpoena Duces Tecum. (See Chapter 14, Section D, for more information.)

At the Order of Examination hearing, the judgment creditor can ask if the debtor has any cash in his possession. If so, this can be taken, using a "turnover order," to satisfy at least a portion of the debt. If the debtor won't empty his purse or pockets, ask the bailiff for help.

There are lots of practical tips on how to find out about a debtor's assets (such as where he banks). See *Collect Your Court Judgment*, by Gini Graham Scott, Stephen Elias & Lisa Goldoftas (Nolo) or "Collecting Your Small Claims Judgment," mentioned above.

JUDGMENT DEBTOR'S STATEMENT OF ASSETS

MAIL TO THE JUDGMENT CREDITOR	SC-133
DO NOT FILE WITH THE COURT	

JUDGMENT CREDITOR (the person or business who won the case) *(name)*:

JUDGMENT DEBTOR (the person or business who lost the case and owes money) *(name)*:

SMALL CLAIMS CASE NO.:

NOTICE TO JUDGMENT DEBTOR: You must (1) pay the judgment or (2) appeal or (3) file a motion to vacate. If you fail to pay or take one of the other two actions, you must complete and mail this form to the judgment creditor. If you do not, you may have to go to court to answer questions and may have penalties imposed on you by the court.	AVISO AL DEUDOR POR FALLO JUDICIAL: Usted debe (1) pagar el monto del fallo judicial, o (2) presentar un recurso de apelación o (3) presentar un recurso de nulidad. Si usted no paga el fallo o presenta uno de estos dos recursos, deberá llenar y enviar por correo este formulario a su acreedor por fallo judicial. Si no lo hace, es posible que deba presentarse ante la corte para contestar preguntas y pagar las multas que la corte le pueda imponer.

INSTRUCTIONS

The small claims court has ruled that you owe money to the judgment creditor.

1. You may appeal a judgment against you only on the other party's claim. You may *not* appeal a judgment against you on *your* claim.
    a. If you appeared at the trial and you want to appeal, you must file a *Notice of Appeal* (form SC-140) within 30 days after the date the *Notice of Entry of Judgment* (form SC-130) was mailed or handed to you by the clerk.
    b. If you did not appear at the trial, before you can appeal, you must first file a *Notice of Motion to Vacate Judgment and Declaration (form SC-135)* and pay the required fee within 30 days after the date the *Notice of Entry of Judgment* was mailed or handed to you, and the judgment cannot be collected until the motion is decided. If your motion is denied, you then have 10 days after the date the notice of denial was mailed to file your appeal.
2. Unless you **pay the judgment or appeal or file a motion to vacate, you must fill out this form and mail it to the person who won the case** within **30 days** after the *Notice of Entry of Judgment* was mailed or handed to you by the clerk.
3. If you lose your appeal or motion to vacate, you must pay the judgment, including post-judgment costs and interest, and complete and mail this form to the judgment creditor within **30 days** after the date the clerk mails or delivers to you (a) the denial of your motion to vacate, or (b) the dismissal of your appeal, or (c) the judgment against you on your appeal.
4. As soon as the small claims court denies your motion to vacate and the denial is not appealed, or receives the dismissal of your appeal or judgment from the superior court after appeal, the judgment is no longer suspended and may be immediately enforced against you by the judgment creditor.

If you were sued as an individual, skip this box and begin with item 1 below. Otherwise, check the applicable box, attach the documents indicated, and complete item 15 on the reverse.

a. ☐ *(Corporation or partnership)* Attached to this form is a statement describing the nature, value, and exact location of all assets of the corporation or the partners, and a statement showing that the person signing this form is authorized to submit this form on behalf of the corporation or partnership.

b. ☐ *(Governmental agency)* Attached to this form is the statement of an authorized representative of the agency stating when the agency will pay the judgment and any reasons for its failure to do so.

JUDGMENT DEBTOR'S STATEMENT OF ASSETS

EMPLOYMENT

1. What are your sources of income and occupation? *(Provide job title and name of division or office in which you work.)*

2. a. Name and address of your business or employer *(include address of your payroll or human resources department, if different)*:

    b. If not employed, names and addresses of all sources of income *(specify)*:

3. How often are you paid?
    ☐ daily ☐ every two weeks ☐ monthly
    ☐ weekly ☐ twice a month ☐ other *(explain)*:
4. What is your gross pay each pay period? $
5. What is your take-home pay each pay period? $
6. If your spouse earns any income, give the name of your spouse, the name and address of the business or employer, job title, and division or office *(specify)*:

(Continued on reverse)

Form Approved by the Judicial Council of California SC-133 [Rev. January 1, 1998]	**JUDGMENT DEBTOR'S STATEMENT OF ASSETS** **(Small Claims)**	Cal. Rules of Court, rule 982.7(a); Code of Civil Procedure, §§ 116.620(a), 116.830

JUDGMENT DEBTOR'S STATEMENT OF ASSETS

CASH, BANK DEPOSITS

7. How much money do you have in cash? . . . . $

8. How much other money do you have in banks, savings and loans, credit unions, and other financial institutions either in your own name or jointly *(list)*:

Name and address of financial institution	Account number	Individual or joint?	Balance
a.			$
b.			$
c.			$

PROPERTY

9. List all automobiles, other vehicles, and boats owned in your name or jointly:

Make and year	Value	Legal owner if different from registered owner	Amount owed
a.	$		$
b.	$		$
c.	$		$
d.	$		$

10. List all real estate owned in your name or jointly:

Address of real estate	Fair market value	Amount owed
a.	$	$
b.	$	$

OTHER PERSONAL PROPERTY *(Do not list household furniture and furnishings, appliances, or clothing.)*

11. List anything of value not listed above owned in your name or jointly *(continue on attached sheet if necessary)*:

Description	Value	Address where property is located
a.	$	
b.	$	
c.	$	

12. Is anyone holding assets for you? ☐ Yes. ☐ No. If yes, describe the assets and give the name and address of the person or entity holding each asset *(specify)*:

13. Have you disposed of or transferred any asset within the last 60 days? ☐ Yes. ☐ No. If yes, give the name and address of each person or entity who received any asset and describe each asset *(specify)*:

14. If you are not able to pay the judgment in one lump sum, you may be able to make payment arrangements with the person or business who won the case (the judgment creditor). State the amount that you can pay each month: $, beginning on *(date)*:   . If you are unable to agree, you may also ask the court for permission to make installment payments by filing a *Request to Pay Judgment in Installments* (form SC-106).

15. I declare under penalty of perjury under the laws of the State of California that the foregoing is true and correct.

Date:

▶

. . . . _____
(TYPE OR PRINT NAME)   (SIGNATURE)

Mail or deliver this completed form to the judgment creditor at the address shown on the Notice of Entry of Judgment form.

SC-133 [Rev. January 1, 1998]   **JUDGMENT DEBTOR'S STATEMENT OF ASSETS**   Page two
                                                                  (Small Claims)

D. Levying on Wages, Bank Accounts, Business Assets, Real Property, Etc.

In this section, I discuss a number of ways to collect a court judgment. One or more may work easily and quickly. However, some judgment debtors hide assets or are otherwise difficult to collect from. If you face this situation and believe the judgment debtor may own or buy real property your best bet may be to establish a lien against that property and wait until the judgment debtor pays you. (See Section F, below, for details on how to do this.)

Think twice before using a collection agency. It is possible to turn your debt over to a real collection agency, but this probably doesn't make much sense, as the agency will often take up to 50% of what it can collect as its fee. And unless you are a regular customer, the agency probably won't treat your debt with much priority unless it believes your judgment will be easy to collect. Of course, if the debt is easy for them to collect, you should be able to do the job yourself and pocket the amount of the collection fee.

If you know where the judgment debtor works, you are in good shape. You are generally entitled to get approximately 25% of a person's net wages to satisfy a debt. (But if a person has a very low income, the amount you may recover can be considerably less than 25%, and possibly nothing at all.)

It is more difficult to garnish the pay of U.S. Government employees. The wages of postal service and federal housing workers may be reached following normal California garnishment procedures set out below. However, wages of other federal employees, including seamen, longshoremen and harbor workers, must be pursued through a special process. See *Collect Your Court Judgment,* by Scott, Elias & Goldoftas (Nolo) for details.

Knowing where a judgment debtor banks can also be extremely valuable, as you can order a sheriff, marshal or constable to levy on a bank account and get whatever it contains at the time of the levy, subject to several exceptions. (See Sidebar, below.) Of course, a bank account levy will only work once at a given bank, since the debtor is pretty sure to move his account when he realizes that you are emptying it.

SOME PROPERTY IN BANK ACCOUNTS IS EXEMPT FROM ATTACHMENT

Bank account levies are subject to exempt property laws—meaning a judgment debtor can take steps to have deposits from several sources returned. Approximately 75% of wages placed in a bank account are exempt (100% if there has been a previous wage attachment involving the same money) for 30 days after payment. Social Security money in a bank account is exempt.

Other types of property are normally much more difficult to grab. Why? Because California has a number of debtor's "exemption" laws that say that, even though a person owes money, certain types of her property can't be taken to satisfy the debt. Major types of protected property include:

- personal residence—up to $100,000 in equity for those who are over 65, blind or disabled, and those over 55 who earn under $15,000 per year ($20,000 if married). Families qualify for a $75,000 equity exemption. All others may claim $50,000

- furniture and appliances

- clothing

- jewelry, heirlooms and art up to $5,000

- public benefits (welfare, unemployment, Social Security, workers' comp.) and

- most pensions.

Again, this means, practically speaking, the only personal property assets (as opposed to real estate) other than wages and bank accounts that are normally worth going after to satisfy a Small Claims judgment are business receipts and property and motor vehicles in which the judgment debtor has equity in excess of $1,900. Theoretically, there are many other assets that you could reach—boats and planes, for example—but in most cases they are not worth the time and expense involved, considering that your judgment is for less than $5,000. Real estate is different. Even if the judgment debtor has little equity in the property, you will still want to record a judgment lien. Most people refinance or sell within a three-year period, at which time you are apt to get paid (your lien will be satisfied).

Amend a judgment to include other names used by the defendant. What if you find the judgment debtor's assets, only to discover that he holds them in a different name from the one you sued him under? If this happens, you must have your judgment amended before you can collect. CCP Sec. 116.560(b) allows you to ask the court to amend its judgment to include both the correct legal name and any other name used by the defendant. Once this is done, you can collect the property held in those names.

1. Writ of Execution

Before you can levy on a person's wages or other property, you must complete a Writ of Execution form and have it issued by the court. You get your Writ from the Small Claims Court clerk, who will help you fill it out. There is a small fee, which is a recoverable cost. (See Section G, below.)

2. The Sheriff (or Marshal or Constable)

Once your Writ of Execution form is issued by the court, take or send it to the sheriff, marshal or constable in the county where the assets are located. The Small Claims Court clerk will do this for you if you request it. Give the officer or Small Claims clerk the following:

- The Writ of Execution (original) and one to three or more copies, depending on the asset to be collected. Keep a copy of the Writ of Execution for your files.

- The required fees for collecting (this will vary as to the type of asset); call ahead to inquire.

- Instructions on what type of asset to collect and where it is located. The sheriff, marshal, constable or Small Claims clerk may have a form they wish you to use when providing these instructions. Or the instructions might be a part of the writ form itself. Normally, however, they will accept a letter if it contains all the necessary information.

Don't delay in serving a Writ of Execution. A Writ of Execution expires in 180 days if it is not served by then. If this time runs out, you will have to go back to the Small Claims clerk and get another Writ of Execution issued.

WRIT OF EXECUTION

ATTORNEY OR PARTY WITHOUT ATTORNEY *(Name and Address)*:	TELEPHONE NO.:	FOR RECORDER'S USE ONLY

☐ Recording requested by and return to:

John Toller   (510) 845-0000
P.O. Box 66

☐ ATTORNEY FOR   ☐ JUDGMENT CREDITOR   ☐ ASSIGNEE OF RECORD

NAME OF COURT: San Francisco Municipal Court
STREET ADDRESS: 400 McAllister
MAILING ADDRESS:
CITY AND ZIP CODE: San Francisco, CA 94102
BRANCH NAME:

PLAINTIFF: John Toller

DEFENDANT: Mildred Edwards

WRIT OF
☒ EXECUTION (Money Judgment)
☐ POSSESSION OF ☐ Personal Property
☐ Real Property
☐ SALE

CASE NUMBER: 123456

FOR COURT USE ONLY

1. To the Sheriff or any Marshal or Constable of the County of:
San Francisco
You are directed to enforce the judgment described below with daily interest and your costs as provided by law.

2. To any registered process server: You are authorized to serve this writ only in accord with CCP 699.080 or CCP 715.040.

3. *(Name)*: John Toller
is the ☐ judgment creditor ☐ assignee of record
whose address is shown on this form above the court's name.

4. Judgment debtor *(name and last known address)*:

Mildred Edwards
17 Valparaiso St.
S.F., CA 94133

☐ additional judgment debtors on reverse

5. Judgment entered on *(date)*: Jan. 7, 2000
6. ☐ Judgment renewed on *(dates)*:

7. Notice of sale under this writ
a. ☒ has not been requested.
b. ☐ has been requested *(see reverse)*.
8. ☐ Joint debtor information on reverse.

(SEAL)

9. ☐ See reverse for information on real or personal property to be delivered under a writ of possession or sold under a writ of sale.
10. ☐ This writ is issued on a sister-state judgment.
11. Total judgment . . . . $
12. Costs after judgment (per filed order or memo CCP 685.090) . . . . $
13. Subtotal *(add 11 and 12)* . . . . $
14. Credits . . . . $
15. Subtotal *(subtract 14 from 13)* . . . . $
16. Interest after judgment (per filed affidavit CCP 685.050) . . . . $
17. Fee for issuance of writ . . . . $
18. Total *(add 15, 16, and 17)* . . . . $
19. Levying officer:
(a) Add daily interest from date of writ *(at the legal rate in 15)* of . . . . $
(b) Pay directly to court costs included in 11 and 17 (GC 6103.5, 68511.3, CCP 699.520(i)) . . . . $
20. ☐ The amounts called for in items 11–19 are different for each debtor. These amounts are stated for each debtor on Attachment 20.

Issued on *(date)*:   Clerk, by _____ , Deputy

— NOTICE TO PERSON SERVED: SEE REVERSE FOR IMPORTANT INFORMATION —

(Continued on reverse)

Form Approved by the
Judicial Council of California
EJ-130 (Rev. July 1, 1996)   **WRIT OF EXECUTION**   Code of Civil Procedure, §§ 699.520, 712.010, 715.010

3.   How to Levy on Wages or Bank Accounts

To seize a person's wages, you need to fill out an Application for an Earnings Withholding Order (you can get one from the Small Claims clerk). Take or send this, along with two copies of the Writ of Execution, a letter of instruction and fee (check with the levying officer), to the levying officer in the county where the assets are located. She will then serve an Earnings Withholding Order on the debtor's employer, and you should get some money soon. An Earnings Withholding Order lasts until the judgment is satisfied or expires.

To levy on a bank account, first contact the sheriff, marshal or constable's office to be sure they handle this work (if not, contact a process server). Assuming they do, you'll need the original and one copy of the Writ of Execution, a letter of instruction and their fee. Under CCP Sec. 700.160, it is even possible to levy on accounts held by the judgment debtor's spouse (or on a business where a fictitious business statement lists the owner as the judgment debtor or the judgment debtor's spouse). However, in both of these latter instances, extra paperwork must be filed. Before sending in your paperwork, ask the sheriff, marshal or constable what they require.

Here is a sample letter of instruction:

                                        P.O. Box 66
                                        Berkeley, California
                                        March 1, 19__

Sheriff (Civil Division)
Alameda County
Alameda County Courthouse
Oakland, California

Re: *John Toller v. Mildred Edwards*
Albany-Berkeley Judicial District
Small Claims Court No. 81-52

Dear Sheriff:

Enclosed you will find the original and one copy of a Writ of Execution issued
by the Small Claims Court for the Oakland Judicial District in the amount of
$ _____ (fill in total due). I also enclose an Application for Earnings
Withholding Order and check for your fee in the amount of $_____.

I hereby instruct you to levy on the wages of Mildred Edwards, who works at
the Graphite Oil Co., 1341 Chester St., Oakland, California. Please serve the
Writ on or before March 15, 19__. (For a bank account, you would simply
substitute "all monies in the accounts of Mildred Evans, located at [address]."
You generally do not need to know the account number [although some
counties may require it]—only the bank and branch.)

                                        Very truly yours,

                                        John Toller

---

4. Business Assets

It is possible to have someone from the sheriff's, marshal's or constable's office sent to the business of a person who owes you money to collect it from the cash on hand. It is done with a "till tap" or a "keeper."

A till tap consists of a one-time removal of all cash receipts from the business. The fees are reasonable. For a "keeper," a deputy from the sheriff's, marshal's or constable's office goes to the place of business, takes all the cash in the cash register and then stays there for a set period of time (an "eight-hour keeper," a "24-hour keeper" or a "48-hour keeper") to take more money as it comes in. Because you must pay the deputy to stay at the collection site, keepers' fees are relatively high; a 48-hour keeper can cost as much as $400. It is also possible for the business's property to be seized and sold. But costs of doing so are usually prohibitive.

Talk to the sheriff, marshal or constable in your area to get more details. He will want an original and three copies of your Writ of Execution, as well as instructions telling him where and when to go. Fees are recoverable from the judgment debtor if enough money comes in to cover them, plus the judgment.

If a business is licensed or bonded, it may be easier to collect. If you wish to sue a business such as a contractor or travel promoter that is required to purchase a bond to cover its legal obligations, there may be an easy way to collect your judgment. In addition to naming the company you have a claim against, name the bonding company. Once you receive a judgment, send the bonding company a copy along with a letter describing the claim and requesting payment.

If you win a judgment against a licensed contractor that stems from her line of work, you can submit the judgment to the Registrar of the Contractor's State License Board, P.O. Box 26000, Sacramento, CA 95826. The judgment will be placed on the licensee's record. If the contractor (licensee) doesn't pay the judgment or file a judgment bond, the contractor's license will be suspended.

5. Levying on Motor Vehicles (Including Planes, Boats and RVs)

Selling a person's motor vehicle tends to be difficult for several reasons, including the following:

- $1,900 combined equity in one or more motor vehicles is exempt from your levy. (CCP Sec. 704.010.)

Example: A judgment debtor has a car worth $4,000 on which he owes $3,000 to a bank. This means that his equity is $1,000—the bank owns the rest. As equity of $1,900 is exempt, you would end up with nothing.

- One motor vehicle is exempt from attachment up to $5,000 if it is a "tool of a person's trade," as it would be if the debtor ran a delivery service or as part of a hauling business. (CCP Sec. 704.060.)

   Example: A judgment debtor has a pickup truck worth $3,000 that she uses every day in her gardening business. The truck would be exempt as a tool of trade.

- The car must be parked in an accessible place, such as a street or driveway, unless you obtain a court order allowing entry into a garage or other private place.

- The judgment debtor may not own the car he drives. It may be in someone else's name, or he may be leasing it.

Finding out if a judgment debtor owns the car he drives can be tricky. You might get this information from the Judgment Debtor's Statement of Assets (Section C1) or by conducting an order of examination (Section C2). In addition, for a small fee, you may be able to find out from the DMV who owns the car, including whether or not a bank or finance company is involved. The DMV will not provide the residence address of an individual owner, but it can release a separate mailing address for the purpose of serving legal papers. (See the discussion about the DMV in Chapter 8, Section F.)

Once you have this information, you can determine whether selling the car is likely to yield enough to pay off any loan you discover, provide the debtor with her $1,900 exemption, cover the costs of sale and still leave enough to pay off all, or at least a substantial part, of your judgment. If you are convinced that the vehicle is worth enough to cover these costs, as would be the case if it is relatively new and owned by the debtor free and clear, have the sheriff pick up the car and sell it. But remember, the sheriff fees to do this are relatively high and must be paid in advance. Also, the sale price at a public auction will fetch far less than at a private sale. Your costs are recoverable when the vehicle is sold.

Call the sheriff, marshal or constable of the county in which the car is located to find out how much money he requires as a deposit and how many copies of the Writ you need. Then write a letter such as this:

P.O. Box 66
Berkeley, Calif.
March 1, 19__

Sheriff (Civil Division)
Alameda County
Alameda County Courthouse
Oakland, California

Re: *John Toller v. Mildred Edwards*
Small Claims Court
Albany-Berkeley Judicial District
No. SC 81-52

Dear Sheriff:

You are hereby instructed, under the authority of the enclosed Writ of Execution, to levy upon and sell all of the right, title and interest of Mildred Edwards, judgment debtor, in the following motor vehicle:

(Enter the description of the car as it appears on your DMV report, including the license number.)

The vehicle is registered in the name(s) of Mildred Edwards, and is regularly found at the following address(es):

(List home and work address of owner. Remember that the car must be in a public place, such as parked on a street.)

Enclosed is my check for $_____ to cover your costs of levy and sale.

Very truly yours,

John Toller

6.   Stocks, Bonds, Mutual Funds and Other Securities

If the judgment debtor owns stock or other securities that are not exempt as part of a retirement plan (see Section D8, below), your collection method will depend on how the ownership is physically represented.

If ownership is manifested in certificates held by the judgment debtor, you can levy against the certificates themselves as tangible personal property. However, you will first need to get a court order allowing you to reach property in a private home. How to do this is covered in *Collect Your Court Judgment,* by Gini Graham Scott, Stephen Elias & Lisa Goldoftas (Nolo).

If, as is common, the certificates are held for the judgment debtor by a broker, you can initiate a third-party levy against the branch office of the stock brokerage firm. The sheriff, marshal or constable will require a Writ of Execution, written instructions and fee to handle the levy.

Sometimes stock or mutual fund ownership is not manifested in certificates, but is recorded in the computers of the company issuing the securities. In this case, it is possible to make a third-party levy at a company's in-state headquarters. If the company's headquarters are out of state, you will need to obtain a court order assigning you the right to the securities.

7.   Other Personal Property

Normally, it isn't worth the trouble to try to levy on small items of personal property, such as furniture or appliances, because they are commonly covered by one or another of the California debtor's exemption laws that prevent certain possessions from being taken to satisfy debts. The exemption laws are found listed in CCP Secs. 704.010 and following, and include furniture, clothing and much more. Even if property isn't exempt, selling it is usually more trouble (and produces less cash) than it's worth. If you identify valuable non-exempt property, you will need a court order to allow a levying officer access to property in a private home.

For a complete list of exempt assets and a thorough discussion of the best ways to collect a California judgment, see *Collect Your Court Judgment*, by Gini Graham Scott, Stephen Elias & Lisa Goldoftas (Nolo).

8.   Pensions and Retirement Benefits

You can only go after the money in individual or self-employment retirement plans (IRAs, Keoghs) if that money is in excess of the amount tax-exempt under federal income tax law. In addition, the judgment debtor may try to claim that non-tax-exempt money is necessary for the reasonable support of her and her family. If the court agrees as part of a Claim of Exemption procedure, you're out of luck.

Private company retirement plans and state or local government retirement plans generally can't be touched until the money is paid over to the employee. And even then, the employee (judgment debtor) could claim those amounts as exempt.

Federal government pension and retirement benefits may not be garnished to satisfy any debts, except those for alimony and child support.

E. Judgments Stemming From Auto Accidents

In certain circumstances, a judgment debtor's California driver's license may be suspended by the Department of Motor Vehicles (DMV) if the debtor doesn't pay the judgment.

- *90-day Suspension:* The judgment must be for $500 or less, arise from an accident on a California road and remain unpaid for more than 90 days from the date judgment was entered. After the DMV is notified, the debtor has 20 days to pay or prove that insurance will cover the damage. (CCP Sec. 116.880, Vehicle Code Sec. 16370.5.)

- *Suspension Until Judgment Paid:* The judgment must be for more than $500 or for personal injury or death, and have resulted from an accident caused by an uninsured debtor's operation of a motor vehicle. Unless the debtor had as much insurance as is required by state law, he is considered uninsured. If the debtor carried insurance at the time of the accident, and the insurance company won't pay the judgment, see an attorney. The suspension continues for six years, or until the judgment is paid or converted to a type of judgment under which payments are made in installments. You cannot immediately renew the suspension after it expires. However, you can follow the suspension process again if you renew your judgment. (See Chapter 24.)

Remember that if the debtor needs to drive to work, license suspension may make her lose her job. To get rid of the debt and therefore avoid the suspension, the debtor might decide to declare bankruptcy. If you intend to take such a drastic step—don't make idle threats—first negotiate with the debtor. You may be able to work out a payment plan.

To get the judgment debtor's license suspended, you must send to the DMV—or arrange for the court that issued the judgment to send:

- a certified copy of your judgment or a docket entry showing the judgment;
- the required fee (check with the DMV)
- a simple one-page form available from the DMV titled Certificate of Facts Re Unsatisfied Judgment (Form DL-30).

Your court may have the Certificate of Facts Re Unsatisfied Judgment form, since it must complete part of the form. Or contact: Department of Motor Vehicles, Financial Responsibility/Civil Judgments Division, P.O. Box 942884, Sacramento, CA 94284-0884, 916-657-7573.

F. Creating Property Liens

The simple act of recording an Abstract of Judgment at the County Recorder's office in counties where the judgment debtor owns or later buys real property gives you a lien against all of his real property in that county. When the judgment debtor wishes to sell his real property, the title will be clouded by your lien and he will have to pay you off to be able to transfer clear title to a third party. Likewise, if he wishes to refinance, it almost certainly will be contingent on all liens being paid off. Thus, sooner or later, you should get your money. One important exception to this rule is that a home on which the judgment debtor has filed a homestead prior to your recording your Abstract of Judgment can be sold by the judgment debtor and the money (up to $75,000 in equity for a family; $50,000 for a single person under 65; and $100,000 for people over 65, the blind or disabled, and those over 55 who earn under $15,000 if single and under $20,000 if married) used to buy another homesteaded home within six months without paying off your lien.

Before you record your lien, make sure you wait until the time to appeal has passed (see the introduction to this chapter). To record your judgment against real property, first get an Abstract of Judgment from the Small Claims clerk's office. The clerk will prepare this paper for you. There will be a small fee for issuing it. Then take or mail the Abstract of Judgment to the County Recorder's office in each county where the property is located or you think the debtor might buy property, and pay the required fee. The Recorder's Office will record your lien and notify the judgment debtor.

G. Recovering Collection Costs and Interest

Costs (including the filing fee, costs of service, etc.) incurred prior to recovering a judgment should be included in the judgment total when it is entered by the judge. I discuss this in Chapter 15, Section D.

Here I am concerned with costs incurred after judgment. These are the costs that result when the judgment debtor doesn't pay voluntarily and you have to levy on her assets. This can be expensive, so you will want to make the judgment debtor pay, if possible. Many costs of collecting a judgment are recoverable; a few are not. Generally speaking, you can recover your direct costs of collecting, which include such things as sheriff, marshal or constable fees; costs to get copies of required papers issued by the court, such as a Writ of Execution or Abstract of Judgment; and recording fees. Indirect costs such as babysitting costs, lost wages or money you pay for postage, photocopying or gasoline or parking can't be recovered.

You are entitled to collect interest on your judgment at the rate of 10% per year. Interest begins to accrue on the date the judgment was entered. To collect, you must first file a form to claim interest (available from the Small Claims clerk). If the judge has entered a judgment to be paid in installments, you can charge interest on the unpaid balance. (CCP Sec. 116.620.) Apply any payments you receive first towards costs you have incurred, then towards interest and finally to the unpaid balance of the judgment. You cannot claim interest on accrued unpaid interest.

There are two main ways to collect your costs and interest:

1. Costs Associated With a Levy

As part of levying on wages, bank accounts, automobiles, businesses, etc., collection fees can simply be added to the total to be collected by the levying officer, with no need for additional court action. These include the fee for issuing a Writ of Execution (Section D1, above) and the sheriff's, marshal's or constable's fee for collecting it. These fees can really add up, as the costs for selling a motor vehicle or placing a keeper at a place of business are considerable. In addition, you can collect interest that has accrued on the judgment from the date the Writ was issued.

2. Memorandum of Credits, Accrued Interest and Costs After Judgment

Other costs, such as money expended for an Abstract of Judgment, County Recorder fees and costs for unsuccessful levies on wages, bank accounts, businesses, motor vehicles, etc., can be recovered only after you file a document with the court. To get these, you must prepare and file a Memorandum of Credits, Accrued Interest and Costs After Judgment. The Small Claims Court clerk will help you prepare this form. File one copy with the clerk and have an adult friend mail another copy to the judgment debtor. Then have your friend fill out a Proof of Service form to be filed with the clerk. (See Chapter 11, Section F.) Unless the judgment debtor objects by filing papers with the court, costs claimed on the Memorandum may be added to the judgment and will incur interest. Interest you've claimed cannot collect additional interest, however. ■

25

Where Do We Go From Here?

Sometimes it almost seems that America's legal system was designed by the Chinese Emperor K'ang-hsi, who said, "...lawsuits would tend to increase to a frightening extent if people were not afraid of the tribunals and if they felt confident of always finding in them ready and perfect justice....I desire therefore that those who have recourse to the tribunals should be treated without pity and in such a manner that they shall be disgusted with law and tremble to appear before a magistrate."

It's easy to criticize America's existing legal system—almost everyone knows it's in trouble. The $1,000-a-day experts, with their degrees, titles and well-funded consulting companies, have studied the problem to death, with few positive results. And this is hardly surprising, since most of the experts are lawyers who, at bottom, are unable to understand a problem of which they are so thoroughly a part.

But instead of my lecturing you about all the things that are wrong at the local courthouse, let's sit down at the kitchen table with a pot of tea and a bowl of raspberries and see if we can't design a better system for handling everyday disputes. After all, this republic was founded by ordinary people taking things into their own hands. And don't forget—since we have already agreed that the present legal structure doesn't work very well, we obviously have little to lose by changing things. Hey, leave a few raspberries for me, and why don't you jot down a few of your own ideas as we go along, so this becomes a two-way communication.

Before we get to specific suggestions for doing things differently, let's take a moment to think about how we Americans look at the fundamental purpose of our legal system. As a society, we clearly have something of a fixation with trying to solve problems by suing one another. Nowhere in the world do people even come close to being as litigious as we are. The result of this love of lawsuits, or perhaps its cause—it's one of those chicken-and-egg problems—is the fact that whenever we Americans get into any sort of spat with anyone, or even think we might get into one in the future, we look for a lawyer. It's gotten so bad that people who suffer an injury have been known to call their lawyer before their doctor. But there is an odd paradox here. At the same time that we tolerate vast numbers of lawyers eating at the top end of our societal trough, and are individually fairly likely to use one, public opinion polls tell us our respect for the legal profession has fallen to an all-time low. Indeed, we rate the trustworthiness of attorneys below that of used-car salespeople, undertakers and loan sharks. It's as if the less we respect lawyers, the more we use them. Perhaps we're afraid that if we don't sue first, someone will get the jump on us. (If you eat one more of those raspberries, I'll see you in court.)

To begin to see how we might design a better dispute resolution system, let's start by considering how people solved their disputes in less complicated societies. Pretend, for a moment, that we are members of a tribe of deer hunters in a pre-industrial age. One fine fall morning, we both set out, bow in hand, you to the east and me to the west. Before long, you hit a high cliff and turn north. My way is blocked by a swift river, and I, too, turn north. Without our realizing it, our paths converge. Suddenly, a great stag jumps from the underbrush and we both pull back our bows and let fly. Our arrows pierce the deer's heart from opposite sides, seemingly at the same instant.

For a moment, we stand frozen, each surprised by the presence of the other. Then we realize what has happened and that we have a problem. To whom does the deer belong? Together, we carry the deer back to the village, each unwilling to surrender it to the other. After the deer is gutted and hung, we take our problem to the chief of our tribe. He convenes a council of elders to meet late in the afternoon to consider it. When this occurs, each of us has his say as to what happened. The deer carcass is examined. Anyone else who has knowledge of our dispute is invited to speak. Tribal customs (laws) are consulted, our credibility is weighed and a decision is made—in time for dinner.

Now, let's ask ourselves what would happen today if you and I simultaneously shot a deer (instead of each other) on the first day of hunting season and were unable to agree on who it belonged to. Assuming we didn't fight it out on the spot but wanted the dispute resolved by "proper" legal procedures, lawyers would have to be consulted, court papers filed and responded to, a court appearance scheduled, words spoken in legalese and a court decision written and issued. (Since the case doesn't involve the payment of money, it wouldn't be appropriate for Small Claims Court.) All of this for a deer that would have long since rotted away unless it had been put in cold storage. If the deer had been frozen, the storage costs would have to be added to court costs and attorney fees, which, all together, would surely add up to a lot more than the value of the deer.

What were the principle differences between the ways the two societies resolved the problem of who owned the deer? Or to ask the same question in a different way, why did the primitive society do a better job of resolving the dispute? The simple answer is that their dispute resolution process was in proportion to the problem—and allowed the disputing parties to participate in and understand what was going on—while ours is so cumbersome and expensive it often dwarfs the dispute.

So the question becomes, why can't our court system do a better job of resolving disputes quickly, fairly and cheaply? The answer is depressingly simple—lawyers who have a vested financial and psychic interest in the present cumbersome way of doing things have neither the motivation nor the vision to make changes.

But isn't my view a bit radical? Isn't there something uniquely valuable about the great sweep of our common law courts as they have evolved through the ages? Doesn't the majestic black-robed judge sitting on his throne mumbling age-old Latin mantras somehow guarantee that God is in heaven, the republic safe and "justice will be done?"

To all three questions, the best answer is, "not necessarily." History is often arbitrary—our dispute resolution mechanisms could have developed in a number of alternative ways. If our present system worked well, imposing it on the future would make sense. As, in fact, it hardly works at all, continuing it is silly. Those who get misty-eyed recounting the history, traditions and time-tested forms behind our present court system are almost always people that benefit by its continuance. Consider, too, that in the United States we have no pure legal tradition, having borrowed large hunks of our jurisprudence on a catch-as-catch-can basis from England, Spain, France, Holland and Germany, as well as various Native American cultures.

Okay, granted there have been legal systems that worked better than ours, and granted at least some change is overdue, what should we do? One significant reform would be to expand Small Claims Court. Like the system followed by the deer hunters, but unlike most of the rest of our legal system, Small Claims Court is simple, fast and cheap, and allows for the direct participation of the disputing parties. Never mind that up to now Small Claims Court has been tolerated as a way to keep lawyers' offices clear of penny-ante people with penny-ante disputes. It's there, it works and we can expand it to play a meaningful role in our lives.

As you know by now, Small Claims Court as it is presently set up has several disadvantages:

- *First:* The maximum dollar amount is far too low.

- *Second:* In most instances, the court only has the power to make judgments that can be satisfied by the payment of money damages. (In most states, a Small Claims judge couldn't divide the deer.)

- *Third:* Most types of cases, such as divorces, adoptions and petitions to raise or lower child support, aren't permitted in Small Claims Court at all.

- *Fourth:* Many states still allow lawyers to represent people in Small Claims Court and by doing so gum up the works.

Why not start our effort to improve things by doing away with these disadvantages? Let's raise the maximum amount for which suit can be brought to $20,000. I would like to suggest $30,000, but that's probably unrealistic given the high likelihood that it would result in vitriolic attorney opposition in our state legislatures. But even an increase to $20,000 would be a significant reform, allowing tens of thousands of disputes to be removed from our formal legal system. One logical reason to pick $20,000 is that people clearly can't afford lawyers to handle disputes for amounts below this.

Example: Randy the carpenter agrees to do $30,000 worth of rehabilitation to Al's home. When the work is completed, an argument develops about whether the work was done properly according to the agreement. Al pays Randy $15,000, leaving $15,000 in dispute. Randy goes to his lawyer and Al to his. Each has several preliminary conferences, after which the lawyers exchange several letters and telephone calls. Eventually, a lawsuit is filed and answered, a court date is obtained many months in the future and then changed several times and finally a two-hour trial is held. Randy's lawyer bills him $4,480 (28 hours x $160 per hour) and Al's charges $4,725 (27 hours x $175 per hour), for a combined fee of $9,205. The dispute takes eleven months to be decided. In the end, Randy is awarded $10,000.

This is a typical case with a typical solution. Between them, the lawyers collected over half of the amount in dispute and took most of a year to arrive at a solution that very likely left both Randy and Al frustrated. Don't you think Randy and Al would have preferred presenting their case in Small Claims Court, where it would have been heard and decided in a month? Of course, either of them could have done worse arguing the case himself, but remember, when the legal fees are taken into consideration, the loser would have had to do a lot worse before he would have ended up poorer. True, Randy recovered $10,000 with a lawyer, but after subtracting the $4,480 lawyer fee, his net gain was only $5,520. Al ended up paying $14,725 ($10,000 for the judgment and $4,725 for his attorney). Thus, if a Small Claims Court judge had awarded Randy any amount from $5,521 to $14,724, both men would have done better than they did with lawyers. Of course, if this sort of case were permitted in Small Claims Court, there would be two big losers—the lawyers.

The second great barrier to resolving disputes in Small Claims Court is that, with minor exceptions, the court is limited to making money judgments. Think back for a moment to our problem of the twice-shot deer. How does the award of money make sense in this situation? In Small Claims Courts, the tribesman who didn't end up with the carcass would have had to sue the other for the fair market value of the deer. What nonsense—if we are going to have a dispute resolution procedure, why not permit a broad range of solutions, such as the judge deciding to cut the deer in half, or the whole deer being awarded to one hunter who then agrees to give the other 12 ducks by way of compensation? Using an example more common at the end of the 20th century, why not allow a Small Claims Court judge to order that an apartment be cleaned, a garage repainted or a car properly fixed, instead of simply telling one person to pay X dollars to the other? One advantage of this sort of flexibility is that more judgments would be carried out. Under our present system, tens of thousands of judgments can't be collected because the loser has no obvious source of income. We need to get away from the notion that people who are broke have neither rights nor responsibilities. To have a decent life, people need both.

Lawyers and judges often contend that it would be impossible to enforce nonmoney judgments. Perhaps some would be hard to keep track of. Certainly it might require some experimentation to find out what types of judgments are practical and which are not; however, since it is often impossible to collect a judgment under the present system, it can't hurt to try some alternatives.

The third barrier to bringing cases in Small Claims Court is the current limitation as to the types of cases that court can consider. Consequently, the next big change I propose, and the one that would truly make over our court system, involves expanding the types of cases that can be heard in Small Claims. Why not think big and take the 20 most common legal problems and adopt simplified procedures enabling all of them to be handled by the people themselves, without lawyers? Why not open up our court-houses to the average person who, after all, pays the bill for the lights and heat?

To accomplish this democratization of our dispute resolution procedures, it makes sense to divide Small Claims Court into several separate divisions, each one responsible for a broad subject area. For example, there could be landlord–tenant and domestic relations Small Claims Courts. Incidentally, there is nothing new about the idea of dividing a court by subject matter. It is already done in our formal trial courts and works well (and in a few states, landlord–tenant and a few other types of cases are already handled separately in Small Claims Court). To see how this approach would improve matters, consider that today, if you have a claim against your landlord (or he against you) for money damages, you can use Small Claims only if the claim is for $5,000 or less. If you want a roof fixed, a tenant evicted or your privacy protected, Small Claims Court can't help you, except possibly to award a money judgment for the intentional infliction of emotional distress.

Following this same general approach, a domestic relations Small Claims Court could adopt simplified procedures to help people safely and cheaply handle their own uncontested divorces, adoptions, name changes, child support and custody disputes and guardianships. And why not? Even with considerable hostility from many lawyers and court personnel—and despite the fact that nonlawyers must deal with the complicated procedures inherent in going to Superior Court—up to 60 percent of the divorces in California are already handled without a lawyer. I'm not advocating that sensible safeguards be dropped. For example, if a divorce involves children, you would want to have someone trained in the field carefully examine the parents' plans for custody, visitation and support to see if they are reasonable.

I also suggest that if we delawyered our domestic relations courts, we would significantly lighten the heavy burden of hostility and anxiety that divorcing spouses must now bear. Clearly our present system, in which anxious and frequently angry parents and children become clients of a hired advocate (the lawyer), is a bad one. By definition, the client role (the Latin root of the word "client" translates, "to hear, to obey") is weak and the professional advocate role is strong. This imbalance commonly results in lawyers making critical decisions affecting their clients' lives—sometimes overtly, sometimes subtly. All too often these decisions benefit the lawyer and his bank balance to the detriment of both the client's psyche and pocketbook. The lawyer, after all, is paid more to fight, or at least to pretend to fight, than to compromise. I have seen dozens of situations where lawyers have played on people's worst instincts (paranoia, greed, ego, one-upsmanship) to fan nasty little disagreements into flaming battles. Perhaps mercifully, the battles normally last only as long as the lawyers' bills are paid.

Let's assume now that the hostility of the legal profession to self-help friendly legal systems can be overcome and the role of Small Claims Court greatly expanded. Here are a few specific ideas to accomplish this change:

1. Let's make Small Claims Court easily accessible. This means holding weekend and evening sessions. This is being done now on a limited basis in our larger counties, but should be routinely available everywhere. When court is held at 9 a.m. on weekdays, it often costs more in time lost from work for all the principals and witnesses to show up than the case is worth.

2. Let's build a mediation alternative right into the Small Claims system. This is already done in Maine (and a couple of California counties), where every contested case is immediately referred to a mediator. The job of the mediator is to help the parties search for areas of agreement and possible compromise, and, even if this proves impossible, to at least help them clearly define the issues in dispute. Only if the dispute can't be resolved through mediation should it be heard by a judge with power to declare a winner and a loser.

3. Let's help consumers better educate themselves about how to use Small Claims Court. Far more comprehensive how-to pamphlets, as well as audio and video materials, should be available from the court clerk. Even more important, the current in-person advisor program should be expanded. As the amounts that can be sued for in Small Claims go up, it will become more important to provide help for people confused by the system. This can easily be done by insisting that a portion of every filing fee go to the advisor program.

4. Let's assure that all Small Claims judges are competent. The present practice of appointing lawyers as "pro tem" Small Claims Court judges must be dropped. No lawyer can put on a robe a few days or a few weeks a year and do a decent job. Sophisticated users of Small Claims Court know this and normally refuse to accept a pro tem judge. Too often, this leaves less knowledgeable people, who don't understand that most pro tem judges have no meaningful training or experience on the bench, at risk of receiving second-class justice.

5. Let's change Small Claims appeal rules so plaintiffs and defendants are on an even footing. The present California system that allows litigants to be represented by lawyers on Small Claims appeals is nuts. All too often corporate defendants who have lawyers on retainer use the present system to frustrate consumers who have won in Small Claims Court. Also, the wacky California law that prohibits losing plaintiffs from appealing at all, while at the same time allowing losing defendants a whole new trial on appeal, should be scrapped. Far better to adopt a system that allows both parties to

appeal, but only if they claim that the Small Claims judge mistakenly applied the law and not to re-argue the facts.

Unfortunately, because of the so-called constitutional right to be represented by a lawyer if you want one, there will be problems barring lawyers from Small Claims Court itself and eliminating the defendant's right to appeal (or transfer) to a court where they can have a lawyer. One way to solve this dilemma is to create a simplified (voluntary) Small Claims procedure with no lawyers allowed that is so desirable that very few defendants will want their cases transferred to a formal court where lawyers are allowed.

I don't mean to suggest that the changes I propose in this short chapter are the only ones necessary. If we are going to put the majority of our routine legal work in Small Claims, it will require turning much of our current dispute resolution process on its head. Legal information must be stored and decoded in a way that makes it easily available to the average person. Clerk's offices and the other support systems surrounding our courts must be expanded and geared to serve the non-lawyer. Legal forms and courtroom language must be translated from "legalese" into English. Computer systems must be developed to bring legal information into our offices and living rooms.

Let's illustrate how things might change by looking at a case I recently saw argued in a Northern California Small Claims Court. One party to the dispute (let's call her Sally) arranged fishing charters for business and club groups. The other (let's call him Ben) owned several fishing boats. Sally often hired Ben's boats for her charters. Their relationship was of long standing and had been profitable to both. However, as the fishing charter business grew, both Sally and Ben began to enlarge their operations. Sally got a boat or two of her own and Ben began getting into the charter-booking business. Eventually they stepped on one another's toes and their friendly relationship was replaced by tension and argument. One day a blow-up occurred over some inconsequential detail, phones were slammed down and Sally and Ben each swore never to do business with the other again.

Before the day of the fight, Sally had organized two charters on Ben's boat. These were to have taken place a week after the phones were slammed down. For reasons unconnected with the argument, the charters were canceled by the clubs that had organized them. Ben had about a week's notice of cancellation. He also had $900 in deposits Sally had paid him. When he refused to refund this amount, Sally sued him in Small Claims Court for $900.

Testimony in court made it clear that charters were commonly canceled and were often replaced by others booked at the last minute. Ben and Sally had signed a "Standard Marine Charter Agreement," which dealt with the issue of canceled charters, because it was required by the Coast Guard, although they had never in the past paid attention to its terms. They had always worked out sensible adjustments on a situation-by-situation basis, depending on whether substitute charters were available and whether the club or business canceling had paid money up front, etc.

When Ben and Sally first presented their arguments about the $900, it seemed that they were not too far apart as to what would be a fair compromise. Unfortunately, the adversary nature of the court system encouraged each to overstate his (her) case and to dredge up all sorts of irrelevant side issues. "What about the times you overloaded my boat?" Ben demanded. "How about those holidays when you price-gouged me?" Sally replied. As the arguments went back and forth, each person got angrier and angrier and was less and less able to listen to the other.

The result was that after half an hour of testimony the judge was left with a confused mishmash of testimony about how maritime charter contracts work, promises claimed to be made (or not made) by each party and industry customs. Against this background, no decision the judge rendered was likely to be accepted by both Ben and Sally as being fair. Indeed, unless the judge gave one or the other everything he or she requested, both of them would probably feel cheated. That is not to say that the Small Claims hearing was all bad. Some good things did occur that would have been impossible in our formal court system. Principal among them, the dispute was presented quickly and cheaply, and each person got to have his or her say and, by so doing, blow off some steam. However, if Small Claims Court were changed along the lines suggested above, a better result might have been reached. For example, if instead of formal courtroom confrontation Ben and Sally were first encouraged to talk the dispute out themselves. If this failed, the next step would be for the two of them to sit down with a court employee who was trained as a mediator and whose job was to help people arrive at a fair compromise—a compromise that in this case would hopefully provide a foundation for Ben and Sally to continue to work together in the future. Only if this process didn't work would Ben and Sally have recourse to a formal court hearing. Incidentally, I am convinced that if this sort of three-tiered approach had been available, Ben and Sally would have worked out a compromise at the first or second stage.

■

Appendix

Major California Consumer Laws

1. Automotive Repair Act
   (Bus. & Prof. Code §§ 9880–9889.68)

2. Consumer Contract Awareness Act
   (Civ. Code §§ 1799.200–1799.206)

3. Consumer Credit Laws
   (Civ. Code §§ 1799.90–1799.102)

4. Consumer Finance Lenders Law
   (Fin. Code §§ 24000–24654)

5. Consumer Legal Remedies Act
   (Civ. Code §§ 1750–1784)

6. Contractors License Law (False advertising, etc.)
   (Bus. & Prof. Code §§ 7000–7191)

7. Contracts for Discount Buying Services
   (Civ. Code §§ 1812.100–1812.128)

8. Credit Services Act of 1984
   (Civ. Code §§ 1789.10–1789.25)

9. Dance Studio Contracts
   (Civ. Code §§ 1812.50–1812.68)

10. Dating Service Contracts
    (Civ. Code §§ 1694–1694.4)

11. California Fair Debt Collection Act
    (Civ. Code §§ 1788–1788.32)

12. Federal Fair Debt Collections Practices Act
    (15 U.S.C. §§ 1692–1692(o))

13. Fraud—Cancellation of Contracts Based On
    (Civ. Code §§ 1572, 1689(b)(1))

14. Health Studio Contracts
    (Civ. Code §§ 1812.80–1812.95)

15. Home Improvement Contracts
    (Bus. & Prof. Code §§ 7150–7168)

16. Home Solicitation Contracts
    (Civ. Code §§ 1689.5–1689.14)

17. Mail Order or Catalog Business
    (Bus. & Prof. Code §§ 17538–17538.5)

18. Minors Cancellation of Contract Rights
    (Civ. Code §§ 34, 35)

19. Personal Loans—Credit Unions
    (Fin. Code §§ 14000–16154

20. Recission of a Contract Based on Fraud, Lack of
    Consideration, Illegality, etc.
    (Civ. Code §§ 1689(b)(1)–1689(b)(3))

21. Rees-Levering Motor Vehicle Sales and Finance Act
    (Civ. Code §§ 2981–2984.4)

22. Retail Installment Accounts
    (Civ. Code § 1810.1–1810.12)

23. Seller-Assisted Marketing Plans
    (Civ. Code §§ 1812.200–1812.221)

24. Song-Beverly Consumer Warranty Act
    (Civ. Code §§ 1790–1797.86)

25. Song-Beverly Credit Card Act
    (Civ. Code §§ 1747–1748.12)

26. Unconscionable Contracts
    (Civ. Code § 1670.5)

27. UCC Warranties
    (a) Express (Com. Code § 2313)
    (b) Implied (Com. Code § 2315)

28. Unfair Trade Practices Act
    (Bus. & Prof. Code § 17000–17101)

29. Unruh Act
    (Civ. Code §§ 1801–1812.20)

30. Unsolicited Goods
    (Civ. Code §§ 1584.5–1584.6)

31. Vehicle Leasing Act
    (Civ. Code §§ 2985.7–2990)

32. Weight Loss Contracts
    (Civ. Code §§ 1694.5–1694.9)

■

INDEX

A

B

written testimony of, sample letter, 14/11

Express warranties. *See* Oral (express) warranties

Extraordinary writ, 23/17

F

Failure to appear
  and bare bones presentation, 15/1–2
  by defendant, 10/11–12
  by plaintiff, 10/11, 10/12–13
  See also Default judgment
Failure to perform a contract. *See* Breach of contract
Failure to return security deposit, defined, 2/4
  See also Security deposit; Security deposit claims
Fair market value
  recovery rules on, 4/10
  replacement value versus, 2/11, 21/2
False arrest cases, 21/7–8
Federal Bankruptcy Act, Chapter 7, 3/3
Federal government, suits against, 8/1, 8/7–8
Federal Trade Commission (FTC), 2/21, 18/9
Fees
  changing court date, 10/9
  collection agencies, 24/13
  expert witnesses, 14/3
  filing Defendant's Claim, 10/1
  filing Notice of Appeal, 23/15
  filing Plaintiff's Claim, 10/1
  for judgments paid to Court, 23/5, 24/3
  process servers, 11/11
  process serving by certified mail, 11/4
  subpoenaed police officers, 14/6
  subpoenaed witnesses, 14/4
  for till tap or keeper, 24/19
  unfiled Satisfaction of Judgment, 23/6
  winner's recovery of, 15/10, 24/25–26
Fictitious business name
  of corporations and LLCs, 8/5
  of individually owned businesses, 7/2, 8/3
Financial Declaration Form, 12/5
Formal court
  Declaration, to transfer to, 10/7

defined, 1/7
for suits against bonding companies, 8/8
See also Municipal Court; Superior Court
Fraud
  to defend bad debt claim, 18/9
  and district attorney's intervention, 17/8
  forms of, 2/23
  proof of, on used car defects, 17/6–7, 17/8
  statute of limitations period, 5/2
FTC (Federal Trade Commission), 2/21, 18/9

G

Garnish. *See* Wage garnishment
General partnerships, named as defendant, 8/4
General release
  necessary items on, 6/18
  sample form, 6/19–20
  validity/enforcement of, 6/17
Good faith dispute, 4/7, 4/9
Government entities. *See* Public entities
Guardian Ad Litem, Petition for Appointment of, 7/5

H

Hearing date. *See* Court date
Holding deposits, on rentals, 20/3–4, 20/21
Homestead Declaration, 1/8, 24/25
Hospital bills. *See* Medical/hospital bills

I

Implied contracts, 18/6
  See also Oral contracts
Implied warranties, 2/19
Individually owned businesses. *See* Businesses
Individuals
  listed as plaintiff, 7/1
  named as defendant, 8/2
  as out-of-state defendant, 9/2
  serving papers on, 11/2–5
Installment contracts
  recovery rules for, 4/6, 18/5
  statute of limitations period, 5/3
  venue for claims, 9/5, 9/9

CATALOG

		PRICE	CODE

BUSINESS

	PRICE	CODE
Avoid Employee Lawsuits (Quick & Legal Series)	$24.95	AVEL
⊙ The CA Nonprofit Corp Kit (Binder w/CD-ROM)	$49.95	CNP
▣ Consultant & Independent Contractor Agreements (Book w/Disk—PC)	$24.95	CICA
▣ The Corporate Minutes Book (Book w/Disk—PC)	$69.95	CORMI
The Employer's Legal Handbook	$39.95	EMPL
▣ Form Your Own Limited Liability Company (Book w/Disk—PC)	$44.95	LIAB
▣ Hiring Independent Contractors: The Employer's Legal Guide (Book w/Disk—PC)	$34.95	HICI
▣ How to Create a Buy-Sell Agreement & Control the Destiny of your Small Business (Book w/Disk—PC)	$49.95	BSAG
▣ How to Form a California Professional Corporation (Book w/Disk—PC)	$49.95	PROF
▣ How to Form a Nonprofit Corporation (Book w/Disk—PC)—National Edition (CA edition also available)	$44.95	NNP
▣ How to Form Your Own California Corporation (Book w/Disk—PC) (NY & TX editions also available)	$39.95	CCOR
How to Write a Business Plan	$29.95	SBS
The Independent Paralegal's Handbook	$29.95	PARA
Legal Guide for Starting & Running a Small Business, Vol. 1	$29.95	RUNS
▣ Legal Guide for Starting & Running a Small Business, Vol. 2: Legal Forms (Book w/Disk—PC)	$29.95	RUNS2
Marketing Without Advertising	$22.00	MWAD
▣ Music Law (Book w/Disk—PC)	$29.95	ML
Nolo's California Quick Corp (Quick & Legal Series)	$19.95	QINC
⊙ Open Your California Business in 24 Hours (Book w/CD-ROM)	$24.95	OPEN
▣ The Partnership Book: How to Write a Partnership Agreement (Book w/Disk—PC)	$39.95	PART
Sexual Harassment on the Job	$24.95	HARS
Starting & Running a Successful Newsletter or Magazine	$29.95	MAG
Take Charge of Your California Workers' Compensation Claim	$34.95	WORK
Tax Savvy for Small Business	$34.95	SAVVY
Wage Slave No More: Law & Taxes for the Self-Employed	$24.95	WAGE
▣ Your Limited Liability Company: An Operating Manual (Book w/Disk—PC)	$49.95	LOP
Your Rights in the Workplace	$24.95	YRW

CONSUMER

	PRICE	CODE
How to Win Your Personal Injury Claim	$29.95	PICL
Nolo's Everyday Law Book	$24.95	EVL
Nolo's Pocket Guide to California Law	$15.95	CLAW
Trouble-Free Travel...And What to Do When Things Go Wrong	$14.95	TRAV

ESTATE PLANNING & PROBATE

	PRICE	CODE
8 Ways to Avoid Probate (Quick & Legal Series)	$16.95	PRO8
9 Ways to Avoid Estate Taxes (Quick & Legal Series)	$24.95	ESTX
Estate Planning Basics (Quick & Legal Series)	$18.95	ESPN
How to Probate an Estate in California	$39.95	PAE
▣ Make Your Own Living Trust (Book w/Disk—PC)	$34.95	LITR
Nolo's Law Form Kit: Wills	$19.95	KWL
▣ Nolo's Will Book (Book w/Disk—PC)	$34.95	SWIL
Plan Your Estate	$34.95	NEST
Quick & Legal Will Book (Quick & Legal Series)	$21.95	QUIC

▣ Book with disk   ⊙ Book with CD-ROM

	PRICE	CODE

FAMILY MATTERS

	PRICE	CODE
Child Custody: Building Parenting Agreements That Work	$29.95	CUST
Child Support in California: Go to Court to Get More or Pay Less (Quick & Legal Series)	$24.95	CHLD
The Complete IEP Guide	$24.95	IEP
Divorce & Money: How to Make the Best Financial Decisions During Divorce	$34.95	DIMO
Get a Life: You Don't Need a Million to Retire Well	$19.95	LIFE
The Guardianship Book for California	$34.95	GB
⊙ How to Adopt Your Stepchild in California (Book w/CD-ROM)	$34.95	ADOP
A Legal Guide for Lesbian and Gay Couples	$25.95	LG
▣ Living Together (Book w/Disk—PC)	$34.95	LTK
Nolo's Pocket Guide to Family Law	$14.95	FLD
Using Divorce Mediation: Save Your Money & Your Sanity	$21.95	UDMD

GOING TO COURT

Beat Your Ticket: Go To Court and Win! (National Edition—California edition also available)	$19.95	BEYT
The Criminal Law Handbook: Know Your Rights, Survive the System	$29.95	KYR
Everybody's Guide to Small Claims Court (National Edition—California edition also available)	$18.95	NSCC
How to Change Your Name in California	$34.95	NAME
How to Collect When You Win a Lawsuit (California Edition)	$29.95	JUDG
How to Mediate Your Dispute	$18.95	MEDI
How to Seal Your Juvenile & Criminal Records (California Edition)	$29.95	CRIM
How to Sue for Up to $25,000...and Win! (California Edition)	$29.95	MUNI
Mad at Your Lawyer	$21.95	MAD
Nolo's Deposition Handbook	$29.95	DEP
Represent Yourself in Court: How to Prepare & Try a Winning Case	$29.95	RYC

HOMEOWNERS, LANDLORDS & TENANTS

California Tenants' Rights	$24.95	CTEN
▣ Contractors' and Homeowners' Guide to Mechanics' Liens (Book w/Disk—PC)	$39.95	MIEN
The Deeds Book (California Edition)	$24.95	DEED
Dog Law	$14.95	DOG
⊙ Every Landlord's Legal Guide (National Edition, Book w/CD-ROM)	$44.95	ELLI
Every Tenant's Legal Guide	$26.95	EVTEN
For Sale by Owner in California	$24.95	FSBO
How to Buy a House in California	$24.95	BHCA
The Landlord's Law Book, Vol. 1: Rights & Responsibilities (California Edition)	$44.95	LBRT
⊙ The California Landlord's Law Book, Vol. 2: Evictions (Book w/CD-ROM)	$44.95	LBEV
Leases & Rental Agreements (Quick & Legal Series)	$24.95	LEAR
Neighbor Law: Fences, Trees, Boundaries & Noise	$24.95	NEI
⊙ The New York Landlord's Law Book (Book w/CD-ROM)	$39.95	NYLL
Renters' Rights (National Edition—Quick & Legal Series)	$19.95	RENT
Stop Foreclosure Now in California	$34.95	CLOS

IMMIGRATION/LEGAL RESEARCH

How to Get a Green Card: Legal Ways to Stay in the U.S.A.	$29.95	GRN
U.S. Immigration Made Easy	$44.95	IMEZ
Legal Research: How to Find & Understand the Law	$29.95	LRES

MONEY MATTERS

▣ 101 Law Forms for Personal Use (Quick & Legal Series, Book w/disk—PC)	$29.95	SPOT
Bankruptcy: Is It the Right Solution to Your Debt Problems? (Quick & Legal Series)	$19.95	BRS
Chapter 13 Bankruptcy: Repay Your Debts	$29.95	CH13

▣ Book with disk   ⊙ Book with CD-ROM

Call 800-992-6656 • www.nolo.com • Mail or fax the order form in this book

		PRICE	CODE
☐	Credit Repair (Quick & Legal Series, Book w/disk—PC)	$18.95	CREP
☐	The Financial Power of Attorney Workbook (Book w/disk—PC)	$29.95	FINPOA
	How to File for Chapter 7 Bankruptcy	$29.95	HFB
	IRAs, 401(k)s & Other Retirement Plans: Taking Your Money Out	$24.95	RET
	Money Troubles: Legal Strategies to Cope With Your Debts	$24.95	MT
	Nolo's Law Form Kit: Personal Bankruptcy	$16.95	KBNK
	Stand Up to the IRS	$29.95	SIRS
	Surviving an IRS Tax Audit (Quick & Legal Series)	$24.95	SAUD
	Take Control of Your Student Loan Debt	$24.95	SLOAN

PATENTS AND COPYRIGHTS

		PRICE	CODE
⊙	The Copyright Handbook: How to Protect and Use Written Works (Book w/CD-ROM)	$34.95	COHA
	Copyright Your Software	$24.95	CYS
☐	Getting Permission: How to License and Clear Copyrighted Materials Online and Off (Book w/disk—PC)	$34.95	RIPER
	How to Make Patent Drawings Yourself	$29.95	DRAW
	The Inventor's Notebook	$19.95	INOT
☐	License Your Invention (Book w/Disk—PC)	$39.95	LICE
	Patent, Copyright & Trademark	$29.95	PCTM
	Patent It Yourself	$46.95	PAT
	Patent Searching Made Easy	$29.95	PATSE
⊙	Software Development: A Legal Guide (Book with CD-ROM)	$44.95	SFT
	Trademark: Legal Care for Your Business and Product Name	$39.95	TRD
	The Trademark Registration Kit (Quick & Legal Series)	$19.95	TREG

SENIORS

		PRICE	CODE
	Beat the Nursing Home Trap: A Consumer's Guide to Assisted Living and Long-Term Care	$21.95	ELD
	The Conservatorship Book for California	$44.95	CNSV
	Social Security, Medicare & Pensions	$24.95	SOA

SOFTWARE

Call or check our website at www.nolo.com for special discounts on Software!

		PRICE	CODE
⊙	LeaseWriter CD—Windows/Macintosh	$129.95	LWD1
⊙	Living Trust Maker CD—Windows/Macintosh	$89.95	LTD3
⊙	Patent It Yourself CD—Windows	$229.95	PPC12
⊙	Personal RecordKeeper 5.0 CD—Windows/Macintosh	$59.95	RKD5
⊙	Small Business Pro 4 CD—Windows/Macintosh	$89.95	SBCD4
⊙	WillMaker 7.0 CD—Windows/Macintosh	$69.95	WMD7

Special Upgrade Offer

Save 35% on the latest edition of your Nolo book

Because laws and legal procedures change often, we update our books regularly. To help keep you up-to-date, we are extending this special upgrade offer. Cut out and mail the title portion of the cover of your old Nolo book and we'll give you **35% off** the retail price of the NEW EDITION of that book when you purchase directly from Nolo.com. This offer is to individuals only.

Prices subject to change without notice.

☐ Book with disk   ⊙ Book with CD-ROM

Order Form

Name

Address

City

State, Zip

Daytime Phone

E-mail

Our "No-Hassle" Guarantee

Return anything you buy directly from Nolo for any reason and we'll cheerfully refund your purchase price. No ifs, ands or buts.

☐ Check here if you do not wish to receive mailings from other companies

Item Code	Quantity	Item	Unit Price	Total Price

Method of payment

☐ Check ☐ VISA ☐ MasterCard
☐ Discover Card ☐ American Express

Subtotal	
Add your local sales tax (California only)	
Shipping: RUSH $8, Basic $3.95 (See below)	
"I bought 3, Ship it to me FREE!"(Ground shipping only)	
TOTAL	

Account Number

Expiration Date

Signature

Shipping and Handling

Rush Delivery-Only $8

We'll ship any order to any street address in the U.S. by UPS 2nd Day Air* for only $8!

* Order by noon Pacific Time and get your order in 2 business days. Orders placed after noon Pacific Time will arrive in 3 business days. P.O. boxes and S.F. Bay Area use basic shipping. Alaska and Hawaii use 2nd Day Air or Priority Mail.

Basic Shipping—$3.95

Use for P.O. Boxes, Northern California and Ground Service.

Allow 1-2 weeks for delivery. U.S. addresses only.

For faster service, use your credit card and our toll-free numbers

Order 24 hours a day

Online	www.nolo.com
Phone	1-800-992-6656
Fax	1-800-645-0895
Mail	Nolo.com
	950 Parker St.
	Berkeley, CA 94710

Visit us online at

www.nolo.com